Lifelong Learning and Social Justice: Communities, Work and Identities in a Globalised World

To Evie, Jacob and Layla
May you live your lives always inspired by a concern to strive for social justice, and by a lifelong love of learning

Lifelong Learning and Social Justice: Communities, Work and Identities in a Globalised World

Edited by Sue Jackson

6237892

Published by niace

© 2011 National Institute of Adult Continuing Education
(England and Wales)

21 De Montfort Street
Leicester LE1 7GE

Company registration no. 2603322
Charity registration no. 1002775

NIACE has a broad remit to promote lifelong learning opportunities for adults. NIACE works to develop increased participation in education and training, particularly for those who do not have easy access because of class, gender, age, race, language and culture, learning difficulties or disabilities, or insufficient financial resources.

For a full catalogue of all NIACE's publications visit http://shop.niace.org.uk/

All rights reserved. No reproduction, copy or transmission of this publication may be made without the written permission of the publishers, save in accordance with the provisions of the Copyright, Designs and Patents Acts 1988, or under the terms of any licence permitting copying issued by the Copyright Licensing Agency.

Cataloguing in Publications Data
A CIP record for this title is available from the British Library

Print ISBN 978 1 86201 454 1
ePub ISBN 978 1 86201 495 4
AER ISBN 978 1 86201 496 1
Online ISBN 978 1 86201 497 8

Designed and typeset by Avon DataSet Ltd, Bidford on Avon, Warwickshire, UK.
Printed and bound in the UK.

Contents

Acknowledgements	viii
Contributors	ix
Lifelong learning and social justice: Introduction Sue Jackson	1

PART ONE – SUSTAINING COMMUNITIES

Sustaining communities: Introduction Sue Jackson	13
Chapter One Lifelong learning and environmental sustainability John Blewitt	18
Chapter Two Literacy, lifelong learning and social inclusion: Empowering learners to learn about equality and reconciliation through lived experiences Rob Mark	42
Chapter Three Women, education and peacebuilding in Northern Ireland Paul Nolan	59
Chapter Four Community engagement and the idea of a 'good university' Sue Webb	82
Sustaining communities: Conclusion Sue Jackson	102

PART TWO – LEARNING AND WORKING
Learning and working: Introduction 105
Sue Jackson

Chapter Five
Welfare to work: Training, benefits, un/employment and
social justice 109
Jacky Brine

Chapter Six
Social justice, inclusion and lifelong learning in Scotland: The
experiences of adult learners 133
Elisabet Weedon and Sheila Riddell

Chapter Seven
Learning to be a good citizen: Informal learning through unpaid
household work among recent Chinese immigrants in Canada 155
Lichun Willa Liu

Learning and working: Conclusion 181
Sue Jackson

PART THREE – IDENTITIES
Identities: Introduction 185
Sue Jackson

Chapter Eight
Transformations: Lifelong learners in the era of globalisation 190
Nataly Tcherepashenets with Lisa Snyder

Chapter Nine
Dialogical processes in adult learning: teacher identity and professional
development in New Zealand's low socioeconomic communities 210
Vicki M Carpenter

Chapter Ten
Challenging constructed learner identities: Women's informal learning 237
Helen Aberton

Chapter Eleven
Love in a cold climate: Mental illness and learning to write 'I love you' 266
Olivia Sagan

Identities: Conclusion 284
Sue Jackson

Lifelong learning and social justice: Conclusion 285
Sue Jackson

Index 291

Acknowledgements

This book derived from a conference on *Lifelong Learning and Social Justice* at Birkbeck Institute for Lifelong Learning, Birkbeck, University of London, although it contains contributions from several authors who were not at the conference, as well as from others who were. However, my thinking about the book, its structure and its key themes began in preparation for that conference, developed during the conference itself, and evolved in the work that took place in preparing this volume. I am, then, very grateful to all those who contributed to the original conference, whether as presenters or as delegates, as academic or as administrative colleagues. My deep thanks too, of course, to all the contributors to this book, who have participated in critically exploring lifelong learning and social justice from a range of international perspectives. It has been a pleasure to work with them in the production of this book. Thanks too to my students and colleagues on my *MSc Education, Power and Social Change*, who have brought new insights into my thinking about education, globalisation, power and resistances. Finally, I am very grateful to NIACE, and especially to David Shaw for making this book possible and for his continued support from conception to completion.

Contributors

Helen Aberton, a doctoral candidate at the University of Melbourne, is completing her study on the informal learning and identity formation of women engaged in rural community activities. Previous research involved a study of older adults learning computer skills in community classes. Formerly a secondary school teacher, Helen's interest is in the relations between lifelong learning rhetoric, educational practices and social justice. Now, in addition to community learning, her research interest includes the learning of older professionals, and in this research, paying particular attention to objects central to the processes and practices of learning and knowing.

John Blewitt is Director of Lifelong Learning at Aston University, UK. He has a wide experience of adult, further and higher education and has fervently advocated of education for sustainability for many years. He is author of *The Ecology of Learning* (Earthscan, 2006), *Understanding Sustainable Development* (Earthscan, 2008) and most recently *Media, Ecology and Conservation* (Green Books, 2010). He is a member of the IUCN Commission for Communication and Education. His research interests include sustainability, urban education and the pedagogy of place and he currently leads the Birmingham based Lifelong Learning Network Consortium in Sustainable Communities, Urban Regeneration and Environmental Technologies.

Jacky Brine is Professor of Education at the University of the West of England, Bristol, England and co-director of the Bristol Centre for Research in Lifelong Learning and Education. She has published widely in journals on the broad theme of EU education, training and related social policy where she focuses primarily on analyses of gender and social class. This includes her current work on the education and training aspects of welfare-to-work policies. She is the author of two monographs: *Under-educating women: globalising inequality* (1999, Open University Press) and *The European Social Fund and the EU: flexibility, growth, stability* (2002, Continuum).

Vicki Carpenter is a principal lecturer in the Faculty of Education, University of Auckland, New Zealand. Her teaching and school leadership background is in urban and rural low SES schools. Vicki lectures in undergraduate and graduate programmes, and supervises Masters, PhD and EdD theses. Her research interests centre on social justice issues, in particular those surrounding schooling in low SES communities, and matters related to sexual orientation. Publications include the co-editing of three texts, a range of book chapters and several refereed journal articles. Vicki sits on journal editorial boards, and reviews papers for international journals.

Sue Jackson is Professor of Lifelong Learning and Gender and Pro-Vice-Master for Learning and Teaching at Birkbeck University of London. She is also Director of Birkbeck Institute for Lifelong Learning, from where this book originated. Sue's research focuses on the intersections of multiple learner identities, including gender, age and social class. Her recent books include *Reconceptualising Lifelong Learning: feminist perspectives* (Routledge, 2007, with Penny Burke), *Innovations in Lifelong Learning: critical perspectives on diversity, participation and vocational learning* (Routledge, 2010) and *Gendered choices: Learning, Work, Identities in Lifelong Learning* (Springer, 2011, with Irene Malcolm and Kate Thomas).

Lichun Willa Liu was an associate professor at a university in China, where she taught for many years. She has recently completed her PhD studies at the Department of Sociology and Equity Studies, Ontario Institute for Studies in Education, University of Toronto, Canada. Her doctoral research focused on Chinese immigrants, unpaid household work (food work, childcare, and emotion work), and lifelong learning. Her other PhD-related publications include two peer-reviewed journal articles, in *Cuizine*, 2009, 1(2) and in the *Canadian Journal for the Study of Adult Education*, 2007, 20 (2), two book chapters, and over 20 conference papers/proceedings.

Rob Mark has recently taken up an appointment as Head of Lifelong Learning at Strathclyde University. He previously worked as Director of

Education at Queen's University Belfast and has also experience working in the further education and community education sectors. He has worked with literacy educators following a range of professional development programmes and was also himself for many years a teacher of literacy. He has contributed to several European projects on research and practice in adult literacy and has published widely in the field. His publications include quality in adult literacy, technology enhanced literacy learning and access to education for excluded groups.

Paul Nolan is the Research Director with the Northern Ireland Peace Monitoring Survey, which is funded jointly by the Joseph Rowntree Foundation and the Joseph Rowntree Charitable Trust to provide ongoing analysis of the peace process in Northern Ireland. Before taking up this position in 2010, Paul's background was in adult education. In the early part of his career he worked for the Workers' Educational Association, first as a Tutor-Organiser in disadvantaged areas of Belfast, and then as the Northern Ireland Director. He took on the Director's role in 1984 and held it until he moved to Queen's University Belfast in 2001. At Queen's he headed up the Institute of Lifelong Learning, a structure which was subsequently merged with the School of Education.

Sheila Riddell is Director of the Centre for Research in Education, Inclusion and Diversity (CREID) at the University of Edinburgh. She is the author of *Policy and Practice in Special Educational Needs: Additional Support for Learning* (Dunedin Academic Press, 2006) and co-author of Improving *Disabled Students' Learning in Higher Education* (RoutledgeFalmer 2009), *Disabled Students in Higher Education: Perspectives on Widening Access and Changing Policy* (RoutledgeFalmer, 2005) and *The Learning Society and People with Learning Difficulties* (Policy Press, 2001).

Olivia Sagan is Head of the MSc in Psychoanalytic Developmental Psychology at University College London. Her PhD won the 2009 Director's prize for Best Doctoral Research at the Institute of Education, University of London, and was a longitudinal, psychosocial study of mentally ill adults' community auto/biographic practices. A firm believer in the role of 1st person narratives in counter-balancing 'culturally sanctioned stories', Olivia makes extensive use of biographic narrative in her research, and uses psychosocial theory to explore the quandaries of learning and creativity.

Lisa Snyder is currently the Coordinator of Curriculum and Instructional Design with the State University of New York, Empire State College. For well over a decade Dr. Snyder has been teaching aspiring teachers as well as conducting research and presenting on topics pertaining to curriculum design, alternative learning environments, and program evaluation models. Her current research interests include examining faculty transformations due to the use of specific modalities in global learning environments along with evaluating approaches for creating cross-cultural experiences in virtual environments.

Nataly Tcherepashenets is Assistant Professor of Spanish and Area Coordinator of Foreign Languages at the State University of New York, Empire State College. She received her Ph.D. in Hispanic Languages and literature from the University of California, Los Angeles. Her research interests include distance language learning and its impact on identity development, and online learning cultures. She is also the author of numerous publications on topics of Latin American, Peninsular, and comparative literature, as well as translation studies.

Sue Webb is Professor of Education, Work and Learning at Monash University, Australia and was formerly Professor of Continuing Education and Director of the Institute for Lifelong Learning at the University of Sheffield. Her research interests are in the areas of lifelong learning and higher education with a focus on widening participation and learner transitions through education and work. Her research engages with the themes of social differentiation and the continued ways that differences such as class, gender, 'race' age and disability impact on learner transitions and learners' decision-making and identities.

Elisabet Weedon is Deputy Director in the Centre for Research in Education Inclusion and Diversity (CREID) at the University of Edinburgh. Her main research interests are in the area of lifelong learning and social justice. She has been involved in research into the experiences of disabled students in higher education, the use of restorative practices in education and dispute resolution in the area additional support needs. Current projects include an investigation of the experiences and outcomes for Muslim pupils, research into lifelong learning in Europe and learning in the workplace.

Lifelong learning and social justice: Introduction

Sue Jackson

Both lifelong learning and social justice are part of the complexities of the twenty-first century, in which individuals find themselves living in a world that is both globalised and localised, homogenised and splintered. The growth of individualism vies against the politics and policies of equity and social justice. Whilst a commitment to 'lifelong learning' is at the forefront of the educational arena both nationally and internationally, what it means is highly contestable, as is the connection (or not) between lifelong learning and social justice. This book argues that there needs to be a sharp refocus to an alignment of lifelong learning with social justice and explores some of the contestations, complexities and challenges that arise from attempts to position lifelong learning alongside social justice, demonstrating the costs of a focus which is solely about economic imperatives. It offers alternative ways of developing and enhancing learning opportunities through the intersections between lifelong learning and social justice.

Lifelong learning and social justice

Policy endorsement of lifelong learning is almost universal (Field, 2000), although its practices and definitions are varied and contested. In the main 'the field' of lifelong learning is described as though it is neutral, ahistorical and uncontestable, with little account given of a wide range of different histories and competing 'fields', including those of adult and continuing education, community based learning, and the personal and political learning that takes place in, for example, trade unions, women's groups, or groups for other marginalised people, such as gay and lesbian groups, black and minority ethnic groups and so forth (Burke and Jackson, 2007; see also Chapter Ten of this book).

Lifelong learning has been defined as

> *the combination of processes throughout a lifetime whereby the whole person . . . experiences social situations, the perceived content of which is then transformed cognitively, emotively or practically . . . and integrated into the individual person's biography, resulting in a continually changing (or more experienced) person* (Jarvis, 2007: 1).

However, as many feminist writers have shown, individual biographies are in part formed through experiencing the gendered, classed and racialised social situations in which we are all located (see, e.g., Leathwood and Francis, 2006; Skeggs 1997; Mirza, 2009). As Louise Archer (2007) has shown, geographies of power, located within the connections and disconnections between the global, national and local, mean that im/mobility becomes central to the reproduction of social inequalities, with it being in the interests of more powerful groups to fix other groups within less powerful spaces (see also Chapters Three and Seven). This in turn may mean that less powerful groups and individuals learn to take their place as (gendered, classed and racialised) neoliberal subjects rather than learning how to become empowered members of communities. Whilst marginalised groups may be able to access learning, they can feel 'little sense of entitlement or belonging' (Archer, 2007: 647). Such positioning shapes choices, experiences and outcomes and there appears to be little or no policy recognition of alternative ways of developing and enhancing learning opportunities. Few questions are asked by policy makers about learner identities or the intersections between lifelong learning and social justice (Burke and Jackson, 2007). And even when policies appear to focus on diverse groups of students, their dislocation from dominant educational structures and cultures is 'a key area of concern for social justice' (Archer, 2007: 647).

Whilst discourses of choice abound in lifelong learning policies and practice, 'choice' is illusory and the unequal participation of non-traditional students in education is indicative of social injustice, even if it appears to be traceable to individual choice (Voigt, 2007). What choices are achievable and thinkable are shaped by structural location and identities (Archer, 2007: 646). Research on widening educational participation has shown that access to learning must be understood in relation to deeply embedded relations of inequality that operate at multiple levels (Burke and Jackson, 2007). Although there is a dominant policy language about widening participation, justified in relation to social equity and justice, it is driven by the changing needs for labour in a globalised knowledge economy (Naidoo and Callender, 2000). Critics have argued that widening participation policies will only work to increase participation amongst the same groups who have historically always benefited from education and is likely to increase the gap between middle class access and working class exclusion (Archer, 2007). As Louise Archer has shown, the causes and patterns of unequal participation are discursively separated from structures and practices that ensure inequalities, with non-traditional groups pathologised and blamed for (seemingly) not participating in learning (2007: 640).

Although lifelong learning has been described as a lifelong, voluntary, and self-motivated pursuit of knowledge for either personal or professional reasons (DfES, 2000) interventions in lifelong learning are designed to improve the skills and flexibility of the workforce (Field, 2000: 21). There is often little that is 'voluntary' or about the 'self-motivated pursuit of knowledge'. There has been a strong and often persuasive movement towards highly individualised learners who are expected to take individual responsibility to continually (re-)train, or (up-)skill for the workplace within globalised knowledge economies (see also Chapter One of this book). Of concern to several authors of this book are the ways in which lifelong learning has increasingly come to mean vocational education and training within a globalised knowledge economy (see, e.g., Chapters Four, Five and Six). There is a clear policy interest in producing an efficient and productive workforce – but this workforce is one where opportunities are still created or denied according to class, gender, ethnicity, disability and age.

When public policy is driven by largely economic concerns then competitiveness becomes a primary focus (Field, 2000, 3). Yet John Field has also pointed out that

> *For the past two decades, the wider policy agenda (. . .) has sought to balance the demands of competiveness with the maintenance of social cohesion* (Field, 2005: 135).

Lines of connection are frequently between policies for social cohesion, lifelong learning and social justice, as social cohesion policies aim to ensure that all citizens have opportunities to participate fully in society, and lifelong learning has a central role in this process. However, whilst equity and inclusion are a part of the equation of social justice, they are not the sum of it. Mapping the connections between lifelong learning and social justice remain under-theorised (Gerwitz, 1998) in part because, like lifelong learning, social justice is a contested territory (Gerwitz and Cribb, 2002). Whilst social justice might be about the equitable (re)distribution of resources, this is not all it is. Social justice is also about the politics of (mis)recognition:

> *intimately tied to culture, particularly social patterns of misrepresentation, interpretation and communication, that result in cultural domination, invisibility and disrespect* (Fraser and Honneth, 2003: 18).

Marginalised groups can become excluded and silenced in the process, leading to the oppression of others, or to a need to play by the rules of those in power (North, 2006). To be 'equal' or included, for example, may mean having to become part of a dominant group, to move from the 'other' to the 'One'. Equity and inclusion are often located in the realm of power, privilege and oppression.

In his development of a pedagogy of and for the oppressed, Paulo Freire has said that it is from reflection by the oppressed on their oppression and its causes that pedagogy will be made and remade (Freire, 1972: 25). His theory of education is closely linked to issues of oppression, struggle and social justice. Education, whilst often promoted in the name of social justice, can become a means of oppression, continually recreating social class and other divisions and perpetuating inequalities (see Chapters Two and Nine of this book).

Some of those inequalities with which Paulo Freire engaged are embedded within language, literacy, and literary practices, which concern several of the authors of this book (see for example Chapters Two, Eight and Eleven). In considering literacy and oppressive practices, Freire uses an example of how Creole was viewed as an antagonistic force that threatened the privileged and dominant position of Portuguese (Freire, 1985, p184/6). The colonisers, he says, had to convince people that the only valid language was Portuguese: they stated that Creole does not contain the necessary vocabulary to enable scientific and technical advancement, for instance, and that Portuguese is far superior as an 'educated' and advanced language (see Jackson, 2004: 24). The colonisers have the power of naming and of constructing those who 'know' and those who do not.

Although for Freire literacy is an essential step on the route to becoming a reflective thinker, others have argues that 'literacy itself is a colonising process that reinforces a modern sense of individualism' (Bowers and Apffel-Marglin, 2005: 3). Bowers and Apffel-Marglin have described how they were at first deeply motivated by Freire's vision of empowerment, which they initially interpreted as a noncolonising pedagogy. But as they learned from indigenous cultures, they became aware that Freire's ideas are based on Western assumptions and that the Freirean approach to empowerment was really a disguised form of colonialism (Bowers and Apffel-Marglin, 2005: 2). Freire, however, suggests that we can only achieve a sense of identity through language, and that through claiming or reclaiming language, people can critically engage in an analysis of their experience which enables them to transform and create the world. Whilst the global provision of literacy skills and development has been embedded in a discourse of equality of opportunity and inclusiveness, the acquisition of key basic skills and qualifications may be useful, but is never good enough.

Throughout his life's work, Freire has viewed education as a political act and has insisted that teaching can never be divorced from critical analysis of how society works. Learners must be challenged to think critically about the social, political and historical realities within which they are a presence in the world, and it is the responsibility of teachers to continually link lifelong learning with social justice. This is especially true today as neoliberal discourse and ideologies become dominant in both policy and practice. Education is always a certain theory of knowledge put into practice, and it is therefore always political (Freire, 2004: 71). Ruling groups are able to exercise control both over *what* is taught and *how* it is taught, maintaining hegemonic control. Although neoliberalism purports to support social justice, embedded within it are discourses of individualism and support for a 'free' market. Judgements are then made and enforced according to those who have the power to enforce, and in relation to 'the market' rather than to social justice.

Neoliberalism, globalisation and postcolonialism

Neoliberalism has led education to be understood as gaining technical knowledge, training learners in skills which enable them to adapt to economic globalisation:

> Then education becomes pure training, it becomes pure transfer of content, it is almost like the training of animals, it is a mere exercise in adaptation to the world (Freire, 2004: 84).

Mark Olssen (2006) argues that neoliberalism 'pertains to the way that practices of economies and discursive patternings of knowledge and learning interact' (217). He claims that lifelong learning is a global discourse for the flexible preparation of subjects to participate in a knowledge economy, involving a 'restructuring of the context of education in the interests of efficiency through flexibalisation' (222). He describes lifelong learning as a form of neoliberal control in its conception, emergence and development. Its apparent but highly limited choices, discussed above, lead to compliance and obedience, far removed from progressive emancipation based on egalitarian politics and social justice. As several authors in this book demonstrate (see especially Section Two), neoliberalism thrives through discourses about the knowledge economy and lifelong learning, leading to shared dominant paradigms of the role of education across the globe.

Globalisation often refers to economic activities across national boundaries: however, it is much more than this. As Olssen *et al.* argue, for example:

> Cultural globalisation involves the expansion of Western . . . culture to all corners of the globe, promoting particular values that are supportive of consumerism and capital accumulation (2004: 6).

Globalisation is an ongoing process by which regional economies, societies and cultures become integrated – or at least inter-related – through globe-spanning activities (Olssen *et al.*, 2004). Lifelong learning is one such activity, tied through policy and discourse to knowledge economies. Thus those countries with the products, skills and resources take advantage of global markets. However, globalisation has significantly increased the gap between rich and poor and has been viewed as a renewed form of colonisation.

Colonialism is about exploitation and power, including the use of a weaker country's resources to strengthen and enrich the stronger country. It is about hierarchies of power, where one form of knowledge is privileged over another, where dominant forms of knowledge are legitimised by transnational systems of power through major global organisations (Spring, 2009). Colonial power continues even after breakup of colonial empires, with the power of previous colonisers re-emerging (Spring, 2009).

To say that we live in a *post*-colonial age, then, does not mean that such exploitation no longer happens. In considering postcolonialism, I am not therefore arguing that colonialism no longer has relevance. On the contrary, the histories and experiences of colonialism continue to impact on the (previously) colonised and the (previous) colonisers (Jackson, 2010). Whilst 'post' can suggest something which supersedes, or comes after, the prefix 'post' can also be used to indicate a process of ongoing transformation or change (see, e.g., Venn, 2006), central to theorisations not just of postcolonialism but also of poststructuralism and feminism (see, e.g., Brooks, 1997, for discussion of postfeminism). In considering the postcolonial, Couze Venn suggests that:

> *The postcolonial can be understood as a virtual space, that is, a space of possibility and emergence. It is thus also potential becoming: it opens towards a future that will not repeat existing forms of sociality and oppressive power relations* (Venn, 2006: 190).

The authors of this book add to such critical endeavours, and open up discussions about the potentials of becoming.

Overview of the book

The authors of these chapters span a range of identities, experiences and disciplinary and institutional positionings. They include doctoral students and professors; researchers, teachers and practitioners. They are currently located in the UK (England, Northern Ireland and Scotland), in Australia and New Zealand, and in North America (Canada and the USA). Whilst these locations indicate a dominant Western paradigm, some of the authors engage in a critique of the domination of Western thought and ideologies. Some base their chapters on empirical work, others on theoretical (and many on both): all are concerned with conceptualisations of lifelong learning and social justice.

The authors develop issues such as those discussed above through the book's three sections. Each section has an introduction to help the reader through some of its key themes, including those discussed above. However, the sections should not be seen as discrete: their chapters engage with inter-related issues including identities, power, constructions of knowledges and the relationships between policies, practices and ideologies.

Section 1, 'Sustaining communities', explores both how communities sustain, and can be sustained. It takes as its central concern the interaction of lifelong learning with sustainable communities, exploring ways in which communities can be sustained to promote social justice through lifelong learning, and ways in which liveable lives (Butler, 2004) can be led. Section 2 takes learning and working as its theme. The chapters are critical of the ways in which social justice is aligned to lifelong learning policies and practices regarding employability and to questions of the 'new unemployed'. The final section turns to learner identities and social justice, and includes debates about subjectivities, identities, power and gender. It explores ways in which identities which to some extent are built around neoliberal ideologies of individualism are nevertheless also constructed through senses of (un)belonging, through intersectionality, and through complex and contradictory biographies and histories.

The conclusion to the book returns to some of the key themes of its three sections and considers the implications for lifelong learning and social justice.

References

Archer, L. (2007) 'Diversity, equality and higher education: a critical reflection of the ab/uses of equality discourse within widening participation', *Teaching in Higher Education*, 12: 5 635–53.

Bowers, C. A. and Apffel-Marglin, F. (eds) (2005) *Rethinking Freire: globalization and the environmental crisis*, New Jersey: Lawrence Erlbaum Associates.

Brooks, A. (1997) *Postfeminists: feminism, cultural theory and cultural forms*. London: Routledge.

Burke, P. and Jackson S. (2007) *Reconceptualising lifelong learning: feminist interventions*. London: Routledge.

Butler, J. (2004) *Undoing Gender*. London: Routledge.

Department of Education and Science (2000) *Learning for Life: White Paper on Adult Education*. Dublin: Stationery Office.

Field, J. (2000) *Lifelong learning and the new educational order*. Stoke-on-Trent: Trentham Books.

Field J. (2005) *Social policy and lifelong learning*. Bristol: Policy Press.

Fraser, N. and Honneth, A. (2003) *Redistribution or recognition? A political–philosophical exchange*. New York: Verso.

Freire, P. (1972) *Pedagogy of the oppressed*. New York: Herder and Herder.

Freire, P. (1985) *The Politics of Education*. Basingstoke: Macmillan.

Freire, P. (2004) *Pedagogy of indignation*. Boulder: Paradigm.

Gewirtz, S. (1998) 'Conceptualizing social justice in education: Mapping the territory', *Journal of Education Policy*, 13: 4, 469–84.

Gewirtz, S. and Cribb, A. (2002) 'Plural conceptions of social justice: implications for policy sociology', *Journal of Education Policy*, 17: 5, 499–511.

Jackson, S. (2010) 'Learning through social spaces: migrant women and lifelong learning in postcolonial London', *International Journal of Lifelong Education* 29: 2, 237–54.

Jackson, S. (2004) *Differently academic? Developing lifelong learning for women in higher education*. Dordrecht: Kluwer Academic Press.

Jarvis, P. (2007) Globalisation, lifelong learning and the learning society: sociological perspectives. London: Routledge.

Leathwood C. and Francis B. (eds) (2006) *Gender and lifelong learning: critical feminist engagements*. London: Routledge.

Mirza, H. (2009) *Race, gender and educational desire: Why black women succeed and fail*. London: Routledge.

Naidoo, R. and Callender, C. (2000) 'Towards a more inclusive system of HE? Contemporary policy reform in higher education', *Social Policy Review*, 12, 224–49.

North, C. (2006) 'More than Words? Delving into the Substantive Meaning(s) of 'Social Justice'', *Review of Educational Research*, 76: 4, 507–35.

Olssen, M. (2006) 'Understanding the mechanisms of neoliberal control: lifelong learning, flexibility and knowledge capitalism', *International Journal of Lifelong Education*, 25, 213–30

Olssen, M., Codd, J. and O'Neill, A. (2004) *Reading education policy in the global era*, London: Sage.

Skeggs, B. (1997) *Formations of class and gender: becoming respectable*. London: Sage

Spring, J. (2009) *Globalisation of education: an introduction*. New York: Routledge.

Venn, C. (2006) *The post–colonial challenge: towards alternative worlds.* London: Sage.

Voigt, K (2007) 'Individual choice and unequal participation in higher education', *Theory and Research in Education*, 5: 1, 87–98.

PART ONE

SUSTAINING COMMUNITIES

Sustaining communities: Introduction

SUE JACKSON

In this first section, whilst considering how communities sustain and are sustained, the authors start to set out some of the key themes which will run throughout the book, including ways in which lifelong learning is both sustained by the communities in which it resides, and sustains communities in their development of social justice and learning, including though both formal and informal learning. John Annette (2003: 140) argues that in contemporary political thinking, 'community has become politically and philosophically significant. He identifies four ways of conceptualising community: as a place, or neighbourhood; as a normative ideal, linked to respect, solidarity or inclusion; through the construction of cultural identities and politics of recognition (see also introduction to this book); and as participation, inclusion and citizenship.

All of the chapters in this section are interested in different conceptualisations of community and in the ways in which social communities are constructed, and social justice developed, through engagement with lifelong learning and through critical pedagogies of place. In particular, the first three chapters are concerned with grassroots actions in communities, and the ways in which social justice can be developed through community engagement with lifelong learning. The authors are interested in developing wider understandings of how people sustain themselves and their communities through engaging with lifelong learning, civic participation and inter-cultural connectedness, as well as through a commitment to social justice. Conversely, they show how a commitment to social justice brings about the development of learning, particularly within and through communities.

However, agendas for sustaining communities through lifelong learning, and sustaining learning through community engagement, have become increasingly dominated by neoliberal discourses and policies driven by a perceived need to participate in knowledge economies, although there is a parallel agenda located in education for sustainable development which is linked to social justice (see Chapter One). As Mike Raco maintains in his consideration of neoliberalism and sustainable communities:

> *The emergence of (sustainable development) ... provides policy makers and a range of communities with alternative ways of thinking about ... social justice and resource use ... The greater attention given to social justice and inclusion which characterised the original foundations of the sustainability movement sit uneasily with neoliberal, trickle-down economics in which development capacities are to be maximised with scant regard for redistribution or social justice* (Raco, 200: 330).

Yet it has been claimed that despite such uncertainties and dichotomous positionings:

> *(a) quiet transformation is taking place in communities ... around the world. Thousands of citizens and their governments are embracing a new way of thinking and acting about their future* (Roseland, 2005: 2).

Nevertheless, John Blewitt begins Chapter One, and therefore the book, by taking a less optimistic stance and arguing that disaster is in the air: our world is changing, he states, and not necessarily for the better. The financial crunch has occurred simultaneously with the climate crunch and the global energy crunch. The critical lack of emphasis on sustainability in both policy and academic discourses highlights the need for a renewal in thinking about lifelong learning. Blewitt argues that debates around the purpose and future of lifelong learning have tended to neglect environmental sustainability and a more ecologically informed lifelong learning. Whilst education and learning are key to enable individuals to live lives they value, he demonstrates that there are still key questions to ask (and to be answered) about how lifelong learning can serve social justice. Key to social justice, for Blewitt, is environmental sustainability, and he develops his chapter by outlining what this means for lifelong learning, and how lifelong learning can help sustain communities. Blewitt demonstrates how where we live, work and play are places of, and spaces for, learning. He gives an example of community gardens as sites for learning combined with practical actions. Community gardens, he says, are frequently important sites for social learning reconnecting urban dwellers with the natural world, other cultures and other people, and hence leading to a greater awareness of social (in)justices. He concludes that lifelong learning and sustainability are inextricably linked and the need to integrate the principles and practices of environmental sustainability and justice to the reality of lifelong learning is more important than ever.

Chapters Two and Three in certain ways make something of a pair, and continue the discussions about sustaining communities which began in the first chapter. In Chapter Two, Rob Mark looks at ways in which members of communities can be empowered to consider social justice by learning about equality and reconciliation. He shows how this develops as learners begin to understand how the inequalities of people living in (sometimes apparently opposing) communities are experienced. He explains that he policy agenda for lifelong learning is significantly different between the two political jurisdictions in Ireland, with a focus on meeting the needs of the economy in the North and a greater emphasis on equality and social cohesion in the South. His chapter is developed from a peace funded action research project in Ireland, which sought to promote reconciliation and peacebuilding through an exploration of equality and social inclusion issues affecting the lives of literacy learners. Mark draws on the work of Paolo Freire, outlined in the introduction to this book, to show how adult literacy needs to be contextualised in a wider debate about struggle against injustice. He shows how non-text/creative methodologies developed in communities can enable learners to expand their understandings of equality through involvement in a participatory process involving critical thinking and problem solving, providing a sense of identity and purpose which can be used to promote greater equality, social justice and mutual understanding. Mark concludes that a more holistic, contextualised approach is required in meeting literacy needs and practices which can transform individuals, neighbourhoods and communities.

Chapter Three extends some of this discussion, with Paul Nolan exploring women, education and peacebuilding in Northern Ireland. He draws by way of example on a campaign focussed on a women's centre located in what he describes as the 'republican heartland of Catholic West Belfast'. He goes on to show how the campaign to save the centre was supported from women's organisations within the Protestant unionist community. Nolan argues that there are three distinct but overlapping domains in women's movements: feminist groups, community-based women's centres and peace campaign groups. The potential of women's education to contribute to social justice has been framed by the relations between the three, which have all contributed in their own ways to the creation of women's spaces which enable the development of alternative political values. Nolan's chapter begins by looking at how feminist politics first came to be expressed in Belfast, considering the growth and significance of neighbourhood-based women's centres, before turning to women's peace campaigns. He concludes that the idea that discourses developed at community level are constitutive of new forms of politics may be part of the inflation of hopes that accompanies the emergence of political settlements, but that such ideas have been useful in considering the ways in which bridges may be built through women's social practices of learning within, through and between communities.

In Chapter Four, Sue Webb moves the discussion from community learning into higher education through a consideration of 'the good university' and community engagement. She explores meanings of 'good', arguing that particular definitions of 'good' predominate in universities in neoliberal times. She analyses the discourses and practices of lifelong learning, exploring how universities construct their social communities and identify with whom they choose to work. Webb argues that although the growth of neoliberalism suggests that conceptions of 'goodness', even in relation to community engagement, may be informed by an audit and managerial culture, some universities have at the core of their missions an engagement with communities that recognises that one of the purposes of a liberal higher education is to develop active citizens who are able to participate in the democratic conversation of the country and society more widely. As Webb points out, some of this struggle was undertaken in the past by women who came together through the suffrage movement and trade union and co-operative movement campaigning for the right to vote, for access to skilled employment, trade union membership, and higher education. She suggests that the current turn towards community engagement may be understood as a strategy of re-visioning missions and reacting against the globalising tendencies of selectivity and exclusivity that so often mark discussions of 'good' universities.

References

Annette, J. (2003) 'Community, politics and citizenship education', in Lockyer, A., Crick, B., and Annette, J (eds), *Education for democratic citizenship: theory and practice*. Aldershot: Ashgate Publishing.

Raco, M. (2005), 'Sustainable development, rolled-out neoliberalism and sustainable communities', *Antipodes* 37: 2, 324–47.

Roseland, M. (2005) *Towards sustainable communities*. British Columbia: New Society Publishers.

CHAPTER ONE

Lifelong learning and environmental sustainability

JOHN BLEWITT

Introduction

There is little doubt our world is changing and not necessarily for the better. The vociferousness of the global warming sceptics has grown increasingly shrill as the scientific consensus around anthropogenic climate change has become firmly established. Disaster is in the air. Global poverty, gender inequity, AIDS and HIV, illiteracy, drugs and human trafficking, deforestation, war, desertification, resource exploitation and alarming rates of species extinction have seen the film industry capture the zeitgeist in a string of dramatic social and eco disaster movies – *The Day After Tomorrow, 28 Days, 2012, The Road*, etc. There have also been many well made environmental documentaries that have proved to be both effective and motivational teaching tools – *An Inconvenient Truth, The End of Suburbia* and *The Age of Stupid*. Grassroots actions in many communities have seen people learning to live, work and produce in new ways designed to respect the ecological integrity of the planet, encourage civic participation, foster intercultural learning and facilitate the emergence of a sense of global citizenship and connectedness. Groups affiliated to the Low Carbon Communities and the Transition Town networks are exploring forms of low carbon living that are powerfully rooted in a sense of place and care for the whole environment of which human beings are seen as an integral part. We are of nature. As John Dewey (2002: 296) writes,

> *Human nature exists and operates in an environment. And it is not 'in' that environment as coins are in a box, but as a plant is in the sunlight and soil. It is of them, continuous with their energies, dependent upon their support, capable of increase only as it affects them, and as it gradually rebuilds from their crude indifference an environment genially civilised.*

Increasing numbers of people from many cultural and ethnic backgrounds are bypassing mainstream political processes and formal education institutions and are learning to do things for themselves. Indeed, a great deal of the learning about our unsustainability has occurred outside the formal education system despite the very real achievements of some ecoschools, the growth of courses directly addressing environmental sustainability within the Higher Education sector and the bringing together of sustainability with skills development, non-formal and informal community based action with cross sector regional alliances in the diverse and multifaceted area known as lifelong learning (Bagnall, 2009).

Education for Sustainable Development (ESD)

The reason why so much Education (or learning) for Sustainable Development (ESD) has occurred informally or nonformally is quite clear. Formal education policy at every level in the UK (and elsewhere) has until recently taken note of, but in no way energetically endorsed, the need for education and training practices to serve the environment, to maintain ecosystem services or in any meaningful sense, lessen our environmental footprint. For many years there have been tentative institutional and policy discussions on sustainability skills development, environmental management and broader social responsibilities. Probably greatest progress has been made in the primary sector but, as businesses are beginning to recognise the need to demonstrate greener credentials and professional associations are requiring their members to be conversant with the basics of sustainability, schools, colleges and universities are engaging in serious curriculum change and implementing estates management practices that aim to reduce the carbon footprint of the institution. There have also been many activities at grassroots community level with organisations such as the non-governmental organisation Groundwork being funded to design and deliver learning and development programmes for community groups, local authorities and other bodies on sustainability, energy conservation, climate change adaptation, empowerment and the like. The Qualification and Curriculum Authority (QCA) now offers extensive advice and guidance on ESD. The Learning and Skills Council (LSC), responsible for non-advanced post compulsory education, has stated that by 2010 'the learning and skills sector will proactively commit and contribute to sustainable development through its management of resources, the learning opportunities it delivers and its engagement with employers and communities'(LSC, 2009: 2). Similarly, in December 2009 the school inspectorate, Ofsted, issued a report (Ofsted, 2009: 6) recommending that all schools should 'make sustainability a priority in their improvement plans to ensure they are meeting their commitment to become a sustainable school by 2020' and 'develop a whole-school approach to education for sustainability in the curriculum to enable it to become firmly embedded in teaching and learning'. Generally though, the skills development that continues to dominate education policy focuses sharply on the needs of the economy as conventionally understood – growth, income, enterprise and development. Building on the 2006 Leitch Review of Skills (Leitch, 2006), the 2009 White Paper, *Skills for Growth: the national skills strategy* (BIS, 2009a) and strategy document Skills Investment Strategy 2010–11 (BIS, 2009b) refers to 'sustainable employment' or 'sustainable work' as meaning paid labour that is neither short term or part time putting faith in a 'business as usual' economic development that will produce more jobs (Thomson, 2009). There remains a possibility that associated education and training will simply raise qualification requirements for existing employments while leaving the most deprived people largely where they are (Gough, Eisenschitz and McCulloch, 2006). Instead, a 'paradigm shift' in education, lifelong learning and economic development thinking needs to occur for, without it, no meaningful progress towards sustainability and social justice can be made (Sterling, 2001; Blewitt, 2004).

However, there are some positive signs. We are, after all, half way through the United Nation's Decade for Education for Sustainable Development. Within UK Higher Education two Centres of Excellence in Teaching and Learning (CETL), funded by the Higher Education Funding Council for England (HEFCE), and the ESD subject centre within the Higher Education Academy (HEA) have been extremely active, although the long term influence of these projects has yet to be evaluated. There are also complementary international developments. The United Nations University initiative establishing Regional Centres for Expertise (RCE) in Education for Sustainability bring together education providers with private, public and third sector bodies to promote sustainability learning in a range of disciplinary, professional and geographic areas (Mochizuki and Fadeeva, 2008). The number of RCEs is growing steadily with currently 66 established throughout the world. The European Union's pronouncements and policies on lifelong learning and sustainability are also leading to the development of valuable networks, knowledge exchanges, curriculum innovations and capacity building opportunities. In 2007, the European Association for the Education of Adults (EAEA) held a conference on the role of continuous education in sustainable development. In 2009, ADAPT (a European Union initiative designed to help the workforce adapt to industrial change and the information society), the University of Modene e Reggio Emilia (Italy) and Etech Germany organised an international conference on the greening of human capital and, in the same year, the Regional Co-operation Council of South Eastern Europe held an International Conference on Fostering and Building Human Capital for Sustainable Knowledge Societies in Bucharest, Romania. In the United Kingdom, the National Institute of Adult and Continuing Education (NIACE) initiated an *Inquiry into the Future for Lifelong Learning* (IFLL) along themes including prosperity and work, poverty reduction, demography and social structure, well-being and happiness, migration, crime and social exclusion, citizenship, technological change and sustainable development.

Understood holistically, all of these areas contribute to processes of sustainable development of which human and environmental well being are central. John Field's excellent IFLL thematic report, *Well-being and Happiness*, sees well-being as one of the most important outcomes of adult learning. He writes (Field, 2009: 14–15),

> *For learners, a positive outlook on the future and a sense of one's ability to take charge of one's life are indispensable to further, continuing successful learning. Well- being is also associated with better health, higher levels of social and civic engagement, and greater resilience in the face of external crises. (. . .) While income does have an impact on well-being, once a society has dealt with extremes of inequality, the obsessive pursuit of economic growth for its own sake may solve few of the problems that individuals and communities face, calling into question the primacy of the economic in determining education and training policy.*

Field makes clear connections between well-being and other IFLL themes – crime, migration, employment, demography, technological change and citizenship – but unfortunately fails to embrace all of these in an overarching discussion of sustainable development of which well-being, justice, participation and equity are essential characteristics. There is, however, a separate IFLL report on Sustainable Development, Citizenship and Belonging (Plant and Ward, 2009).

Social capital, family relationships, community cohesion and cultural diversity are significant elements in what David Halpern calls 'the hidden wealth of nations' for they often have a greater instrumental value than tightly focused vocational training and skills development. For example, markets work more effectively when there is also a significant level of trust and a higher level of educational achievement is often recorded in schools and communities where both children and parents tend to know one another (Halpern, 2009). A sense of community based 'collective efficacy', most useful when confronting neighbourhood crime and maintaining community health, often develops in areas with high degrees of social capital (Sampson, Morenoff and Gannon-Rowley, 2002; Sampson, 2004). Social capital creates freedoms and possibilities which can be seen as forming the basis for sustainable development and social justice. As Field (2009: 38) writes, '[T]he entire workforce requires skills, resilience and flexibility to cope and thrive in the changing landscape of work' and, of course, present day skill needs must be met but 'a broad portfolio of capabilities for the future' also needs to be generated. What these capabilities are, or could be, are being debated vigorously. IFLL discussions of citizenship have identified four fundamental capabilities that encompass finance, health, digital inclusion and civic participation which could provide learners with enhanced learning and social opportunities. However, future social and economic well-being cannot ignore the environment and as we discuss the need for a just and ecologically sustainable society it is useful to turn to the work of John Dewey, Amartya Sen and Martha C. Nussbaum.

Sustainability, skills and capabilities

Education is not, and never has been, value-free. There are well entrenched habits, beliefs and emotional proclivities, socioeconomic structures, events and power relationships that mediate the effectiveness of formal education as an agent for change. For John Dewey, human conduct concerns both habits and routines and the interpellation of values, intentions, desires, intelligence, impulses and judgments in action and it is human conduct that is at the core of the educative process. Human actions are in effect 'invasions of the future' but it is the present which is ours for the future has to be made through present actions. Therefore, in order to act, it is important to know what to do and what the quality of that act is and the likely consequences which will follow. These consequences may be difficult to determine but through deliberation and learning, it should be possible to appraise proposed actions on the basis of perceived tendencies and current circumstances. This makes education and learning an important capability (or freedom) helping individuals understand what lies before them and what type of lives they will have good reason to value (Sen, 1999; Nussbaum, 2002). If considered as 'ends in view' with each action, each means, being an end en route to other ends these lives constitute; in effect, the aims of education and learning. What we learn and how we learn shape the future. They are, like means and ends, two names for the same reality and just as for Dewey, pragmatism and deliberation are fully complementary so is education and learning for both are relational. Learning is frequently situated, oscillating in practice between the informal, non-formal and formal, turning means into ends and vice versa. Dewey (2002: 36) writes,

> *Means and ends are two names for the same reality (. . .). We must change what is to be done into a how, the means whereby. (. . .). Only as the end is converted into means is it definitely conceived, or intellectually defined, to say nothing of being executable.*

The capabilities approach, initially emerging from a dialogue between development economics and philosophy, is also about human conduct, about what is desirable and what needs to be done to secure a better quality of life although there is no exact consensus regarding what these may be. However, Nussbaum has identified ten fundamental threshold capabilities essential for human dignity, freedom and flourishing. These are not by any means a final statement for they are open to practical revision and conceptual refinement. They include:

Lift – to live a natural human lifespan and a life worth living
Bodily health and integrity – food, shelter, good health (including reproductive health)

Bodily integrity – being able to move about freely, being secure against violent (including sexual) assault, having opportunities for sexual satisfaction
Senses, imagination, thought – to be cultivated through education – literacy and numeracy, etc., – but also through expressive creativity music, science, religion, art, film
Emotions – being able to have attachments with others, to love and care for
Practical reason – being able to form a conception of the good and to reflect critically on the planning of one's own life
Affiliation (a) being able to live for and in relation to others; (b) having the social bases of self-respect and non-humiliation.
Other species – being able to live with concern for and in relation to animals, plants and the natural world.
Play – enjoy laughter, play and recreation
Control over one's environment (a) political – liberal freedoms of speech and participation; (b) material – being able to own property, have gainful and meaningful employment, enter into positive mutual relationships with others, etc.

These capabilities are quite anthropogenic and Holland (2008) has argued that an additional *meta-capability*, a *sustainable ecological capacity*, is required. For Holland, ecological systems are unique in being a meta-capability because unlike social, political, and economic systems, the functioning of ecological systems is absolutely necessary for the exercise of the central human capabilities. They cannot exist outside, or independent of, ecological systems for without them, all organisms (including humans) would lack the bio-, geo-, and chemical conditions that make life possible. This ecological meta-capability is consequently a component of an individual's opportunity set in the same way that property and shelter are components of having control over one's own environment or of bodily health. Ecological conditions also contribute to those wider environmental experiences that make life meaningful, fun and just. Sen (2009) also discusses the power of humans to intervene constructively to improve the environment and further sustainable development. This can empower individuals and communities enhancing the quality (and standard) of life by encouraging people to acknowledge that they can flourish without constantly accumulating material goods. Sen therefore sees education as both an important capability and as a functioning i.e. something enabling individuals to realise the freedom to choose one type of life experience rather than another.

Saito (2003) sees education as having the joint role of enhancing capabilities and opportunities but for Gasper (2002) as well as 'capabilities' it is also important to identify those skills and potentials that will facilitate their realisation which goes beyond having the freedom to choose or even access to appropriate resources like books, computers, school rooms and university libraries. Potential, and its realisation, is linked to power and agency and as the sociologist Zygmunt Bauman (1990: 113) writes, the more power individuals have will increase the range of genuine choices they have and the wider the range of possible decisions that are both realistic and reasonably certain to lead to the consequences they want: 'to have power is to act more freely; but having no power, or less power than others have, means having one's own freedom of choice limited by decisions made by others'. Power is a necessary element of agency and agency is best understood as being both the ability to give direction to one's own life-course and the capacity to influence the conditions that shape the context for action. Knowledge, skills and learning are therefore important aspects of agency.

Human agency should also be understood ecologically. People occupy space and are located within a whole web of relations with which they interact and which interacts with them. A particular environment may be more conducive to some actions than other meaning that humans also act by means-of-an-environment rendering them more 'agentic' in some situations than others. Education, for instance, can be a site of power and power relationships which can be either productive or repressive. The origins of these power relationships will be found in institutional policy, the curriculum, teaching, learning and assessment and in the structure of society and the economy that informs them. Formal education still seems to reproduce social inequalities and cannot by itself restructure society or successfully overturn the still hegemonic business as usual, bottom line, economic growth mentality. As Walker (2008: 155) writes,

> *Becoming an agent through learning is not straightforward for those who are different from the norm that an education system assumes.*

Of course, certain critical pedagogies may raise awareness of social, economic, racial and political inequalities together with the ecological frailties of our world but a blanket call to improve access to education, or raise skill levels, is no guarantee that students will learn to be sustainably literate in either an intellectual or practical sense. Learning takes place in broader social and economic context(s) and individuals tend to shape their preferences to those cultural, consumerist, materialist and competitive values articulated within them. ESD on the other hand, is not business as usual. It articulates norms contrary to the economistic ones dominant in mainstream education and where sustainability and lifelong learning can most productively combine is where the values, habits and motivations of learners derived from their own lived experiences embrace ecological practices, green skills development and community empowerment initiatives achieving a form of agency that will be transformative. There is a pragmatic learning revolution currently taking place and the places where this is happening are shifting temporal perspectives, developing alternative frames of reference and encouraging considerable degrees of reflexivity and reflectiveness.

Knowledge, justice and the green economy

Nico Stehr has written extensively about knowledge and the emergence of knowledge societies. For Stehr (2002: 43), knowledge is a 'capacity for action' and comes largely in three forms: meaningful knowledge affecting mainly the social consciousness of members of society; productive knowledge such as scientific work being converted into ways of directly appropriating natural phenomena; and, action knowledge in which knowledge is an immediate productive force. Information can lead to knowledge but information travels more easily and is less likely to be situated or restricted to specific groups, individuals or organisations. This means that although information can be communicated, diffused and transferred, the acquisition of knowledge is more complex. Stehr (2002: 62) writes,

> *The 'transfer' of knowledge is part of a learning and discovery process that is not necessarily confined to individual learning. Knowledge is not a reliable 'commodity'. It tends to be fragile and demanding, and it has built-in insecurities.*

Formal education and training is clearly important but apart from taking place in a variety of settings and spaces, learning also involves a broad constellation of emotional and cognitive experiences that occur throughout the life course. Climate change is both an economic and an emotional imperative and what is beginning to shape skills development, skills demand and skills requirements are dynamic processes that include our attempt to grapple with the destructiveness of our own unsustainability. Environmental technologies, bioscience and green energy have been identified by Government departments, labour organisations and think tanks as future economic growth areas (BERR, 2009; TUC, 2009). Selwyn and Levett (2006) of the UK Centre for Economic and Environmental Development have forecast that the UK market for Environmental Goods and Services will grow from £25 billion in 2005 to £34 billion in 2010 (42 per cent growth from 2005) and on to £46 billion by 2015. There is money to be made by protecting rather than trashing the environment and apart from opportunities to earn a living many new technologies and technical skills, including those related to ICT, are beginning to rehumanise workforce development after decades of 'Fordist' work practices. The new learning and development needed for a green knowledge economy requires a considerable degree of participation and engagement, autonomy and trust, co-operation and collaboration between professions, trades, disciplines and communities. The dematerialisation of the economy has clearly been underway for some time as knowledge workers of various descriptions have replaced more traditional occupations (Wernick *et al.*, 1996). It has also loosened the bonds between the material dependence of an individual and his/her occupational status or occupational role perhaps leading to a relative emancipation from the labour market. After all, many people seem to be re-evaluating what constitutes for them personal and household wealth, social well-being and meaning.

As Paul Hawken, Amory and Hunter Lovins (1999), Bill McKibben (2007), Lester Brown (2006) and others have argued, dematerialisation and immaterialisation can enhance the lifestyles and well-being of those living in the wealthy countries without being detrimental to the social and economic development of other nations. Immaterialisation may lead to the replacement of material things we once valued with immaterial ones – social relationships, friendship networks, information services and so on. Formal, non-formal and informal learning frequently interconnect and small scale sustainability projects are useful ways of seeing the interconnections develop. Farmers markets are a fast growing sector in the food economies of many nations and because the food sold in them is locally produced, bought and then taken to nearby homes far less energy is consumed than when consumers drive to out of town supermarkets and buy produce in bulk – produce frequently imported from overseas.

Additionally, people tend to socialise more at farmers markets than in supermarkets building relationships with both fellow-shoppers and producers, learning more about food and their locality in the process. Similarly, localised energy generation from renewable sources can engage whole communities in the planning, development and operation of particular schemes. In their review of community renewable energy in the UK, Walker and Devine-Wright (2008) suggest that the issues of equity in the distribution of costs and benefits are extremely important for local people for if they feel they are getting nothing from the project resentment, division and bad feeling will result. Local involvement in renewable community energy projects are therefore nurturing learning experiences that are witnessing a growing support for renewable energy and a growing understanding of the need to lower a community's carbon footprint while being an object lesson in the paramount importance of social equity and democratic participation. Research by Shum and Watanabe (2008) on the local deployment of solar photovoltaic systems also indicates that new technical learning can occur in all types of grid connected small PV projects and, when certificated, learning in renewable energy installation can help build the educational infrastructure necessary for further developments. New media technologies also have a major role in promoting a green, knowledge based economy (GeSI, 2008; SCF Associates, 2009), although job creation in hi tech areas will not compensate for job losses in the old industrial ones, our future economic dependence on green knowledge is clear. Economic growth and full employment have been predicated on cheap and abundant fossil fuels for a long time but climate change and resource depletion is urgently requiring new thinking, new learning and new business models.

Two recent reports have outlined how 'a green new deal' could create prosperity without growth but would necessarily place significant demands on formal education and lifelong learning to articulate the conservation of eco-system services as its primary goal. The Green New Deal Group (2008; 38–39) writes,

> *There will be a need for a training, education, research and development programme for the 'carbon army' of workers needed to bring about a low-carbon future. To reduce carbon dramatically will require expertise ranging from energy analysis, design and production of hi-tech renewable alternatives, large-scale engineering projects such as combined heat and power, and offshore wind at the high skilled end; through to medium and unskilled work making every building*

energy tight, and fitting more efficient energy systems in homes, offices and factories.

Tim Jackson, Economics Commissioner with the UK Sustainable Development Commission, goes further (Jackson, 2009). Growth, he writes, was once the dynamo of industrialisation but it was growth that has been the ultimate cause of the recent credit crunch and economic downturn. Although some economists may argue that growth can continue if we become more resource efficient this would be to dangerously conflate the *relative* with the *absolute* decoupling of the economy from resource consumption. Thus, although global carbon intensity has fallen from one kilo per dollar of economic activity to just under 770 grams per dollar, there is little evidence to suggest that the global economy has witnessed any overall reduction in resource throughput. The world is using more energy and producing more 'stuff'. With the global population rising and with social aspirations following suit, the need to stabilise and drastically reduce carbon emissions to limit global temperature rise is obvious but, for this to occur, Jackson estimates that by 2050 global carbon intensity must be around 6 grams per dollar of economic output – 130 times lower than it is today. And, this is to say nothing about incomes being distributed more equitably among nations. So, although small scale individualistic lifestyle changes are important – driving less, insulating the home, walking more, etc. – only fundamental structural and cultural changes can really make a difference. Jackson (2009: 11) identifies two ways in which this could be done:

The first is to dismantle the perverse incentives for unproductive status competition. The second must be to establish new structures that provide capabilities for people to flourish – and in particular to participate meaningfully and creatively in the life of society – in less materialistic ways. The advantages in terms of prosperity are likely to be substantial. A less materialistic society will enhance life satisfaction. A more equal society will lower the importance of status goods. A less growth-driven economy will improve people's work-life balance. Enhanced investment in public goods will provide lasting returns to the nation's prosperity.

These approaches will also address significant and unacceptable inequalities in many communities' access to public goods, environmental services and experiences of high environmental risk and poor health. Social deprivation is invariably accompanied by environmental injustice for the most deprived communities are frequently the poorest economically, un- or underqualified, workless, living in dirty rundown urban areas with substandard housing, inadequate heating and poor insulation. They invariably experience high crime rates, bad air quality, constant noise, and are often near or on contaminated land. Poor nutrition and ill health are common too because of limited or no access to fresh, healthy and affordable foodstuffs. Agyeman (2005) sees urban poverty in the United States, and elsewhere, as frequently coinciding with racial segregation, low land values and unwanted land uses. Polluters often seek to pollute in areas that will provoke the least political resistance. Many deprived communities are unable to contest these environmental injustices themselves because they are struggling with too many other problems relating to day to day survival. Lucas, Walker, Eames, Fay and Poustie (2004: 111) in their review of research and evidence concerning social and environmental justice in the UK conclude that:

> *Where a neighbourhood or area experiences one environmental problem, this is rarely in isolation; ill health and reduced quality of life is usually the result of an accumulation of these problems over an individual's lifetime or even over a number of generations.*

> *Some sectors of the population groups are consistently more adversely affected than others and these are almost always those that are already recognised as the most vulnerable; environmental ills may not only self-perpetuate, but also lead to other environmental, economic and social problems if left unaddressed.*

Unfortunately, the increasing social polarisation of urban spaces has sometimes led to greater tensions between the needs of disadvantaged groups and government and community initiatives seeking to enhance the overall sustainability infrastructure of urban areas. Pol (2002: 10) writes:

> *The conditions of modern life, especially in the cities, are a major obstacle to the adoption of sustainability values. Social realities differ widely from place to place, but social malaise is emerging in many cities as an expression of dissatisfaction. This situation is characterized by an increase in poverty, the presence of deviant behaviors, a lack of social cohesion in its social fabric, and the implementation of 'individual survival strategies' (...). In these contexts, sustainable development does not appear to be viable.*

Social equity and environmental justice are consequently central tenets of sustainable development and lifelong learning must be ethically and practically more than economistic skills development. A greener economy and a socially sustainable society are interdependent and interconnected for, as Agyeman, Bullard and Evans (2002: 78) argue,

> *Sustainability ... cannot be simply a 'green', or 'environmental' concern, important though 'environmental' aspects of sustainability are. A truly sustainable society is one where wider questions of social needs and welfare, and economic opportunity are integrally related to environmental limits imposed by supporting ecosystems.*

Thus the social environment, including the economy, is part of, and dependent on, the actual physical one. As Hugh McDonald (2004) shows in his book *John Dewey and Environmental Philosophy*, it is extremely important to see the environment as a web of interconnecting relations vital for the maintenance and sustenance of human, social and ecological well-being. The world is always changing, is always 'in the making' and it is the biosphere that ultimately enables human individuals to thrive, grow and flourish. Ethically, this means the environment, perceived both holistically and naturalistically, has a greater moral significance than any individual desire for increased material wealth, status or profit. For sustainability practitioners, educators and others, economic activity, skills development and social learning comes firmly within the scope of moral or right conduct and the realisation of those threshold capabilities that can fashion a more sustainable world. In other words, the triple crunch of climate, energy and recession must help concentrate our minds on the fact that sustainability and lifelong learning is not only about educating engineers, scientists, city planners, designers, etc. in colleges and universities but also entails the non-formal and informal learning of citizens, cultural groups and community members living and working in a whole array of places and spaces which have their own pedagogic import.

Places of learning and a critical pedagogy of place

Where we live, work and play are places of, and spaces for, learning (Blewitt, 2006). They are part of us, of what we are and of how we perceive the world but these places and spaces are rarely static. They do not remain the same for ever, or even for long. As the economy changes and urban areas become redeveloped, gentrified or ghettoised, as new media technologies alter the way we communicate with each other or access learning and information, new demands are placed on us to adapt, accommodate and act. Economic migration has changed the social, political and cultural complexion of many urban areas spatialising life chances and opportunities. Stephen Nathan Haymes (1995: 114) has written powerfully of the need for black urban communities in the United States to establish pedagogical conditions which will enable them 'to critically interpret how dominant definitions and uses of urban space regulate and control how they organise their identity around territory' and resist oppression and disadvantage. Part of this process involves retrieving a black popular vernacular through the telling of stories and narratives that are not encoded or assimilated completely by the wider consumerist [white] culture or the glossy images of urban regeneration with its private-public spaces, shopping malls and surveillance cameras. These new private-public spaces socially segregate the physical urban environment correlating not so much with a fear of crime but with a fear of difference and a fear of strangers that is inimical to the generation of social trust, associational democracy and sustainable community (Mitchell, 2005; Minton, 2009). Issues of power, discrimination and inequality are linked to the broader ecological challenges by the actions of environmental justice campaigners and have been discussed by sustainability educators such as Chet Bowers (2001). His writing on eco-justice education develops our understanding of the relationship between ecological and cultural systems, environmental racism, the revitalisation of non-commodified social traditions and the development of sustainable lifestyles. Gruenewald (2003) writes of a critical pedagogy of place enabling learners to appreciate more fully how struggles against human oppression and the experience of being in connection with others and the natural world are again two sides of the same reality. Critical pedagogies may emerge from the particular attributes of a given location. They are invariably transdisciplinary, experiential, reflective, intergenerational and potentially intercultural. Critical pedagogy may also mean engaging in some unlearning to enable the emergence of an individual's or community's ecological identity and socioecological values. He writes (2003: 7):

> *Human communities, or places, are politicized, social constructions that often marginalize individuals, groups, as well as ecosystems. If place-based educators seek to connect place with self and community, they must identify and confront the ways that power works through places to limit the possibilities for human*

and non-human others. Their place-based pedagogy must, in other words, be critical.

There have been a number of popular education initiatives in the US and the UK pursuing Frierian goals of 'conscientisation', social action and environmental justice (Scandrett, 1999; Scandrett, O'Leary and Martinez, 2005). Organisations like the London Sustainability Exchange work in culturally diverse urban neighbourhoods combining learning with practical action that individually and collectively enhance community members' capacity to realise those capabilities that will improve their standard and quality of living. Community gardens are frequently important sites for social learning reconnecting urban dwellers with the natural world, other cultures and other people. Sharing takes place as a matter of course and a sense of well-being, personal growth and community identity can develop through the organic growing of food, the caring of a small plot of land and, more than just occasionally, fighting against urban development (von Hassell, 2005). The implementation of design-led scenarios for a sustainable everyday urban living can also fashion learning and transform experience in new directions. The Italian designer Ezio Manzini (2004) has outlined a wide range of enticing possibilities ranging from the flexible use of space in existing buildings, the development of food tasting groups, co-operative energy generation, ICT connectivity hubs, transport rental systems, sustainable micro-enterprises, co-operative networks, the extended home and many more. The role of newly designed and constructed green buildings including social housing, universities and schools as well as larger iconic structures have immense pedagogic potential (Alfieri, 2009). More broadly, the Transition Town movement is composed of communities and neighbourhoods developing their own grassroots responses to peak oil and climate change. The movement has spread to over 250 communities worldwide and embraces small villages, affluent market towns and multi cultural inner city districts such as Brixton and Tooting in London. Community groups explore and develop how their own energy descent plans marry into new and more sustainable ways of securing food, health, transport, business opportunities, local currencies and so on. These transition communities are creating a pedagogy of place that in their intended ecological resilience could prefigure wider systemic social changes (Hopkins, 2008).

Culture, memory and intangible heritage is an important part of lifelong learning and sustainable development too. Brick Lane is a street in the Whitechapel district of East London that over three centuries has welcomed successive waves of immigrants escaping political or religious persecution or just seeking better opportunities for making a living. Immigrants have included French Huguenots in the eighteenth century, east European Jews in the nineteenth century and Bangladeshis in the twentieth and twenty first centuries. Brick Lane has seen many trades practised, diverse political views espoused, and even places of worship shifting ecumenical allegiance.

Discussions, disputes and deliberations about the character of the neighbourhood – what it is, what it was, what it might become – have been subjects of television documentaries, feature films, novels, memoirs, local history projects, art exhibitions, planning inquiries, architectural design briefs, poems, pub talk and community education classes. Deliberation is a public learning experience, as the debates around the proposal to erect an illuminated 30 metre tall steel minaret outside the Jamme Masjid Mosque testify. The mosque was formerly the Machzike Hadath Synagogue, and before that a Methodist Chapel and the Huguenot Church La Neuve Eglise. The minaret is now part of the locality's 'cultural trail' which local councillors hope will boost tourism and attract new business. Urban development money has been allocated for the improvement of parks, streets and other open spaces, the construction of a new purpose build Osmani Youth Centre and the restoration of 17 Grade 2 listed buildings which combined with the restoration of other privately owned but once decrepit Georgian dwellings serve to retrieve another architectural and cultural past. Asian restaurants and takeaways have replaced Jewish tailors, bagel shops and haberdashers and new chic stores have encouraged an influx of customers from outside the neighbourhood who themselves collude in changing the sense of a place.

Urban development, the growth of hi-tech dot.com and fashionable design businesses together with attendant gentrification may be a way of modernising Brick Lane, making it fitter for the purpose of making money and improving local image. Place marketing means Brick Lane is now 'Banglatown' – a place where yuppies can find a good curry. But not everyone agrees. In searching for her own roots, Rachel Lichtenstein (2007) tells the stories of many residents, of many pasts, of many gains and losses including those of organic community and historic identity. The assumption that development benefits everyone, that a trickle-down effect will result from the gentrification and economic development process, is disputed by many of those to whom she gives voice.

These views are substantiated by the academic research of Loretta Lees (2008) who argues that gentrification does not usually lead to social mixing. Incoming middle classes prefer to self-segregate and gentrification is really a revanchist attempt of the more affluent to retake the city from its poorer neighbours. Brick Lane seems to be no exception but the story is not that simple or straightforward. In nearby Spitalfields there is a city farm where the Green Fair and Spitalfields Show regularly exhibits locally produced and often organic foodstuffs, sells Fairtrade goods, provides information on climate change, energy conservation and much more. The old meat market has been redeveped with attractive energy efficient lighting and in May 2009 it hosted an 'Alternative Fashion Week' whose aim was to raise environmental awareness, support recycling and promote ethical sourcing. 10,000 people attended. Brick Lane and its surrounding area, like many others, is a social, ecological, cultural and political area replete with vibrant learning possibilities. Lichtenstein (2007: 253–4) quotes the cultural critic Sukhdev Sandhu as saying,

> *I think of Brick Lane as a model for the rest of the country or even the rest of the world. I have learned to live with otherness here in so many different ways. People try to shield themselves away in most places – look at new gated communities, double glazing – but here you hear the ethnic samples, the laughter, the tears, you are forced to interact with what's happening and there is still variety, it's a place of echoes of the past but not in a sentimental way. (. . .) It is suggestive and haunting in terms of what you can learn from a place.*

Ellsworth (2005) also writes of anomalous places of learning such as streets, movies, art installations, buildings, museums, theatrical spaces, multi-media sites and so on. Each one has a pedagogic import that is not readily recognised by many educators in the formal education system but is real nonetheless for these places focus on the experience of learning by the groups or individuals. They deal with change, sensation, intentional and unintentional thinking and the emergence of transitional spaces where new opportunities and capacities can be developed which relate our inner to our outer worlds – to others, to the environment, to the past and to the future. One such intentional place of learning has been provided by the ecological drama-documentary *The Age of Stupid*, directed by Franny Armstrong in 2008 and seen and discussed in a wide range of different locations and pedagogic contexts. The film was premiered in

March 2009 in a solar powered tent in Leicester Square (London) and was linked by satellite to 62 other screens across the UK. An independent audit conducted by Carbon Accounting Systems found the event's carbon emissions to be 1 per cent of those produced by a normal blockbuster premiere. From May 2009 the filmmakers launched their Independent Screening model of distribution enabling anyone to buy a license to screen the film at a price based on the purchaser's means. Campaign groups, educators and others consequently organised screenings which were followed by audience debate and commitments to act on what they had seen. By the time of the film's international release in September nearly 700 local screenings had been booked in the UK. In New York a green carpet cinema tent was set up in the downtown area and was linked by satellite to 442 other screens in the USA and to over 200 others in over thirty different countries. Thirty three countries hosted independent screenings with no satellite link. The film was financed by the 'crowd funding' method – donations were invited from individuals and groups who then became investors in the film and entitled to a share of its profits once costs were covered. 228 donations were made totalling £535 000. All this makes *The Age of Stupid* not just another disaster movie but an opportunity for new learning and prefigurative action being part of the 10: 10 campaign which advocates individuals and organisations cut their carbon emissions by 10 per cent in 2010.

The film text itself offers the viewer a scenario of a world in 2055 where ecological disaster has already occurred because we did too little and learnt even less. An archivist, played by Pete Postlethwaite, uses a touch screen, which is in fact the screen through which we see him to retrieve footage shot in the first decade of the twenty-first century, to relate five personalised stories of global warming: survivors' experiences of Hurricane Katrina, the launch of a cheap airline in India, oil exploration in Nigeria and global environmental degradation. Everything depicted is based on current scientific knowledge and predictions and whatever Stupid's merits as a work of art or as an edutainment, its pedagogic purpose is clear and distinct and its impact is both intellectual and visceral. The film has inspired grassroots activity and has engaged national and international figures with special screenings being requested by the United Nations, the World Bank, the US Environmental Protection Agency and President Obama's think-tank. It has become a pedagogic intervention in the public sphere at a local and global level aiming to stimulate green knowledge, democratic deliberation, participation and political action without the controlling influence of government and the big corporations. As Jamison (2003: 715) writes, it is:

> ... crucial that there remain open in our societies other spaces, non-corporate spaces for social learning and cognitive praxis. We need a public sphere that means something; we need to have opportunities for coming together, for sharing what we know, for discussing freely and critically the challenges that confront us collectively, as communities and societies. Effective public engagement in environmental politics needs, of course, people who are willing to be involved, who, in one of its various forms, have an 'ecological consciousness'; but there are also a number of supportive conditions, or social innovations, that are even more important if that consciousness, so to speak, is be cultivated and contribute to cultural transformation.

Conclusion

The financial crunch has occurred simultaneously with the climate crunch and the global energy crunch. We live in a world where eco systems are collapsing and our industrial mode of economic growth and development can only exacerbate the situation. Greener ways of living, working and producing wealth have been identified and are possible. In some areas environmental technologies are available to ease the path to immaterialisation, greater resource efficiency, renewable energy generation and social justice. Lifelong learning and sustainability are inextricably linked for lifelong learning is about empowerment, formal and informal learning, skills development and the realisation of individual and collective capabilities that will enable us to lead lives we can value. Education and learning is a capability, a freedom that can unlock a sustainable future so long as that is something we desire and work for.

Clearly then, a more sustainable world must be an end in view for education and learning too. If it is not, then we are certainly living in the age of stupid. But how we get there is important too. Grand plans and utopian dreams are fascinating but taking practical, incremental and pragmatic action that values the whole of the environment, and not just one element of it, is key to this future. Professional education, vocational training and community learning and skills development are essential to this process. Lifelong learning must enable individuals to be citizens and community members as well as economically productive workers. Schools, colleges and universities are places where people must learn skills and knowledge that will make a sustainable world but formal educational institutions are not the only or even the most significant ones where this will or is taking place. So, if there is to be a paradigm shift in our formal education system there must also be one in the wider society. Without it, educational institutions cannot, and will not, change enough. Thus, it is human nature and conduct in all its spheres, intricacies and complexities that is the ground on which a lifelong learning practice for sustainability and environmental justice has to be built. It means changing our existing habits, impulses and routines, applying our intelligence in new ways and deliberating democratically on how we wish to live our lives. One rigidity must not replace another. We must appraise present and proposed actions and continually do so pragmatically and imaginatively. 'Even the most comprehensive deliberation leading to the most momentous choice only fixes a disposition which has to be continuously applied in new and unforeseen conditions, re-adapted by future deliberations' (Dewey, 2002: 208). We must continually learn and relearn throughout life. Only by so doing, we will change ourselves and our world in a more sustainable direction.

References

Agyeman, J. (2005) *Sustainable communities and the challenge of environmental justice*. New York: New York University Press.

Agyeman, J., Bullard, R. and Evans, B. (2002) 'Exploring the nexus: bringing together sustainability, environmental justice and equity', *Space and Polity*, 6, 77–90.

Alfieri, T. (2009) *Sustainable buildings as teaching tools: 4 strategies for integrating buildings into experiential learning*. Available at: http://www.ohlone.edu/org/collegeadvancement/articles/20092010/20090924sustainablebuildingsasteachingtools.html .

Bagnall, R. G. (2009) 'Lifelong learning as an idea for our times: An extended review', *International Journal of Lifelong Education*, 28: 2, 277–85.

Baumann, Z. (1990) *Thinking sociologically*. Oxford: Blackwell.

BERR (2009) *New Industry, New Jobs*. London: HMSO.

BIS (2009a) *Skills for growth: the national skills strategy*. Available at: http://www.bis.gov.uk/wp-content/uploads/publications/Skills-Strategy.pdf

BIS (2009b) *Skills investment strategy 2010–11*. Available at: http://www.bis.gov.uk/wp-content/uploads/publications/Skills-Investment-Strategy.pdf .

Blewitt J. (2004) 'Sustainability and lifelong learning', in Blewitt, J. and Cullingford, C. (eds) *The sustainability curriculum*. London: Earthscan.

Blewitt, J. (2006) *The ecology of learning*. London: Earthscan.

Bowers, C. A. (2001). *Educating for eco-justice and community*. Athens GA: The University of Georgia Press.

Brown, L. R. (2006) *Plan B 2.0: rescuing a planet under stress and a civilization in trouble*. New York: Norton.

Dewey, J. (1922/2002) *Human nature and conduct*. New York: Prometheus Books.

Ellsworth, E. (2005) *Places of learning: media architecture pedagogy*. London: RoutledgeFalmer.

Field, J. (2009) *Well-being and happiness*. IFLL Thematic Paper 4. Leicester: NIACE.

Gasper, D. (2002) 'Is Sen's capability approach an adequate basis for considering human development?' *Review of Political Economy*, 14: 4, 435–57.

GeSI (2008) *SMART 2020: enabling the low carbon economy in the information age*. Available at: http://www.gesi.org/LinkClick.aspx?fileticket=tbp5WRTHUoY%3D&tabid .

Gough, J., Eisenschitz, A. and McCulloch, A. (2006) *Spaces of Social Exclusion*. London, Routledge.

Green New Deal Group (2008) *A Green New Deal*. London, New Economics Foundation.

Hawken, P., Lovins, A. B. and Lovins L. H. (1999) *Natural capitalism: the next industrial revolution*. London, Earthscan.

Haymes, S. N. (1995) *Race, culture and the city: a pedagogy for black urban struggle*. New York: State University of New York Press.

Holland, B. (2008) 'Capacity is a meta-capability: justice and the environment in Nussbaum's 'Capabilities Approach': why sustainable ecological capacity is a meta-capability', *Political Research Quarterly*, 61: 2, 319–32.

Hopkins, R. (2008) *Transition town handbook*. Totnes, Green Books.

Jackson, T. (2009) *Prosperity without growth: the transition to a sustainable economy*. London: Sustainable Development Commission.

Jamison, A. (2003) 'The making of green knowledge: the contribution from activism', *Futures*, 35, 703–16.

Lees, L. (2008) 'Gentrification and social mixing: towards an inclusive urban renaissance?' *Urban Studies*, 45: 12, 2449–70.

Leitch, S. (2006) *Prosperity for all in the global economy – world class skills*. London: HMSO.

Lichtenstein, R. (2007) *On Brick Lane*. London: Penguin Books.

LSC (2009) *LSC sustainable development action plan 2009/10*. Available at: http://readingroom.lsc.gov.uk/lsc/National/LSC_Sustainable_Development_Action_Plan_2009-10.pdf .

Lucas, K., Walker, G., Eames, M., Fay, H. and Poustie, M. (2004) *Environment and social justice: rapid research and evidence review*. London: Policy Studies Institute/Sustainable Development research Network.

Manzini, E (2004) *Scenarios of sustainable ways of living: Local and global visions*. Available at: http://www.sustainable-everyday.net .

McDonald, H. P. (2004) *John Dewey and environmental philosophy*. New York: State University of New York Press.

McKibben, B. (2007) *Deep economy: the wealth of communities and the durable future*. New York: Times Books.

Minton, A. (2009) *Ground Control: fear and happiness in the twenty-first century city*. London: Penguin Books.

Mitchell, D. (2005) 'The S.U.V. model of citizenship: floating bubbles, buffer zones, and the rise of the "purely atomic" individual', *Political Geography*, 24: 1, 77–100.

Mochizuki, Y. and Fadeeva, Z. (2008) 'Regional centres of expertise on education for sustainable development (RCEs): an overview', *International Journal of Sustainability in Higher Education*, 9: 4, 369–81.

Nussbaum M. (2000) *Women and human development: the capabilities approach*. Cambridge: Cambridge University Press.

Ofsted (2009) *Education for sustainable development: improving schools – improving lives*. Available at: http://www.ofsted.gov.uk/Ofsted-home/Publications-and-research/Browse-all-by/Documents-by-type/Thematic-reports/Education-for-sustainable-development-improving-schools-improving-lives .

Plant, H. and Ward, J. (2009) *Lifelong learning, citizenship and sustainable development*. Leicester: NIACE.

Pol, E. (2002) 'The theoretical background of the city-identity-sustainability network', *Environment and Behavior*, 34: 1, 8–25.

Saito, M. (2003) 'Amartya Sen's capability approach to education: a critical exploration', *Journal of Philosophy of Education*, 37: 1, 17–34.

Sampson, R. J. (2004) 'Neighbourhood and community: collective efficacy and community safety', *New Economy*, 106–13.

Sampson, R. J., Morenoff, J. D. and Gannon-Rowley, T. (2002) 'Assessing

"Neighbourhood Effects": social processes and new directions in research', *Annual Review of Sociology*, 28, 443–78

Scandrett, E, O'Leary, T. and Martinez, T. (2005) 'Learning environmental justice through dialogue', in *Making knowledge work*. Leicester: NIACE.

Scandrett, E. (1999) 'Cultivating knowledge: education, the environment and conflict', in Crowther, J. Martin, I. and Shaw, M. (eds) *Popular education and social movements in Scotland today*. Leicester: NIACE.

SCF Associates (2009) *A green knowledge society: an ICT policy agenda to 2015 for Europe's future knowledge society*. Available at: http://ec.europa.eu/information_society/eeurope/i2010/greenknowledgesociety.pdf.

Selwyn, J. and Leveret, B. (2006) *Emerging markets in the environmental industries sector*. UK CEED.

Sen, A. (1999) *Development as freedom*. New York: Alfred Knopf.

Sen, A. (2009) *The idea of justice*. London: Allen Lane.

Shum, K.L. and Watanabe, C. (2008) 'Towards a local learning (innovation) model of solar photovoltaic deployment', *Energy Policy*, 36: 2, 508–21.

Stehr, N. (2002) *Knowledge and economic conduct: the social foundations of the modern economy*. Toronto: University of Toronto Press.

Sterling, S. (2001) *Sustainable education*. Totnes: Green Books.

The Age of Stupid (2009) d. Fanny Armstrong, GB. http://www.ageofstupid.net/

Thomson, A. (2009) 'New strategy, same old story', *Adults Learning*, December, 8–10.

TUC/Impetus Consulting Ltd (2009) *Unlocking green enterprise: a low-carbon strategy for the UK economy*. London: TUC.

von Hassell, M. (2005) 'Community gardens in New York City', in Bartlett, P.G. (ed) *Urban place: reconnecting with the natural world*. Cambridge MA: MIT Press.

Walker, G. and Devine-Wright, P. (2008) 'Community renewable energy: What should it mean?' *Energy Policy*, 36: 2, 497–500

Walker, M, (2008) 'Human capability, mild perfectionism and thickened educational praxis', *Pedagogy, Culture and Society*, 16: 2, 149–62.

Ward, J. (2009) 'Lessons from Copenhagen', Wednesday, December 23, Available at http://www.niace.org.uk/news/lessons-from-copenhagen.

Wernick, I. K., Herman, R., Govind, S. and Ausubel, J. H. (1996) 'Materialization and dematerialization: measures and trends', *Daedalus*, 125: 3, 171–98.

CHAPTER TWO

Literacy, lifelong learning and social inclusion: Empowering learners to learn about equality and reconciliation through lived experiences

Rob Mark

Introduction

This chapter examines the relationship between literacy, lifelong learning and social inclusion. It looks at ways in which learning from personal experiences can empower learners through an exploration of inequalities affecting their lives. The chapter draws from learner experiences which were recorded through a peace funded action research project in Ireland, The Literacy and Equality in Irish Society Project (LEIS: 2004–6), which sought to promote reconciliation and peacebuilding through an exploration of equality and social inclusion issues affecting the lives of literacy learners. Grounded on theories of literacy that focus on power relations and inequalities, the chapter describes how learners engaged with the process through exploring equality and social justice issues which affected their lives. Inspired by the post-conflict situation in Ireland, the project argues that learners can develop an understanding of conflicting or fractured relationships which have affected their lives. This can in turn promote a better understanding of the peacebuilding process and the need for reconciliation in Ireland. Through the promotion of learning for reconciliation and peace building learners can also be empowered to further participate in a process of critically engagement and citizenship. To enable learners to learn from their experiences, the project experimented with the use of non-text methods of learning. The chapter argues that these approaches can be effective in enabling learners to improve their understanding of equality issues.

The discourse outlines the processes involved in reconciliation and peace building, examining a framework for dialogue and reflexive practice for adult literacy learning. Finally, it explores the potential role which civic education (whether formal, non-formal or informal) can play in overcoming barriers to learning (intellectual, attitudinal, cultural, physical) and in creating an environment where people feel comfortable and motivated to learn. Such an environment can in turn create the kind of opportunities which promote more sustainable, peaceful relationships and structures for promoting a culture of peace. The findings have a powerful message for the development of adult literacy education. The process and methodology are relevant not only for the development of literacy provision in areas of conflict, but also in all societies where there is a desire to promote improved inter-community relations and an inclusive citizenship based on democratic dialogue. The message arising from the research has local and global relevance. It demonstrates how learners can develop new knowledge and skills based on a greater understanding of inequalities affecting their lives. It also shows how creative approaches can empower learners to change their lives in different ways, e.g. through gaining employment, through engaging in learning for their own personal development or through enabling them to effect change in the everyday life experience at community level.

Connecting literacy, equality and creativity

Many writers in the field of radical literacy, most notably Paolo Freire (1985), have argued that adult literacy needs to be contextualised in a wider debate about struggle against injustice. As an integral part of the equality agenda, literacy becomes an important tool in the construction and development of a more just and equal society. This chapter focuses on the empowering potential of literacy and its ability to transform society through increased understanding of inequalities in learners.

If one examines the concept of literacy and what it means to be literate, very many different meanings are found. Popular usage of the term extends from the simple notion of the ability to read and write to a host of other ideas including the possession of complex multi-literacy skills such as computer, technical, information, media, visual, cultural, financial, economic, emotional and environmental skills. A glance at the literature shows that there is no single universally effective or culturally appropriate way of teaching or defining literacy. Rather definitions of literacy can be seen as a function of social, cultural and economic conditions. In addition, different discourses may be dominant at different times and in different places.

Throughout the industrialised world, the problem of illiteracy has advanced to the top of the policy agenda, largely as a result of the International Adult Literacy Survey (IALS: 1994). There has been a radical rethink of the need to confront the issue of illiteracy in national policies, which now recognise the importance of improving literacy for citizens who wish to actively participate in modern, industrial, democratic societies. However, while there is almost complete acceptance that literacy has a profound impact on life chances around the world, there is somewhat less agreement on how adult literacy learning should develop.

Some writers have emphasised the need to move towards an understanding of literacy which encourages critical thinking about the conditions adults find themselves in. For example, Freire (1970) in *Pedagogy of the Oppressed* emphasised the need for conscientisation of adult learners and more recently, new paradigm shifts have emphasises the need for local everyday life experience to be included in our understanding of literacy needs. (Crowther *et al.*, 2001). Despite attempts of theorists and practitioners to locate literacy within broader sociocultural contexts, the functional view of literacy as a skill to be mastered, still appears to have currency within policy-making. Within recent literacy policy documents, there is little evidence of literacy being considered as a critical practice. In many countries, policies refer to the sociocultural relationships which frame literacy, couched in terms of family, community, citizenship and democracy, but there are few references to the need to examine issues of equality, power relations and identities.

Models of literacy

Street (1984) identified two models which can assist with understanding literacy which he referred to as the autonomous and ideological model. Each of these models has developed discourses which generate very different ways of thinking about literacy. The autonomous model postulates that literacy is a set of normative, unproblematic technical skills that are neutral and detached from the social context in which they are used. The correct skills are defined or fixed (by a powerful group) and learning becomes focused on a mechanical reproduction of correct skills learned in the classroom and which it is assumed may be easily transferred to real life situations. The other alternative ideological model, sometimes called the social practices model, recognises the sociocultural, diverse nature of literacy. With this model, power to determine content and curriculum lies primarily with the learner and the social and communicative practices with which individuals engage in their life-worlds rather than an educational organisation. The development of this model to include a critical approach adds a further dimension to an understanding of literacy by linking it to social and political issues in society. Shor (1999: 15) noted that *a* critical approach to literacy points to providing students not merely with functional skills, but with the conceptual tools necessary to critique and engage society along with its inequalities and injustices.

Equality perspectives and lifelong learning policies

Lifelong learning policies in both parts of Ireland have emphasised the importance of literacy and basic skills as part of lifelong learning strategies, but with somewhat different emphasis. In Northern Ireland, the lifelong learning strategy stressed the development of basic and key skills in the context of skills, knowledge and understanding essential for employability and fulfilment (DEL, 1999: 1). In contrast, the White Paper on Adult Education in the Republic of Ireland (DES, 2000: 26) emphasised the need for social cohesion and equity as well as the skills requirement of a rapidly changing workforce in the emergence of an inclusive civil society.

The policy agenda could therefore be said to be significantly different between the two political jurisdictions in Ireland – North and South – with a particular focus on meeting the needs of the economy in the North and a greater emphasis on equality and social cohesion agenda in the South (Lambe et al., 2006: 18). In addition, the emergence of a Peace and Reconciliation process in Ireland, not tied to existing funding structures, provided renewed opportunities to try out new ways of working in adult literacy practice.

The ideas discussed in this chapter emerged from one such peace project, known as the Literacy and Equality in Irish Society (LEIS) project. The project was one of a number funded by the European Union

(EU) Programme for Peace and Reconciliation (2006). The funding body, noted the twin objectives of the EU Special Support Programme as boosting economic growth and promoting social inclusion for those on the margins. A key objective of the LEIS project, was to explore the links between adult literacy and equality issues and to examine how creative/non-text methodologies might be used to enhance learners understanding of equality issues identified which have affected in their lives. The project adopted a social practices model of literacy development which acknowledged the social, emotional and linguistic contexts that give literacy learning meaning, and which includes a critical approach to literacy. It held the view that literacy programmes should be grounded in the everyday life situations of learners and should embrace issues of equality and social justice and brought together a range of people from the field of literacy practice with different types of expertise to promote dialogue about equality as an issue in adult literacy learner's lives. More than one hundred tutors and learners were involved in the project.

Peacebuilding and equality

Although peacebuilding is a commonly used concept, it is difficult to identify a common understanding of the term. The United Nations Secretary General Boutros-Ghali first used the term in the early 1990s to announce his agenda for peace and in general, definitions seem to varying depending on the particular group who use the term – thus definitions for example, between community and voluntary groups and policy makers can vary. A distinction must also be made between peacemaking, which can be interpreted as a means to tackle some concrete problem in a process that generally begins with a difference of interests and has the goal of achieving some kind of agreement and peacebuilding which can aim at change the social structures underlying the conflict or change in the attitude of those involved in the conflict. The LEIS project was based on the view that peacebuilding and improvement of learner's literacy skills could be closely linked.

The LEIS project was also based on the view that poor literacy skills can be viewed as a manifestation or symptom of inequality and it acknowledged the complexity of the task of helping tutors and learners understand the concept of equality. Baker *et al.* (2004: 47) noted that equality has a complex range of interpretations and like literacy, is a complex issue to define. In simplistic terms they noted that equality is a relationship of some kind or other between two people or more regarding some aspect of their lives. The project set out to develop clearer links between theories of inequality and practical approaches to including equality issues through the development of creative and non-text methodologies using an equality framework developed by Baker et al. (2004), one of the project partners. The underpinning model outlined by Baker (2004: 34) is based on the belief that that there are clear patterns in the structure and level of inequality experienced by individuals and groups.

To understand the implications of equality for adult literacy practice, the project used a contextual framework analysed through four key dimensions of equality. Proposed by Baker, Lynch and Cantillon (2004), the model is underpinned by the belief that there are clear patterns that structure the level of inequality experienced by individuals and groups. The framework identified four interrelated dimensions of equality namely respect and recognition, love care and solidarity, resources, and power relations. These dimensions of equality can be used to describe and analyse key patterns of inequality – the economic, political, cultural and affective systems in society are considered to be particularly important in generating equality and inequality, the affective system referring to the area of the emotions (Baker et al., 2004: 227). These dimensions provided an opportunity to look at the economic, political and cultural dimensions of inequality as well as how the affective or emotional realm. The theoretical framework and its connections with the methodological approaches is discussed in greater detail in the resource guide (2006, Lamb et al.).

Even within this theoretical model, equality can be viewed through different lens along a continuum ranging from a basic concept of equality to a liberal or radical understanding of the condition of equality. The concept of basic equality focuses merely on the availability of goods and services. There is no particular concern for barriers experienced by particular groups, or the support they might need to overcome such barriers. On the other hand, liberal equality assumes basic equality moving beyond it to a concern for distribution of resources and to removing any legal impediments to accessing services which would include education. Rather than questioning competition which gives advantage, the concept of liberal equality focuses on regulating the competition for the advantages that society offers. The radical approach to equality focuses on equality of condition which seeks to eliminate the inequalities altogether or at least massively reduce the current scale of inequality. (Baker et al., 2005: 33).

The dimensions of equality examined in the project are important in that they provide a framework for understanding equality and inequality and are discussed below. The first of these principles is respect and recognition. Underlying this principle is a commitment to social equality by recognising the unequal status of all citizens and of tolerating individual and group differences, so long as they respect basic rights. Every member has a right to the status of citizen, but social esteem has to be earned by achievement. Respect and toleration is based on the idea that recognition of diversity without critical dialogue allows for a sense of superiority of belief that the tolerated view is deviant. The dominant group are not open to having their own culture and ideas critically interrogated (Baker *et al.*, 2004: 34). This dimension therefore inevitably leads to inequalities. In adult literacy and learning, curriculum design, assessment methods and organisational structures are some of the areas where diversity of culture, experiences and learning style should be accommodated and embraced.

Baker *et al.* (2004: 37) noted that caring and being cared for are vital components of what enables people to lead successful lives and an expression of our fundamental independence. Emotions are central to the process of teaching and learning and so love, care and solidarity is an important principle of equality and of the framework adopted by the researchers in this study. Lack of love and care often are intertwined with insufficient access to resources and have in many instances contributed to adults not reaching their full potential. In Ireland, the National Adult Literacy Agency (NALA) acknowledge that literacy encompasses aspects of personal development – social, economic, emotional (2005: 2). However, despite this acknowledgement, it must be recognised that the emphasis on the development of the curriculum has been on the cognitive to the detriment of the emotional realm. Much more could be done within the adult literacy field to help tutors and learners facilitate the development of emotional skills. Equality of condition requires that people have access to the care they need to feel included and respected in society, and have the right to give and receive love and care, and that the work involved in providing love and care is properly recognised, supported and shared. Resources is the third principle of the equality framework. Baker *et al.* (2004: 36) talk about the need to move beyond meeting basic needs and towards a world in which people's resources are much more equal than they are now, so that people's prospects for a good life are more similar. Within this context, economic redistribution is insufficient to address inequality and what is needed is a paradigm shift and a recognition that adult literacy learners require access to a wide variety of provision. Much educational research points to inadequate resources as being one of the primary explanations for poor educational attainment. While income and wealth are clearly important, resources including leisure time, safe environment, access to public facilities and cultural and social capital are also paramount. In adult literary practice there is therefore a need to think about resources not just in terms of resources to set up provision, but also in terms of providing provision at suitable times and places and in surroundings which will enable and empower learners. In addition, imposed curricula and inflexible assessment methods all contribute to resource inequality for literacy learners. The understanding of various forms of power relations which sustain inequality between privileged and oppressed groups is also said to be an important factor to take account of in promoting equality. Power is not a characteristic of individuals in isolation, or something they possess, but is exercised as a result of social relationships within institutional structures. These structures provide meaning to their actions and also constrain them. Unequal power relations between tutor and learner have sometimes been addressed in literacy education, through for example, the adoption of Freirean approaches. Adult literacy provision needs to ensure that adults views are fully represented in decision making at all levels. Decision-making structures should facilitate learner participation especially in relation to decisions affecting their lives. In this way, provision is best able to respond to learner needs, empowering them to learn by taking control of their own destiny.

Understanding equality and inequalities through creative approaches

In keeping with the empowerment and inclusive focus of the framework, the approach used to all development activities was based on an emancipatory research approach. (Baker *et al.*, 2004). This involved an inclusive, participatory approach in which tutors and learners were invited to engage as equal partners with the project development team at all stages in the project. A particular inequality in adult literacy education could be said to be the privilege of using text-based work. There is a constant struggle to have other non-text creative methods recognized as having validity in themselves as opposed to acting as a support or lead into text-based work. The use of alternative methods is in itself an issue of equality in an area where there is acceptance of, and reliance on, text-based teaching and learning. The project therefore focused on the use of a range of creative methodologies to create spaces for the exploration of equality issues within adult literary practice. The methodologies were also intended to empower tutors and learners to engage with equality issues relevant to their lives, in particular those arising from the experience of conflict in Ireland.

Non-text/ creative methodologies can enable learners to develop an understanding of equality through involvement in a participatory process involving critical thinking and problem solving. Fegan (2003: 2) notes that these methodologies can provide a sense of identity and purpose which can be used to promote greater equality, social justice and mutual understanding. He also notes they can transform individuals, neighbourhoods, communities and regions. Greene (1988: 125) claims the passivity and disinterest prevalent in classrooms, particularly in the areas of reading and writing, is a result of a failure to educate for freedom. Instead she argues that we should focus on the range of human intelligences, the multiple languages and symbol systems available for ordering experience and making sense of the lived world. Her theory provides a pluralistic view of intelligences and a holistic picture of how humans learn and can be taught, thus providing further justification for the development of non-text approaches to adult literacy education. Tisdell (2003) also emphasises the need to take a more holistic view of education arguing for culturally relevant approaches to adult education, which outline the value of power of symbol-making and symbol-manifesting activities and the importance of these cultural experiences through creative activity. In a similar way, Mary Norton (2005) suggested the use of music and visual arts in adult literacy education as a way of providing an alternative way to engage learners.

As the project unfolded, the need to explicitly emphasise the value of the creative process within each person through access to multiple forms of education became clear.

The methodologies included Image Theatre, Music, Visual Arts and Storytelling, used as codes to explore equality issues. A participatory approach, where tutors and learners engaged as equal partners was used. Through stakeholder dialogue, equality issues seen as important to learners were raised.

Learning from an intra-cultural research process

The creative learning methods employed encouraging learners to express feelings which were often too difficult to put into words. Images sound and stories were used to highlight real experiences and to construct meaning around them. Learners told stories about past experiences – for example, their inability to access jobs and training due to what were described as discriminatory practices or the effects of political and social unrest. They also recounted experiences of discrimination arising from their religion, gender and sexual orientation. Often these experiences had given rise to feelings of great hurt and resentment which had been difficult to deal with. The opportunity to recall and open them up a safe learning environment provided for many the first real opportunities to acknowledge hurt and losses and to discuss a shared understanding of such issues. Old prejudices were confronted, thus providing the opportunity to build positive relationships and to create real change. The participants also spoke about the methods as being inclusive, encouraging imagination, improving self-esteem, creating a bond between groups and leading to improved listening skills. Through the use of non-text methods learners began to question previously held assumptions on a range of equality issues affecting their lives as a result of low literacy skills.

Various forms of artistic representation were also found to be good ways of introducing experiences and feelings to difficult to express in words alone. The use of sculpture was also found to be a good stimulus to discussion, with learners using the art of sculpture to tell stories about hurtful experiences. By talking about their experiences through artistic representations, learners were able to get right to the heart of things and reported that they were able to speak honestly about experiences. Some learners used collage to encourage representing their views about inequalities in their lives. The collage provided a means for them to think deeply about issues that had affected them, without being inhibited by the need to write down their thoughts. They used collage to talk about their individual experiences as a media for the discussion. Issues discussed included lack of education opportunities, feelings of powerlessness in creating change, and a lack of understanding arising from the religious and political division in society. Participating in making the collage increased the learners understanding of equality and enabled them to talk about themselves honestly without having to put pen to paper. Enhanced understanding of the causes of conflict resulted from linking their own lives as well as the lives of others and to resolving conflicts. The workshops also provided spaces for groups from both communities to explore equality issues impacting on their lives which lead to a common understanding of how a lack of literacy skills can created inequalities.

Evidence from the use of creative/non-text methods revealed both educational and social benefits. The methods provided opportunities to develop increased understanding about inequalities, their causes and effects on individual's lives. They also challenged learners assumptions about what literacy is and showed how learning can arise through examining so many individual situations and through so many different media and in particular non- text modes of knowing, being and doing. The methods also enabled learners to develop new skills as well as creating greater levels of co-operation and understanding. Responses from learners showed that many had learned new skills in communicating and felt more confident talking about the issues affecting their lives. Comments showed that adults with low levels of reading or writing literacy were able to actively participate in learning, thus contributing to the broader goals of social inclusion and citizenship in lifelong learning.

Exploring equality issues in adult literacy education

Some learners expressed criticism of the creative methodologies indicating that activities were childish, while others questioned the value of activities. For some, education and learning was perceived as a serious activity and it is was not always easy to equate this as synonymous with a high level of enjoyment associated with the creative methodologies. The new methodologies placed less emphasis on skills of reading and writing and more on the ability to express views in an open and non-judgmental way, shifting the balance of power between tutor and learner in an new direction and creating a new power dynamic in the learning process. The workshops helped learners embrace equality issue through examining these issues in their own lives. By challenging a 'literacy as skills' approach, the framework helped learners understand and articulate a non-deficit perspective for understanding inequalities in their everyday lives. Through the advocacy of creative methodologies, learners understanding of literacy were widened to include visual literacy, oral literacy and situated learning within creative processes (storytelling, drama, music and visual arts).

The equality framework was used as a tool to initiate discussion about inequalities. In the ensuing discussions tutors also raised issues around structural and institutional inequalities that create barriers to using creative approaches, such as the difficulties in working within rigid curricula and the privilege of learning through text-based work. The project also explored the potential to examine and discuss power relationships through the use of non-text methodologies. A range of issues such as health, housing, welfare and family were all discussed. By introducing tutors to non-text methods, learners were able to open up spaces to question previously held assumptions in the area of politics, economics, religion and culture and also empower them to challenge and question the deep structural societal inequalities that have contributed to the inequalities in their lives, including those related to literacy. The use of creative methods allowed for the development of what Freire (2004) calls generative themes, which raise issues that are important to different groups or individuals within the group and lead to discussion of conflict or social problems in people's lives (Degener, 2001: 36).

The findings from the study showed that complex issues could be discussed and represented through creative methods such as drama, storytelling, image theatre etc., giving literacy learners to opportunity to understand the dynamic of the society within which they live and read their world. (Freire, 1972)

Understanding inequalities through a process of reconciliation and peacebuilding

A central aim of the research was to examine how a focus on equality and social inclusion could contribute towards a process of peace and reconciliation. Hamber and Kelly (2004) have conceptualised a process for peace and reconciliation which highlights different strands involved in such a process. They suggest that a reconciliation process generally involves five interwoven and inter-related strands as follows:

- development of a shared vision of an independent and fair society;
- acknowledging and dealing with the hurts, loses, truths and sufferings of the past;
- building positive relationships following violent conflict by addressing issues of trust, prejudice, intolerance and accepting commonalities and differences with individuals accepting and learning from it in a constructive way and embracing and engaging with those who are different to us;

- developing significant cultural and attitudinal change through devel‑ oping a culture of respect for humans rights and human difference;
- creating substantial social, economic and political change by identify‑ ing reconstructing and transforming existing structures.

Peacebuilding is considered a process at the level of community, individual and polity, and reconciliation is considered as a component of peace building.

The research acknowledged that forcing groups or individuals to enter into joint activities can be counter-productive, as co-operation and integration cannot be enforced. Attention was given to providing safe spaces for groups from both communities to explore equality issues which they consider to have had particular impact on their lives with a view to raising awareness of the commonalities that exist in relation to literacy and equality (such spaces took account of neutral venues for discussion maintaining confidentiality of information and identities providing appropriate support for individuals when dealing with hurtful issues etc.)

Through the process, individuals from both the Roman Catholic and Protestant communities in Ireland were able to open up and talk about hurtful experiences and issues and through addressing these issues they were able to build more positive relationships which lead to attitudinal changes. The research showed that participants appreciated addressing these issues in safe environments which also included participants from different communities. They indicated that by meeting and sharing their experiences and points of view on divisive issues which, they had come to understand better the different points of view of others. They also indicated that as a result they had developed a much better understanding of issues which divide communities.

The workshops also enabled them to understand better issues of equality and inequality which had affected their own lives and through a process of mutual understanding they developed more positive relationships towards each other's points of view.

The innovative methodologies were found to have assisted learners to engage and talk about past experiences experienced during a period of conflict in a way which was often difficult using standard text-based approaches. The non-text/creative methods were found to serve as codes to explore issues for initiating reflection and discussion on equality issues, followed with more critical thinking and action. They provided a way for participants to introduce a problem or issue with a purpose of promoting critical thinking and action. The methods, which can promote socially or emotionally related responses, were also found to lead to a deeper understanding of a range of equality issues affecting learner's lives.

While the research showed that it was possible to effect change in the lives of individuals, which in turn might assist with creating change at community level, wider social, economic and political changes were also needed to reconstruct and transform society and the lives of individuals and communities. While individuals could have some effect in creating changes through participation in democratic processes, for the most part individuals felt powerless to bring about real change and transformation of social, economic and political structures which give rise to estrangement and conflict.

Conclusion

In summary, the research has shown that adult literacy can provide a valuable role in supporting the process of peace and reconciliation, e.g. in breaking down fear and mistrust, creating a space where individuals can hear and be heard and creating a context where each citizen becomes an active participant in society and feels a sense of belonging. In addition, the innovative methodologies employed had helped engage and empower marginalised literacy learners, from both Roman Catholic and Protestant communities who had been deeply affected by years of conflict. The development of new approaches and methodologies are therefore to be welcomed for supporting and enhancing the process of reconciliation and peace building in Ireland.

The equality framework provided a mechanism for talking about equality issues though offered a more democratic process which is also relevant across national and global networks. While it offers an opportunity to enable learners to engage as citizens, it also offers an opportunity to improve their skills and competences and to contribute not only socially but also economically to their own and societies betterment. Ultimately, through personal and community engagement, it provides a way of changing how learners understand inequalities in their lives and the lives of others.

One of the project's lasting achievements was building greater insight and understanding of the causes and consequences of inequalities and the possibilities that exist for change.

The action research model used has challenged the widely held view of deficit among learners and instead focuses on people's ability to do what they want in their lives.

The work was based on the premise that literacy is far more than a set of basic skills, but rather, are a set of social practices. Adult literacy education is in itself an issue of inequality since adults with low literacy skills are more likely to be unemployed, be living on low incomes and experiencing poor health and early morbidity.(Brynner and Parsons, 2001; Hammond, 2004; Raudenbush and Kasim, 2003). Using a social practice account of adult literacy means that instead of literacy being viewed as a de-contextualised, mechanical, manipulation of letters, words and figures, literacy can be located in social, emotional and linguistic contexts. Literacy practices can be seen as integrating routines, skills, and understandings, that are organised within specific contexts and also the feelings and values that people have about these activities. By focusing on equality and creativity, the LEIS project has shown how theories of equality and non-text creative methodologies can be used to develop new skills and understanding for adult literacy learners. It has empowered adult learners to critically examine some of the many issues affecting their lives. Finding ways of addressing these inequalities has no easy answers, but this should not be seen as a reason for denying learners the opportunity to examine and discuss these issues within literacy programmes and practices. The research has shown how a focus on both equality and creativity can develop new skills and understanding that can empower learners through promoting understanding of inequalities which affect their lives.

Speaking about this Shor (1999: 1) argues:

> *This kind of literacy . . . connects the political and the personal, the public and the private, the global and the local, the economic and the pedagogical . . . A key dimension of literacy is that it reflects wider inequalities in society. In the past, political, cultural and religious elites, as well as the wealthy business classes, have all used literacy to assert their dominant positions and maintain the subjugated positions of those with low-level literacy skills.*

Today, a lack of access to literacy is an indicator of widening local, regional and global inequalities, mirrored in inequalities of gender, race, employment status and so forth. The impact of unmet literacy needs is acknowledged in national and international studies and is part of the accepted wisdom that underpins policies on education, poverty and social exclusion. Much less clarity exists in relation to casual and transformational aspects of unmet literacy needs. Illiteracy is not something that occurs in isolation, without any recognisable pattern or root, and research has pointed to the need for a more holistic, contextualised approach. A major challenge in the future, not just in Ireland but in other areas of conflict, will be to find ways of aligning literacy policies and practices to the wider goals of promoting reconciliation, through equality and social justice.

References

Baker, J., Lynch, K., and Cantillon, S. (2004) *Equality from theory to action*. Dublin: Palgrave Macmillan.

Bynner, J. and Parsons, S. (2001) 'Qualifications, basic skills and accelerating social exclusion', *Journal of Education and Work*, 14, 279–91.

Border Action (2006) *Consortium with responsibility for the implementation of the Peace and Reconciliation Projects in Ireland*. http://borderireland.info/.

Bruner, J, (1986) *Actual minds, possible world*. Cambridge, MA: Harvard University Press.

Crowther, J., Hamilton M. and Tett, L. (2001) *Powerful literacies*. Leicester: NIACE.

Degener, S. C. (2001) 'Making sense of critical pedagogy in adult literacy education', in J. Comings, B. Garner, and C. Smith (eds) *Annual Review of Adult Learning and Literacy*, vol.2. San Francisco, CA: Jossey-Bass.

Department for Employment and Learning (2002) *Essential skills for living: equipped for the future: building for tomorrow. a framework and consultation paper on adult literacy*. Belfast: DEL.

Department of Education and Science (2000) *Learning for life*: White Paper of Adult Education. Pn. 8840 Dublin: DES.

Fegan, T. (2003) *Learning and community arts*. Leicester: NIACE.

Freire, P. (2004) *Pedagogy of the oppressed*. New York: Continuum Books.

Greene, M. (1988) *The dialectic of freedom*. John Dewey Lecture Series. New York: Teachers College Press, Columbia University.

Hamber, B. and Kelly, G. (2004) *A working definition of reconciliation*. Belfast: Democratic Dialogue.

Hammond, C. (2004) 'Impacts on well-being, mental health and coping', in Schuller, T. et al., *Wider benefits of learning*. London: Routledge - Falmer, 37–56.

Hardy, B. (1974) 'Narrative as a primary act of mind', in Meek, M.,

Warlow, A. and Barton, G. (eds), *The cool web, the pattern of children's reading*. London: The Bodley Head.

Lamb, T., Mark, R., Murphy, P and Soroke, B. (eds) (2006) *Literacy, equality and creativity. resource guide for adult educators*. Belfast: Queen's University Belfast.

National Adult Literacy Agency (NALA) (2005) *Guidelines for good adult literacy work*. Dublin: NALA.

Norton, M, (2005) 'Welcoming spirit in adult literacy work', *RaPAL Journal*, 58 www.literacy.lancaster.ac.uk/rapal .

Organization for Economic Co-operation and Development *International Adult Literacy Survey* http://www.oecd.org .

Raudenbush, S. and Kasim, R. (2002) *Adult Literacy, social inequality and the information economy, findings from the national adult literacy survey, Ottawa and Hull*: Statistics Canada and Human Resource Development Canada.

Shor, I. (1999) 'What is critical literacy?' *Journal for Pedagogy, Pluralism and Practice*, 1 (4).http://www.lesley.edu/journals/jppp/4/shor.html.

Tisdell, E, (2003) *Exploring spirituality and culture in adult and higher education*. San Francisco: Jossey-Bass.

CHAPTER THREE

Women, education and peacebuilding in Northern Ireland

Paul Nolan

Introduction

In December 1989 Northern Ireland's Belfast City Council withdrew its £2,000 annual grant to the Falls Women's Centre. In the resource wars of that period, such a 'blatantly sectarian'(Ward, 1991: 162) decision was not that unusual; the Falls Women's centre is in the republican heartland of Catholic West Belfast, and at the time the decision was taken the Council had a unionist majority. What did attract attention however was the fact that the campaign to save the centre drew support from the Shankill Women's Centre and other women's organisations from within the Protestant unionist community. Such a display of solidarity excited the interest of the Basque feminist scholar, Begona Aretxaga, who was at that time conducting ethnographic research into the experiences of republican women in West Belfast. In her book, *Shattering Silence: Women, Nationalism and Political Subjectivity in Northern Ireland* she describes the alliance of working-class women from both sides of the sectarian divide as 'a new approach to feminist politics' (Aretxaga, 1997: 170–71). Certainly there were some new features to the protest – principally the unity that sustained the campaign right through to International Women's Day the following March – and although the campaign failed to reverse the council's decision, one practical outcome did emerge in the form of a new organisational structure, the Women's Support Network, set up to provide underpinning strength to all locally-based women's centres.

In many respects though this incident fits comfortably within a well-understood meta-narrative, in which women reject the posturing of their male leaders, put aside their communal identities and enter the public space as a united presence to affirm the shared values of women. Perhaps the most famous instance occurred in 1976 with the spontaneous creation of the Peace People. On the 10th August that year a wounded gunman's getaway car crashed into pedestrians at Finaghy in South Belfast. Anne Maguire had been accompanying her four children along the pavement; two of the children were killed instantly, a third child died the following day, and Mrs Maguire was herself badly injured. Her sister Mairead Corrigan, and another woman who had witnessed the tragedy, Betty Williams, organised a vigil at the spot where the incident had taken place. A thousand people turned up to the 12 August rally, and two days later several busloads of women from the Shankill crossed the city's sectarian boundaries to join a further rally at the same spot. The campaign instantly seized the popular imagination; twenty thousand people attended a peace rally in Belfast's Ormeau Park on 21 August, and a similar number marched up the Shankill a week later. It may be the case, as Jonathon Bardon suggests, that the Peace People campaign was 'largely directed by the journalist Ciaran McKeown' (Bardon, 1992: 727) but the potency of the myth surrounding the campaign attaches to the idea that it was an assertion of women's life-affirming values, and that these values transcended the sectarian divide.

This same narrative was rehearsed in September 1998 during President Clinton's visit to Northern Ireland when Hillary Clinton addressed the four hundred female participants at the Vital Voices conference in the Grosvenor Hall in Belfast. These women, according to the Vital Voices website, had come together to 'establish new relationships, expand partnerships, and secure resources to strengthen the roles of women in democracy' (Vital Voices, 2005). It seemed a propitious moment to launch such a claim. In June 1996 the Women's Coalition, a political party that was then just two months old, had secured two seats in the new Northern Ireland Assembly having, by common consent, played a significant role in facilitating the series of political accommodations that led to the signing of the Good Friday Agreement. With hindsight it is clear that the women's political intervention had already peaked: writing in 2002 Rooney reflects on its decline: 'The community women's sector may be viewed as being less important now than it once was. It is possible that the sector has served its political purposes' (Rooney, 2002: 44). However, the idea that women might in other ways be the pioneers of a new form of radical politics, one that can transcend ethnic antagonisms, is by no means dead; in fact in 2008 many of those who had been active in earlier stages of feminist politics in Ireland came together to launch a new project called Hanna's House. Using the name of the pacifist feminist, Hanna Sheehy Skeffington, as an emblem of intent, this project aims to create a residential centre for women. The mission statement presents a clear political purpose: 'To create home for an active feminist community in Ireland, working for a non-violent, just society that embraces diversity' (Hanna's House website, 2010).

The thread that ties all these initiatives together is an essentialist thread. It is the belief that women possess, in Carol Gilligan's influential phrase, 'a different voice' (1982), and that this voice is one best suited to peace-making. In foreshortened histories of women in the conflict, such as the one I have provided above, that thread can bind together experiences from the feminist campaign group, the local women's centre and the peace rally to suggest that they are all of a piece, that an organic relationship has been forged between the discursive practices of the adult education class in the local women's centre, the accommodation of difference within feminist thought, and the fostering of constructive political dialogue between ethno-nationalist groups. The spirit that bubbles up through these is one that Elisabeth Porter, drawing upon Hannah Arendt's ideas of civic republicanism and Seyla Benhabib's theory of democratic dialogue, claims as the distinctive contribution of women in Northern Ireland to the peace process: ' generally there is more emphasis on accommodation, flexibility, negotiation, process and striving to establish workable solutions.' (Porter, 2007: 88).

The evidence suggests to me that the organic wholeness of women-led initiatives in Northern Ireland can only hold true from a particular normative perspective; once empirical realities are admitted what becomes apparent is that the picture is much more complex and, in fact, much more interesting. What I shall try to demonstrate here is that rather than a united women's political movement there are three distinct, but overlapping domains: feminist groups, community-based women's organisations and peace campaigns. The potential of women's education to contribute to improved community relations has at every point been framed by the relations between the three. This not a static typology, but a force field in which alliances and antagonisms are restlessly shifting within the dynamic of the triad. What holds the three together is the underpinning belief that women acting together can be a force for good.

That is not of itself an essentialist assumption but, like any attempt to contain women within a bounded category, it finds itself in an inescapable tussle with essentialism. It is an argument that takes on a different dimension in each of the three domains I have mentioned. Let us now take each in turn to see the ways in which they relate to each other and the possibilities and limitations they provide for women's education. I will begin by looking at how feminist politics first came to be expressed in Belfast, then consider the growth and significance of neighbourhood-based women's centres, before turning to women's peace campaigns.

Feminism in Belfast

In their summary of research into the Northern Ireland Troubles Hargie and Dickson identify as a major theme the exceptionalism–particularism spectrum, which allows the politics of the place to be seen either as fitting with international patterns or to be seen as wholly exceptional (Hargie and Dickson, 2003: 289–91). At the exceptionalism end of the spectrum, the tendency has been to emphasise the unique features of Irish history and, by extension, the uniqueness of the Irish character. This has met a response from revisionist historians and social scientists who wish to map the Irish experience onto the history of postcolonialism, its patterns reflecting larger historical and societal processes at work elsewhere: what Connolly describes as the 'not that different' paradigm (Connolly, 2003). Both tendencies are at work in the accounts given of the feminist movement in Northern Ireland. For outside writers especially, the tendency to exoticise, and to an extent ethnicise, women-led movements in Ireland has led to a focus on the more extreme expressions of feminist action, such as the dirty protests of female republican prisoners in Armagh or the relationship with paramilitary groups (see Aretxaga, 1995, Cockburn, 1998, Belfrage, 1987). Perhaps one should not be surprised by attention being given to such dramatic, and indeed, attention-seeking expressions of political conviction. It is also the case that the involvement of women in paramilitary structures has magnetised the attention of local writers like Ashe (2006), Loughran (1987), and Fairweather, McDonough and McFadyean (1984).

Other accounts of the origins of feminist politics in Northern Ireland, however, as relayed by those who were most directly involved (Evason, 1991; Ward, 1991), describe a mimetic relationship with the development of feminist groups elsewhere – most notably within a United Kingdom context. Those who involved themselves in the first feminist groupings had a sense of coming late to something that had developed greater momentum elsewhere (Morgan and Fraser, 1994: 5). To use an old Marxist trope, it is no coincidence that the first event to bring feminists together, a women's film weekend at Queen's, took place in 1975, the International Year of Women, when awareness was developing of autonomous women's activity in Europe and the United States. Small feminist groupings had been set up the previous year in both Belfast and Coleraine, based in each case within university-based networks, with another anarchist-inspired group meeting in the Lower Ormeau area in Belfast. An umbrella organisation was formed in 1975, the Northern Ireland Women's Rights Movement, to unite these small fragmentary groups and to offer the superordinate identity of feminist to women who wished to escape the force field of local sectarian politics. Unity had been built around a reform programme designed to bring the more progressive legislation in Britain on sex discrimination and reproductive rights over to Northern Ireland, and the constitutional issue – the core problem of the national identity of the state – was kept off the table. The starting point for the NIWRM was that women could make real gains 'within the existing political framework' (Roulston, 1989: 27).

As the nationalist population became more radicalised a contradiction became very apparent for republican feminists: if the eventual goal was to achieve political independence from Britain, then further legislative and cultural integration was a journey in the opposite direction. The first split came in October 1976 with the creation of the Socialist Women's Group, which took as its foundational belief the view that British imperialism was at the heart of the conflict and that the struggle for women's liberation would have to be part of the struggle for national liberation. The Socialist Women's Group stopped short of endorsing the IRA campaign, but they were quickly challenged by an even more radical group, Women Against Imperialism, who gave explicit support to the armed struggle, and demanded that other feminists respond to the existential challenge faced by women then on the dirty protest in Armagh prison. A small group of middle-class women took up that challenge and went to live in West Belfast. Others took off in a different direction. A lesbian group organised its first conference in Belfast in 1997, while the Women's Law and Research Group continued the campaign begun by the NIWRM for parity with more liberal parts of English legislation. There was a Women in Media group, a campaign group on abortion, and so many other particularist concerns at work that by the mid-1980s the idea of a united women's movement had been surrendered. A conference organised by the Workers Educational Association (WEA) in 1986 to build unity only managed to reveal the nature of divisions. The record of the conference shows a series of bitter exchanges opening up, the flavour of which are captured by these closing remarks by the Chair, the trade unionist Inez McCormick:

> *If we cannot articulate that difficult dangerous honesty between us that we are beginning to touch on, because what we are beginning to touch on is a bit of hate which is surfacing* . . . (Ward, 1987: 58).

For some, the fissiparous nature of the women's movement at this time was a dismaying confirmation of the belief that the backward nature of Irish society and the malformations of sectarianism had combined to halt the growth of feminism, and that Ireland, north and south, was doomed to lag behind developments in other liberal democracies. In fact, the contestations over identity issues did not point to the exceptionalism of the Irish experience but rather the opposite: its conformity to the norm, as throughout Europe, Canada, America and Australia the 'politics of identity' emphasised the differences between women in racial, ethnic and sexuality identities rather than their commonalities. The articulation of 'promoting the needs of women' and 'reducing inequalities' had given way to the disaggregation of the single concept of 'women' and allowed for what Angela Wilson called a 'cacophony of voices'(Wilson, 2007: 32) challenging the essentialist assumptions of the first wave feminists, and allowing for multiple clashing and overlapping identities to assert themselves. What transformed the scene and allowed feminism to regain its energy and vision was the growth of locally-based women's centres. From the mid 1980s on, feminism in Northern Ireland had a new base.

Community-based women's centres

The growth of community-based women's centres throughout Ireland, North and South, has been a remarkable phenomenon, for which there is no comparison anywhere in Europe, or indeed anywhere else in the world. Writing in the year 2000, which may well have been the high tide of the movement, McMinn estimated there were well over 1,000 geographically-based women's groups in the Republic of Ireland and 450 in the North (McMinn, 2000: 35). A subsequent estimate by the Department of Social Development put the number of women's groups or projects in Northern Ireland at the very exact figure of 383 (DSD, 2005). Coulter says the exact number in the Republic has always been impossible to estimate, but refers to the occasion when a meeting of women's groups was convened in the west of Ireland, to be addressed by President Mary Robinson. A hall was hired for 250 people: 'Over one thousand people, representing forty-two women's groups turned up'(Coulter, 1993: 48). This development has not proceeded in accordance with any centralised strategy or roadmap; on the contrary, its growth was not even predicted – nor could it have been. The fuel that drove it in Northern Ireland was the money that flooded in through the EU Peace and Reconciliation Programmes, which funding agencies channelled into women's centres in deprived areas in the belief that women could act as a stabilising force in communities beset by violence. This fed into a well-established narrative: ever since Sean O'Casey's great trilogy of plays set around the rising of Easter 1916, women have been cast as clear-eyed, grounded and compassionate, and as such, seen to be in opposition their vainglorious, violent and destructive menfolk. To many observers, particularly to outsiders watching the activities of women peace campaigners, the Troubles were a version of this drama played out in modern dress. That is not how women saw themselves, and the centres have catered to much more practical and workaday needs through the provision of crèches, shared cooking facilities and recreational activities. Grand ideological projects were left strictly outside the door.

However domesticated the activities may have appeared, the fact was that they brought women out of the domestic sphere into the 'neighbourhood interstices between the public realm of politics and the private realm of the home' (Rooney, 2002: 37). It was in those interstitial spaces that working-class women came into contact with a new cadre of professional community workers, many of whom were feminist in their orientation. In the study conducted by Rooney and Woods (1995) these women are categorised as Professional Organisers, and they are attributed with the establishment and organisation of local groups. Morgan and Fraser (1995) are chary about attributing much influence to feminism in traditional forms of women's organisations but, as others make clear (Cockburn, 1998; Aretxaga, 1995; Connolly, 1999; Abbott and Frazer, 1985), the framework of community development that gained dominance within disadvantaged areas during the Troubles was one that allowed a shared agenda to emerge. For women concerned about issues in their local neighbourhoods, access was given to resources and the professional expertise necessary to create committee structures, write funding applications and the like: the crucial networks described in social capital theory as 'linking capital'(Woolcock, 1998: 13–14) For the Professional Organisers, and particularly those with socialist politics, the newly emerging women's centres provided a bridge to authentic working-class experience and an opportunity to escape the middle-class feminist ghetto. As Cockburn observes: 'Doing women's development enabled them to look to their own interests as women while also furthering the interests of impoverished working-class families and communities' (Cockburn, 1998: 61–2).

The pact between the feminist organisers and government departments was built, like so much else in the Northern Ireland peace process, on ambiguity: top-down governmental concerns about the maintenance of public order met with bottom-up radicalism about the political space available to women. The incorporation of feminist ideas and social organisation into the machinery of local government has been described elsewhere as 'state feminism'(Hernes, 1987). In Northern Ireland's women's centres another name was suggested, 'family feminism'. The term was first coined by a notable community activist, Joyce McCartan, whose drop-in centre on the Lower Ormeau Road offered a range of facilities to women, with a strong emphasis on the everyday experiences of working class women's lives: childcare, nurturing, relationships and consumer and welfare issues. In American feminism, this goes under the name of 'maternal feminism' (Reardon, Offen, Elshtain) and links to an essentialist perspective that sees women as 'naturally' inclined towards peace. In Britain, the Greenham Common protests of the 1980s played off the same 'woman-centred' values, using the American bases to set up a symbolic opposition between women as nurturers and carers, and the most visible manifestation in that period of the male military/industrial/nuclear complex. Lister (1997: 149) points to other political struggles where women have entered the public arena, not to seek equality with men, but to assert their identities and concerns as mothers, caught up in political conflict. She cites the Madres (Mothers) of the Plaza de Mayo in Argentina who occupied the public square to protest against the disappearance of their husbands and children, and also an example more pertinent to the women's centres of Northern Ireland, the struggles of African-American women whose 'community activism has often been prompted by concern for their own children and those in the extended family and community' (p. 149).

The extension of concern into the lives of other women, and the networks that developed across the sectarian divide, gave hope to the idea that the forms of co-operation experienced at community level could shift from the grassroots up into the political arena. The Women's Coalition, created in April 1996, following the paramilitary ceasefires, saw itself as a direct offshoot of the ferment created in the women's centres, as two of its leading figures acknowledge:

> *It is generally recognised that large numbers of women have for many years involved themselves with grassroots and voluntary sector campaigns, holding the fabric of society together while the conflict threatened to tear itself asunder.* (Fearon and McWilliams, 1999: 1254).

Through the Women's Coalition the co-operative and accommodationist practices nurtured in the women's centres and in women's education classes were given an organised political form. This was not only a test for conventional politics, it was a test also of how far working-class women would allow their shared identity to supersede their existing communal loyalties.

Women's Peace Initiatives

The peace process in Northern Ireland is now seen as having begun in the late 1980s with backdoor contacts between the IRA and the British government (see, for example, Hennessy, 1999 and Moloney, 2007). In fact, from the first outbreak of violence there has been a peace process running alongside the war process, one usually led by women. As early as 1970 the first female protest against violence had taken place. Ruth Agnew, a Protestant cleaner at the Belfast Gasworks, had organised a protest against a shooting of a young man in the area, one of the very first deaths of the Troubles. She was contacted by an English Catholic called Monica Patterson, and together they formed a new organisation called Women Together, which set the template for many of the peace campaigns that followed. A first public meeting in September of that year showed a rush of support with 400 women from all areas of Belfast in attendance. Enthusiasm dwindled as the political violence spiralled out of control and the organisation's offices were bombed and burned in 1976, obliterating all their records. The following minute though gives a flavour of Women Together's activities in the first flush of enthusiasm. These included:

> *separating rival gangs in riots by using themselves as human shields (in Andersonstown and Ardoyne), stopping children and youths from setting fire to property (Broadway), dispersing a gang of youths with knives who were attacking a boy from the 'other side', defending neighbours who were having windows broken, and going out night after night talking to tartan gangs, giving sympathy and practical help when it is needed, and showing concern generally.* (Women Together minutes, private collection).

In 1972 the Derry Peace Women formed – a spontaneous reaction to the killing of young Catholic man from the city, Ranger Best, who had joined the British Army and made the fatal mistake of making a visit home. The IRA killed him, seeing his involvement with the British army as a form of treachery. To the women of the city, he was no more than an innocent boy, and they took to the streets. Their campaign to end the violence had at least a partial success in that it helped to contribute to the ceasefire declared by the Official IRA three weeks later, but the spiralling violence and the alienation experienced by the nationalist community after Bloody Sunday soon eclipsed their efforts. In time, the same fate overtook the Peace People. Initially, their moral passion proved inspirational to many, not least the Nobel Prize jury who awarded the Peace Prize to the campaign's founders, Mairead Corrigan and Betty Williams. Moral passion proved an insufficient guide to political life however, and the Peace People lost their way, trying to navigate between the conflicting claims of peace and justice. It simply proved too difficult a juggling act to balance nationalist grievances about the security forces against unionist outrage at the IRA's military campaign. Their failure was also a demonstration of the inability of informal social movements to effect real social change. Surveying various forms of women's activism, Lister (1997) concludes that, Foucault notwithstanding, real power lies in formal political structures. The judgment made by Stacey and Price in their classic study, 'Women Power and Politics' is the one she chooses to endorse: 'If women wish to make changes in the societies they live in, they must seek and achieve power positions' (Stacey and Price, cited in Lister, 1997: 154).

In this way, the Women's Coalition was different. It did not position itself outside the political process as a moral conscience, but made a direct play for electoral power. The prospectus was not based on 'women's issues', but rather on women's way of doing things. This was presented in the essentialist terms of universalist women's peacebuilding, as described here in Elizabeth Porter's 2007 survey, *Peacebuilding: Women in International Perspective*:

Some women become peace activists, advocating strongly for non-violent ways of relating. Other women are mediators, trauma healing counsellors and policymakers working to address the root causes of violence and ways to transform relationships. Many women are educators and group facilitators, contributing to building the capacity of individuals, communities and nations to resolve conflicts and prevent further surges of violence. Some women are humanitarian aid workers or peacekeepers. Many women facilitate dialogue between warring factions, tribes, clans or ethnic groupings by convincing husbands, brothers, uncles and sons to lay their spears, machetes or guns aside. (Porter, 2007: 3–4).

The Women's Coalition acted in just such a manner, mediating, facilitating and working for consensus in the talks leading up to the Good Friday Agreement. As an elected party, the Women's Coalition was entitled to be involved in the talks behind closed doors, and the representatives used the opportunity not to press on 'women's issues, but rather to facilitate consensus on the vexed constitutional problems at the heart of the Agreement. For some this represented a betrayal of sorts, for others it represented an exciting new way for feminists to experiment with dialogic democracy. Perhaps ironically (perhaps not), the strongest attack on the Coalition for deserting feminist values comes from a male academic, Alan Bairner, who sees the focus on reaching political accommodation as a betrayal of gender politics:

Far from initiating such a debate, however, the NIWC appears content to measure the empowerment of women and general social improvement in terms of their own access to (male-dominated) corridors of power. In addition, once seated at the political table, their leading representatives have tended to devote their attention to the details of how to make political institutions work rather than directly confront those dynamics which, if left unchecked, are almost certain to ensure the persistence of male hegemony in the north of Ireland. (Bairner, 137–8).

The academic support for the Women's Coalition approach, from feminist writers like Roulston (2000), Porter (1998, 2000) and, to a lesser extent, the radical democracy advocate Adrian Little (2004), tend to emphasise not so much the contribution that party politics has made to the position of women, but the contribution that women have made to party politics. The idea of dialogic democracy which they seek to promote is linked very closely to the sort of radical pluralism that seeks to recognise the validity of different world views and that seeks accommodation, and to encourage the input of divergent groups into decision-making. It is, above all, anti-elitist and attentive to grass roots movements, and in some ways more concerned with processes than outcomes. As Little puts it: 'it is fair to say that radical democracy is more concerned with how we actually understand the 'political' than the technicalities of the design of political institutions' (Little, 2004: 6). That broader definition of the political, in Porter's analysis, must take in everyday communicative practices such as talking with friends, relating stories, learning to understand the perspectives of others – the types of practice that are in fact best exemplified in women's education classes. (Porter, 2007: 191). An organic model can be constructed which sees reconciliation and peacebuilding being nourished at the roots through community-based women's education, and the flowering of that process taking place at the negotiation table.

It is however by no means the only way in which women's education can feed into the body politic, or into increased understanding at local level, and I will now turn to the specific forms of women's education and assess their likely effects to see if they live up to the larger claims put forward by Porter and Little.

Women's education

In its quotidian form, as evidenced by statistics, brochures and syllabi, the reality of women's education in Northern Ireland falls short of the rhetoric of some of its more theoretical supporters who have viewed it only from the windows of the academy; the poetical gives way to the prosaic when everyday practices come under inspection. There are however particular forms of educational practice which do bear out the idea that shared interests allow for a transcendence of sectarian barriers – described in Cynthia Cockburn's study of the women's movement in Belfast as 'transversal politics' – and, moreover, there is evidence that these contacts have allowed for the promotion of an alternative set of values in which tolerance and mutual respect are key. In this sense community-based women's learning can be seen as an adumbration of the eventual political settlement and as a stabilising and sustaining force for community relations in the post-conflict period. To make this idea more concrete I will use as a case study the work of the Belfast-based Women's Information Group which has since 1984 provided a forum for cross-community exchanges between women.

First though it is important to gain a definition of women's education, which might be seen as a set of cultural practices operating in the interstices between 'community', 'feminism' and 'education' without ever being owned by any of them. There is a body of literature which offers both normative and descriptive accounts of women's education in the UK (Thompson, 1980, 1983, 1993; Coats, 1994; Barr, 1999; McGivney, 1993) and also in the Republic of Ireland (Ryan, 2001; Aontas, 2003) and in these various accounts issues of curriculum, pedagogy and context are problematised. All of these debates shed light on developments in Northern Ireland, but an initial starting point might be the simple definition put forward by the Equal Opportunities Commission for Northern Ireland when it took women's education to be 'basically concerned with education for women, about women, by women' (EOC, 1986: 30). The first moves in this direction were broadly in line with the Second Chance form of compensatory education, followed quickly by the more unstructured curriculum of Women's Studies groups which allowed women's lived experiences to become the content of the course. It was here, in the resemblance to the feminist consciousness-raising group, or to the Freirean 'conscientisation' process, that women's education took on its distinctive character – not, as Barr says (1991: 41) 'education for the disadvantaged' but something *sui generis* that presents a challenge to existing epistemologies by drawing directly on women's own lived experiences to create, at least in idealised form, a 'feminist way of knowing'. Barr gives the example of women's health courses which 'produced a kind of knowledge about medical phenomena different than that produced by medical science and experts – knowledge and skills which drew on women's own experiences and needs' (ibid: 40). For this to happen women's education had to slip outside the college gates and take root in the community, and into those organisations, like the Workers' Educational Association, which were prepared to allow traditional disciplines to be broken down, curricula to be negotiated, and most important of all, self-organisation in the form of women's studies branches.

Did Northern Ireland follow the same pattern? The answer is essentially, yes, at least in its early days. The later developments that emerged from the women's centres eventually gave it its own distinctive character, which I will go on to explore, but the early shaping influences came directly from developments in England This is not surprising given the indebtedness to British feminism described earlier, and also because the most important vehicle for women's education was the Workers' Educational Association (Munby, 2003; Coats, 1994; Barr, 1999), the Northern Ireland version of which tended to follow the agenda set at national level. This was no slavish adherence – on the contrary, the Northern Ireland WEA was enthusiastic in its promotion of women's education, offering its first women-only classes in 1979 and in 1982 setting up the first Women's Studies Branch with the aim of creating provision 'geared to women's needs, encouraging women to develop greater self-confidence and self-knowledge' (WEA Annual Report, quoted in Hope, 1992: 20). Soon there was an entirely independent, entirely feminist Women's Education Project which allowed women to organise education completely outside the recognised institutions.

In which ways did these programmes reflect the specific Northern Ireland circumstance of an ethnically divided society? Those looking for course titles which explicitly address that central political problem will be disappointed. A breakdown of all the women-only classes offered by the WEA and the women's centres in the period since the first IRA ceasefire shows that the most popular titles are ones which would be equally familiar in women's education programmes in Glasgow, Cardiff or Newcastle. The most popular by far is Computer Studies, followed by Aromatherapy, Head Massage and the other popular personal development courses. There are also some 'empowerment' programmes, with titles such as *Time For Me* or *Assertiveness Training*, but the focus is still on individual change, not social change. Conspicuous by its absence is any activity that suggests an engagement with community relations, sectarianism or the creation of shared political understandings. It is not a complete absence – the Women Into Politics project, for example, does offer programmes in some of the centres, and there are occasional appearances of the WEA *Us and Them* course, which allows the issue of sectarian division to be tackled directly. Taking the curriculum as a whole though, it would be reasonable to conclude that the connection between women's education and peacebuilding is, at best, tenuous. That is not the conclusion I intend to draw. There is another perspective which allows us to see how the real connections to community relations work are built, but it takes us into a paradox. The paradox is that the most important bridge-building activities between Protestant and Catholic women have been followed on from educational activities that are usually characterised as individualistic, such as personal development courses, as opposed to the traditional forms of education for social purpose which focused on collective rights or concerns (Field, 2000: 49). In fact, it has been by blocking off the larger political issues that women have found a space in which commonalities could be explored. It is, admittedly, a limited space but it is one that has allowed for significant developments in cross-community contact and understanding. The peacebuilding which has occurred has resulted from the way in which the provision has converted a form of bonding social capital into a potent form of bridging social capital — in other words, turning the networks of trust *within* communities into networks of trust *between* communities. That has been possible because of the dedicated efforts of the Women's Information Group and other linking agencies which between them have created a central nervous system keeping local women's groups in contact with each other.

I will now describe how that has worked in practice, and how it has affected two local women's groups, one in a Catholic area, the other in a Protestant area. The account that follows is based on a series of interviews I conducted with women from these centres in 2007 and 2008. In both cases the names of the centres and the women involved are disguised. Before turning to them however I will first describe the activities of the main umbrella body, the Women's Information Group.

The Women's Information Group

The Women's Information Group celebrated its 30th anniversary in 2010. It was the anniversary of an accidental birth. The first meetings were convened by a group of social workers who were conscious of the fact that the grassroots mother-and-toddler clubs, play groups and community associations in Belfast were operating with very little state support, and that they were all in pursuit of the same information. What they needed, in the traditional language of adult education, was 'really useful knowledge'. This meant knowledge of the benefits system, of the law and how to access educational resources form the WEA, the FE colleges and the Open University. It was more economic to generate this knowledge by bringing women to a central venue — more importantly, a 'neutral' space — in the city centre and inviting speakers from the various agencies to attend. The days were known as Information Days, and the loose collective who regularly attended constituted themselves as the Women's

Information Group – a necessary step in order to receive grants to cover running costs.

As trust developed greater risks were taken. Residentials became a feature of the Women's Information Group calendar, and more significantly, the decision was made to move away from neutral venues and to rotate the meetings around the city with each group taking a turn to host the sessions. Given the social composition of the membership, this meant travelling into ethnically defined space where the manifestations of the 'other' in terms of wall murals, kerb paintings, bunting and political graffiti were very much in evidence. Bridie McGrath recalls the first time the group agreed to go to the community centre in the then notorious Divis Flats:

> It was in the middle of the flats, right in the middle. One of the women put her hand up, and that's where we were going, we were going to Divis, and we daren't, well, one of the women put her hand up and she says 'we're not going to Divis'. I said 'Oh, that's fine, that's fine', I said 'I know you're a bit nervous, like. Do you know the women from Divis feel a bit nervous going into your area? Oh, I said, when they're travelling it's just the same, they're fearful the way you're fearful'. And when we pulled the shutter up for lunch, I pulled up the shutter in the kitchen and there were the women from Knocknagoney with their arms on their hips saying 'We're here' – the first in the queue for lunch (interview, 9 August 2007).

The apprehension of travelling into another area was one Bridie experienced directly herself on a regular basis. She describes a particular experience when she was very conscious of being a Catholic woman in a Protestant area, in this case the loyalist Rathcoole estate:

> I remember being in Rathcoole and it was the youth hall and there were windows high up right round, wee small windows that run the whole length around the whole building . . . and there was a figure, a shadow went round the windows and it was definitely a male figure, tall, dark, and he was carrying something over his shoulder . . .
> Q: That looked like a gun?
> . . . That looked like a gun. Sure, you knew which one was which in the hall because all the Catholics' eyes was following this figure right round the hall whereas the Protestants were quite at ease – that's only a workman with a plank! So I know that if I felt fear then every woman that was the same background as me knew the area was (pause) different, and she felt it.

Testing the bonds in situations like this led to a shared trust and there is an unqualified acceptance from all commentators that the Women's Information Group succeeded in creating bonds of trust for women from the two ethnic communities (see, for example, Edgerton: 17; McMinn, 2000: 34; Sales, 1997: 192; Taillon, 1992: 45; Rooney, 2002: 37; Evason, 1991: 50). It has, moreover, acted as the incubator for a number of political campaigns, beginning with the protest against the rent increases, and going on to campaigns on issues such as the dependence of working-class women on tranquillisers, the cost of living in Northern Ireland and the need for healthy eating. And, of course, the campaign mentioned at the start of this chapter when in 1990 all the women's groups in Belfast, including the Shankill Women's Centre, came out in support of the Falls Women's Centre and in opposition to Belfast City Council which was then imposing cuts in its funding. It also crucially acted as a linking agency that allowed co-operation to develop on a one-on-one basis between women's groups in Protestant and Catholic areas. The Churchwell Women's Group and the Ballymac Women's Group are an example of such a partnership.

Churchwell is a Protestant area in south Belfast with traditional terraced housing in a network of narrow streets, and strong associations with urban decline, unemployment and paramilitary violence. The presence of the loyalist paramilitaries is strongly asserted through wall murals and graffiti, and in recent years attacks on immigrant communities have added to the area's general notoriety. The electoral ward where the Women's Centre is situated has very low records for educational attainment: approximately 60 per cent of the population possess no formal qualifications, and for women aged between 18 and 65 that figure rises to 71 per cent. Only 7.5 per cent of these women have a qualification at A-level or above. Given these circumstances, it is striking that the area should also be known for its very busy programme of adult education classes, and the strength of its cross-community programme. Both of these developments have been the creation of the Churchwell Women's Centre. The educational classes have been nurtured over a thirty year period; with the links between the women in the Catholic Ballymac and the Protestant Churchwell developed fifteen years ago, beginning not long after the IRA ceasefire in 1994. It was a big step for the Churchwell women to go on their first visit to Ballymac, an area notorious for the strength of the IRA presence. The Coordinator of the Women's Centre there relates a story which is almost a parable of how women in the area related to the violence:

> *Well the Republican movement fired a mortar over the roof of here, they were actually aiming at a police land rover passing the shops just beside us, and, em, I have a vivid memory of that day because one of the women who was a sort of family woman stood at the sink – we were expecting visitors that day for something to eat. One of the women stood at the sink continuing to wash and prepare food as if it hadn't happened. Another woman who would have had family very involved in the conflict darted out the door to find it, literally chased it to see where it was going to land. And another one just went hysterical.*

The awareness of internal diffe[rences within] frontline communities like this leads to the appreh[ension that] in the sense of the larger politics of republi[canism] could fragment the unity of women in exac[tly the way] th Centre Coordinators feel that they were given very [clear sig]nals by the local women not to allow the politics of any party or paramilitary group to enter the centre because of the fear that the fissures that divided the neighbourhood would break up the women's group.

Does that extend to the cross-community politics promoted by the Northern Ireland Women's Coalition when it entered the electoral arena? To the disappointment of the Professional Organisers, the women did not follow their lead into support for organised politics. As Joanne McCauley, the Churchwell Women's Centre Coordinator explains:

> *The Women's Coalition tried to forge a partnership with the women's sector but the women's sector, the working-class women's sector, rejected that. It was nearly expected by the Women's Coalition when they set up that it would be automatic support but it wasn't.*

The two Women's Coalition candidates who were elected to the Assembly in 1998 won their seats in the leafy suburbs of South Belfast and North Down, and those who stood in predominantly working-class wards failed to rally the vote. Class is not in itself however an adequate explanation – those same working-class constituencies returned other candidates drawn from the professional classes. The concept that most illuminates the manner in which the women from the women's centres make their choices is Bourdieu's idea of *habitus* (Bourdieu, 1977). This habitus constitutes the taken-for-granted assumptions of any group of people; it is not a conscious set of beliefs nor is it a formulated set of rules. It is rather a way in which the parameters of possibility are set for people at different layers of social stratification. Bourdieu had developed the concept when first trying to understand the barriers that kept working-class people from entering higher education, and concluded that the not-for-us mindsets he was encountering were to do with a tacit recognition of the real distribution of social power. Habitus then is the way in which social groups become complicit in limiting the horizons of possibility for themselves – the process is neither voluntary nor involuntary, but the unconscious negotiation of a social space

It has no better illustration than the following vignette from Sally Belfrage's sharp-eyed account of women in Northern Ireland, *The Crack – A Belfast Year*. Recalling a series of telling moments she refers to:

> *The residents at a battered wives' refuge, Protestant and Catholic living together not only contentedly but with a sense of true, almost miraculous discovery of each other. When presented with the notion that they might try to find permanent housing together, they vetoed it solidly: 'I feel safer in my own area'* (Belfrage, 1987: 288).

This captures the two truths about women and peacebuilding in Northern Ireland: it has been possible to build bridges across the sectarian divide, but those who build the bridges accept the existence of the two blocs as the permanent reality.

Conclusion

The women's centres, the women's peace initiatives and the feminist movement have all contributed in their own ways to the creation of neutral spaces and alternative political values. In their different ways they fit with radical pluralist ideas of politics which hold that women's political identity is different from, rather than less than, that of men. Certainly the style of openness, co-operation and dialogue developed by the women's centres has been markedly different from the aggressive and antagonistic politics in male-dominated organisations and some remarkable forms of cross-community solidarity have developed as a result. The type of feminism that has resulted – family feminism – fits with the theoretical models of maternal feminism articulated by writers like Ruddick (1990), Offen (1998) and Elshtain (1990, 1993), and in terms of geopolitics can also be aligned with women's peace movements elsewhere. The reality, as I have shown, is that women's centres have been chary of Northern Ireland peace initiatives, including even those, like the Northern Ireland Women's Coalition, that would wish to claim their support. The idea that the discourses developed at community level are constitutive of new forms of politics may be seen with hindsight as part of the inflation of hopes that accompanied the emergence of a political settlement, but they have been useful in drawing attention to the special character of women's social practices in the working-class communities of Northern Ireland, and in particular to the educational activities of organisations like the Women's Information Group, or local centres like the Churchwell Women's Centre or the Ballymac Women's Centre.

Ultimately though, the best tribute to women's education is that painted on a wall in the Markets area of Belfast. Friendly Street which, despite its name, has played host to a number of brutal killings, also conveyed messages of militant republican resistance on the wall that faces out towards Belfast's central station. In 2005 a new mural went up in Friendly Street which remains in place to this day. Instead of presenting images of masked men the mural sets out to celebrate women's education. The painting is divided into two in a 'before and after' sequence. The left hand side shows a woman in 1905 holding aloft a rolling pin while all around her are images of domesticity: a pram, weighing scales, a young baby. The other side of the painting shows a woman, the same woman in fact, but as the liberated woman of today she is surrounded with icons of adult learning: a neat pile of books, various computer symbols and a mortar board. She herself is wearing a graduation gown and is jubilantly holding aloft a degree parchment. The message is clear: liberation has been achieved through education.

There can be few other examples in Europe of a form of adult learning receiving such voluntary and sincere endorsement from a working-class community.

References

Abbott, M. and Frazer, H. (1985) *Women and community work in Northern Ireland*. Belfast: Farset Community Press.

Aretxaga, B. (1997) Shattering silence: women, nationalism and political subjectivity in the North. Princeton, NJ: Princeton University Press.

Ashe, F. (2006) 'The Virgin Mary connection: reflections on feminism and Northern Irish politics', *Critical Review of International Social and Political Philosophy*, 9: 4, Dec., 573–88.

Bairnier, A. (1999) 'Masculinity, violence and the Irish peace process', *Capital and Class*, 23, 123–44.

Bardon, J. (1992) *A history of Ulster*. Belfast: Blackstaff Press.

Barr, J. (1999) *Liberating knowledge: research, feminism and adult education*. Leicester: NIACE.

Belfrage, S. (1987) *The Crack – A Belfast Year*. London: Andre Deutsch.

Bourdieu, P. (1977) *Outline of a theory of practice*. Cambridge: Cambridge University Press.

Cockburn, C. (1998) *The space between us: negotiating gender and national identities in conflict*. London: Zed Books.

Connolly, L. (2003) 'Theorizing Ireland: social theory and the politics of identity', *Sociology* 37(1), 173–82.

Coulter, C. (1993) *The hidden tradition: feminism, women and nationalism in Ireland*. Cork: Cork University Press.

Edgerton, L. (1986) 'Public protest, domestic acquiescence: women in Northern Ireland', in R. Ridd and H. Callaway (eds), *Caught up in conflict: women's responses to political strife*. London: Macmillan.

Elshtain, J. B. (1990) *Power trips and other journeys: essays in feminism as civil discourse*. Madison: University of Wisconsin Press.

Elshtain, J. B. (1993) Public man, private woman: women in social and political thought Princeton, NJ: Princeton University Press.

Evason, E. (1991) *Against the grain: the contemporary women's movement in Northern Ireland*. Dublin: Attic Press.

Fairweather, E., McDonough, R. and McFadyean, M. (1984) *Only the rivers run free: Northern Ireland and women's war*. London: Pluto Press.

Fearon, K. and McWilliams, M. (2000) 'Swimming against the mainstream: the Northern Ireland Women's Coalition', in: C. Davis, and C. Roulston (eds), *Gender, democracy and inclusion*, 174–240. Basingstoke: Palgrave.

Field, J, (2000) *Lifelong learning and the new educational order*. Stoke-on-Trent: Trentham Books.

Fraser, G. and Morgan, V., (1994) *The company we keep: women, community and organisations*. Coleraine: Centre for the Study of Conflict, University of Ulster.

Gilligan, C. (1982) *In a different voice* London: Harvard University Press.

Hanna's House *Strategic plan* at www.wrda.net/wrdanews/data/upimages/HH_strategicplan_2006. pdf.

Hargie, O. and Dickson, D. (2004) *Researching the Troubles: social science perspectives on the Northern Ireland conflict.* Edinburgh and London: Mainstream.

Hennessy, T. (1999) *The Northern Ireland peace process: ending the Troubles?* Dublin: Gill and Macmillan.

Hernes, H. (2000) *Welfare state and women power.* Oslo: Norwegian University Press.

Hope, A. (1992) 'Sharing and learning: non-vocational education for women in Northern Ireland', M Ed thesis. Belfast: University of Ulster.

Lister, R. (1997) *Citizenship: feminist perspectives.* Basingstoke: Macmillan.

Little, A. (2002) 'Feminism and the politics of difference in Northern Ireland', *Journal of Political Ideologies*, 7 (2), 163–77.

Loughran, M.C. (1987) 'The origins and development of feminist groups in Northern Ireland', PhD thesis. Belfast: Queen's University Belfast.

McMinn, J. (2000) 'The changers and the changed: an analysis of women's community education groups in the north and south of Ireland', Dublin: Equality Studies Centre, University College Dublin, PhD thesis.

Morgan, V. and Fraser, G. (1994) *The company we keep: women, community and organisations.* Coleraine: The Centre for the Study of Conflict, University of Ulster.

Moloney, E. (2007) *A secret history of the IRA* 2nd edition. London: Penguin.

Munby, Z. (2003) 'Women's involvement in the WEA and women's education', in S. K. Roberts (ed.) *A ministry of enthusiasm: centenary essays on the Workers' Educational Association.* London: Pluto Press.

Offen, K. (1988) 'Defining feminism: a comparative historical approach', *Signs: Journal of Women in Culture and Society* 14: 1, 119–57.

Porter, E. (2000) 'Women in Northern Irish politics: difference matters', in Davis, C. and Roulston, C. (eds) *Gender, democracy and inclusion in Northern Ireland*, pp 164–186. Basingstoke: Palgrave.

Porter, E. (2007) Peacebuilding: women in international perspective. Basingstoke: Palgrave.

Reardon, B. (1993) *Women and peace; feminist visions of global security.* New York: State University of New York Press.

Rooney, E. (2002) 'Community development in times of trouble: reflections on the community women's sector in the north of Ireland', *Community Development Journal*, 37:1, January, 34–46.

Rooney, E. and Woods, M. (1995) *Women, community and politics in Northern Ireland: a Belfast study*. Belfast: University of Ulster.

Roulston, C. (2000) 'Democracy and the challenge of democracy: new visions, new processes', in C. Davis, and C. Roulston (eds) *Gender, democracy and inclusion in Northern Ireland*, 24–48, Basingstoke: Palgrave.

Ruddick, S. (1990) *Maternal thinking: towards a politics of peace*. London: The Women's Press.

Taillon, R. (2000) *The social and economic impact of women's centres in Greater Belfast*. Belfast: Women's Support Network.

Vital Voices website at www.vitalvoices.org/desktopdefault.aspx?page_id.8 .

Ward, M. (ed) (1986) *A difficult dangerous honesty: 10 years of feminism in Northern Ireland*. Belfast: Women's book Collection.

Ward, M. (1991) 'The women's movement in Northern Ireland: twenty years on', in S. Hutton and P. Stewart, *Ireland's histories*. London: Routledge.

Wilson, A. (2007) 'Theoretical underpinnings: women, gender, feminizing and politics', in C. Annesley, F. Gains and K. Rummey (eds) *Women and New Labour*. Bristol: The Policy Press.

CHAPTER FOUR

Community engagement and the idea of a 'good university'

Sue Webb

Introduction

Community engagement has become an increasingly significant strand of activity for many universities in the UK over the past decade (UUK, 2007). Yet, it is not a new idea. Community engagement has had a long history of association with universities, both in the UK and worldwide, although the activities encompassed by this term vary extensively. For some it is a concept that is embedded in the core purposes of higher education, for example, where it played a central role in the establishment of the Victorian civic universities in the UK and the Land Grant universities in the USA (Watson, 2007). For others, it is a more recent idea used to describe relationships built around teaching and research between universities and their communities whether these are local, regional, national or international (Boyer, 1990). In both of these accounts it is presented as a good thing and as an indicator of the contribution of the university to 'public good'.

This chapter provides a conceptual contribution to this debate. It begins with a discussion of what being good might mean and will explore this in relation to distinct purposes, missions and histories of different universities. It will draw on political philosophy to identify different understandings of good to provide a framework for an educational policy analysis of the rhetorical use of the term 'good' in current rankings and benchmarking of universities. It argues that this is increasingly relevant given the growth of leagues tables in higher education and the growth of benchmarking and measurement of the scale of community engagement. Comparison of these different notions of 'good' will raise questions for further empirical work to examine how community engagement contributes to 'public good' and to the making of a 'good university'.

In addition, by focusing on conceptions of a 'good university' the chapter will engage with a central concern of this book, that is the intersections of lifelong learning, social justice and conceptions of community. This is because there are two ways in which universities relate to the concept of lifelong learning: on the one hand, there is their role in preparing young adults to become lifelong learners, and on the other hand, there is their role in encouraging and supporting lifelong learning and the widening of access to higher education opportunities for adults across the life course. Arguably, in order to assess the relationship between universities' lifelong learning practices and social justice, it is important to understand how universities undertake these activities, how they define and determine with which communities they will engage and how they conceptualise being 'good'.

The 'good university' in neoliberal times

Good is a normative term that is used frequently to value and categorise activities and practices to which professionals and organisations aspire. It is a particularly crucial value laden term when it is applied to activities, such as education, that are the subject of public policy and funding from the public purse. In the organisational cultural language of universities we can recognise some commonsense usages of the term. Teachers and professionals will aim to undertake 'good practice' in teaching and research, students to learn well and do 'good work' and institutions aim to produce good outcomes for the economy and fulfil objectives for society more widely.

At the same time, in this era of globalisation, universities compete, not only nationally, but also worldwide, to position themselves within various national and international league tables. A number of these league tables indicate the positional value of their measurements and rankings through the use of adjectives such as 'good' or 'top'.[1] Whilst the use value

---

[1] Examples of university league tables include: 1. World-wide tables such as the *Times Higher Educational Supplement* QS World University Ranking, see www.thes.co.uk/worldrankings, and the Academic Ranking of Top 500 Universities, see http://www.ed.sjtu.ed.cn/ranking.htm; and at national levels, *The Times Good University Guide* (UK); and the *Australian Good University Guide*.

of these two adjectives may be interchangeable, as evidenced by the juxtaposing of the results of many such tables on university web-pages in order to show the institution in the best possible light, arguably philosophical they have very different meanings. The term 'good' might include ideas of ethical commitment and reasoning, behaviour and intent, and benefit and outcome for private individuals or the public, as well as, a position in a hierarchy. In contrast, the term 'top' suggests simply a place in a social ranking. Given the malleability of these terms in everyday usage, and their underpinning philosophical distinctiveness, an exploration of the diverse meanings of 'good' will be important in order to understand how the term 'good university' is being used in neoliberal times.

Another way of understanding whether or not education is a public or a private good is to consider its place in the political economy and the debates that determine good outcomes by identifying its sources of funding. From a commonsense point of view we might assume that definitions of public or private good equate with public and private distinctions in the funding and organisation of higher education institutions and in the benefits they provide for individuals and for the state. In other words, if the state is the prime funder then it might be assumed that the outcome produced will be for the public good, and vice versa, private funding would be solely for private good.

Arguably, underpinning these commonsense understandings that public universities are engaged in producing public goods, which also might maximise individuals' private goods, are liberal philosophical notions associated with utilitarianism. Galbraith's (1996) precepts for a 'good' society are an example. These precepts were based on utilitarian notions of the importance of assigning to the state one's individual natural rights to freedom of action, and thereby enabling the state to maximise the common good, whilst creating the conditions in which one's own private good also benefits. These are consequentialist definitions of good. They assume that public or common good is an outcome from participation in political debate in a liberal democracy when such debates result in consensus about how the state should organise conditions for individual freedoms to prosper. These definitions assume that the contract people make with the state carry rights and responsibilities to participate in social democracy, and, at the same time, notions of the social responsibilities of the state to create the fair conditions under which individuals can flourish. In this form of collectivist or classic liberalism the state is expected to take responsibility for maximising public good by, for example, creating the conditions for economic growth, universal access to education, protection of the young, the old, the disabled and the environment.

However, the nation states within which many institutions are located today are often characterised as neoliberal market based economies in which the state has withdrawn somewhat from its social responsibilities (Giroux, 2002; Olssen and Peters, 2005). Consequently, the landscape of higher education is increasingly varied with different mixes of public and private funding and various public and private beneficial outcomes. As Marginson (2007c, 316–17) notes,

> *The ownership of higher education can be exclusively public, or mixed, or exclusively private. But almost everywhere in the world, what is produced is a variable mix of public and private goods . . . Thus, free state-controlled universities produce certain private goods; while at the same time even the most expensive Ivy league private universities contribute to public goods, collective goods and externalities.*

What is understood here by 'good' and how is it possible for 'good' to be distributed in these counter-intuitive ways so that public funding can produce private goods and private funding produce public goods? For Marginson (2007c) this is possible because higher education providers can be privately or publicly funded or a mixture, but the measure of goodness relates not to their sources of funding, but to their outputs and activities and the relationship of these to civil society and the state. In this way, private providers can produce public goods just as easily, or not, as public providers. Private providers are able to produce public good outcomes through, for example, the spill-over effects between sectors so that overall their efforts enhance knowledge, collective literacy and a common culture. Equally, under the conditions of neoliberal market economies, publicly funded institutions may focus on producing and increasing private goods such as individual status differentials through qualifications that attract individual rewards and benefits. Indeed, some would argue that this is the crux of today's neoliberal project, as opposed to its idealised nineteenth century forms. In this narrative, publicly funded university education is regarded as part of a wider neoliberal project that 'undoes past collective gains, privatises public goods, uses state expenditure to subsidise profits, weakens national regulations, removes trade barriers, and so intensifies global market competition' (Levidow, 2002: 228). Tellingly, Slaughter and Rhodes (2004: 7) document many examples from the United States in which public and private funding of universities, and their faculty and students are increasingly intertwined, with the effect that they are 'shifting from a public good knowledge/learning regime to an academic capitalist knowledge/learning regime'. As such, these practices could be seen as simply reinvigorating the central ideology of liberal free market, laissez faire individualism, albeit with a different model of the role of the state and the organisations the state chooses to fund to facilitate enterprise (Olssen and Peters, 2005). In this analysis of neoliberalism, the state is recognised as assuming some social responsibility to foster public goods through establishing the social, political and economic conditions to develop private goods, such as freedom, choice and individual enterprise. Higher education and lifelong learning policies and the practices of universities become some of the tools and apparatus the state uses to identify policy problems and fashion solutions.

In other words, these policy problems and their solutions are framed through a language of lifelong learning that promotes public good and social justice but operate in a context where market competition and reputational hierarchies undermine the extent to which private goods can be equitably distributed. For example, it is widely recognised that economic concerns and the dominance of human capital theory, which are central to the neoliberal policy conceptualisation of the problems and solutions to globalisation, are being imposed on the field of education, including higher education (Olssen and Peters, 2005). In addition, this includes an understanding that the field is increasingly globalised because of the influence of international agencies such as the Organisation for Economic Co-operation and Development (OECD) and the World Bank on national policies (Lingard, Rowelle and Taylor, 2005). And this has resulted in universal trends in higher education to commodify teaching, learning and research, and manage this through a new emphasis on Lyotard's concept of 'performativity' and audit (Barnett, 2000) of institutions and the employability of those being worked upon, the students.

The growth of league tables is just one facet of this shift towards valorising economic benefits. Increasing global competition between universities is leading to steeper hierarchies between institutions within and between countries and a concentration in the main, in the United States and the UK, of what (Marginson, 2004: 175) calls the 'winner takes all' institutions. It is a competition in which position in the pecking order denotes a positional good that brings rewards for some and greater disadvantages for others at both the level of institutions and the level of individuals, their staff and students.

Increasingly, the two major international league tables that confer these rewards or goods are provided by Times Higher Education (THE) in the UK and the Shanghai Jiao Tong University, China, which date only from 2003 and 2004 respectively, but now are quoted widely. In spite of their ubiquity, there is much dispute as to whether or not league tables are valid and objective measures of the good practices or outcomes of universities (Berry, 1999; Tight, 2000), and much argument about the significance of the different measurement tools and scales employed. The UK *Times Higher Education Supplement*'s (THES's) World University Rankings are regarded as the brand leader and the most subjective (Watson, 2007). Until 2010 their criteria gave the greatest weighting to peer judgements by including academic peer review comprising 40 per cent of the weighting and employer ratings, first introduced in 2005, comprising 10 per cent. In 2010 a new set of criteria were developed with the commercial publisher Thomson Reuters, which is experienced in producing citation indices, and has led to their claiming to have attained the 'gold standard' in international performance comparisons.[2] In contrast, the Shanghai Jiao Tong top 500 has always been based more on publicly available indicators, such as research citations and prizes that skew the focus towards particular ways of measuring research output. Therefore, the criteria for doing well in these competitions are partial and dominated by indicators that favour universities with a history and mission of high volume 'good' research and operate in a global knowledge market. The obverse is that the criteria place less emphasis on public goods, such as equal opportunities and community engagement that might require more qualitative measures of social change and arguably fit more closely the history and missions of many newer institutional higher education players.

Nevertheless, taking part in the competition is so important to institutional reputations that few opt out regardless of the appropriateness or not of these criteria to measure the effects of distinct missions (Proven and Abercromby, 2000). Employing the concept of governmentality from Foucault, participation in these competitions means that all university players (regardless of their different missions and aspirations to produce

---

[2] In 2010 the THEs introduced a new set of performance indicators 'designed to capture the full range of university activities from teaching to research to knowledge transfer' (http://www.timeshighereducation.co.uk/world-university-rankings/)

public or private goods) subject themselves to valorising research. By this practice other goods or objectives (whether they be for public or private benefit), that some universities might aspire to, are devalued and positioned outside the game of what is a 'good university'. Or as a Foucauldian might say, they are rendered 'other'.

In contrast, at the national level there are examples where a wider definition of good is used. For example, within the UK, the *Times* 'Good University Guide' utilises performance measures that highlight individualised and privatised conceptions of 'good' outputs for the institutions, for students and for staff. For example, the measures include student satisfaction, research quality, entry standards, staff-student ratios, services and facilities spending, completion rates of good honours degrees and graduate prospects. However such indicators of 'goodness' foreground the auditing activities that shape and within which we complicity organise our universities as entrepreneurial (Barnett, 2003), displaying market behaviour (Delanty, 2001) and new public managerialism (Deem, Hilyard and Read, 2008). Therefore rather than being seen as indicators of a broader view of public good, the 'good university' in this neoliberal discourse 'is construed in terms of our identities as consumers' (Bryman, 1995: 195 adapted from a citation in Giroux, 2002: 430).

A further issue with this neoliberal view of the public and private goods produced by this notion of a 'good university' is that these outcomes are often concomitant with reducing equitable access (Marginson, 2007c) because league tables result in institutional differentiation and hierarchical ordering. A further consequence for individuals is that a university education, which appears to provide a level playing field in the human capital neoliberal discourse becomes differently valorised and positioned in the competition for 'good' jobs. In the world of mass higher education, argue Brown and Hesketh (2004), a degree is no longer a badge of distinction. Instead, drawing on data from the UK, they argue that in the competition for employment graduates find themselves having to draw on other resources and their personal social capital to secure scarce positions whilst the recruiting companies and universities play the same reputational games to secure their positions in their respective hierarchies. The effect is that access to the lifelong learning of a university education continues to reproduce social differentiation rather than social justice. In contrast a 'good university' in a Galbraithian good society would be regulated and steered by state intervention and funding drivers to counter these tendencies of markets to under-provide equitable access and outcomes. Clearly, the conception of 'good' that predominates in the UK with the reward systems of the market-focused league tables seems far from this Galbraithian view.

Nevertheless, within the UK there are some examples of state interventions to modify the workings of the market. In England, for example, the Higher Education Funding Council (HEFCE) sets policies and institutional benchmarks for Widening Participation and Fair Access.[3] From 2009 universities and other providers of higher education have been required to develop widening participation strategic assessments and evaluation of practice measurements. At national level, the funding council produces annual performance rankings that include measures for the recruitment and retention of students from low participation neighbourhoods and lower social economic groups, and these are used to determine part of the institutional funding. However, these measures of public goods are not included in commercial rankings such as the *THES* 'Good University Guide'. And, at the global level there are no such regulating bodies or even spaces for publicly debating goodness, argues Marginson (2007c) with the consequence that global patterns of domination and subordination are barely modified by any conception of global public goods. Another exception however, is Australia where there is a growing debate about these matters, particularly the methodologies and measurement indices of league tables (Williams, 2008) and the Bradley Report even suggested that Australia should reject the 'influence of university rankings as a driver of public policy making' (Sheil, 2010: 70).

Such questioning of the role of league tables is somewhat limited though. Instead, where there appear to be spaces for international cross border spill-over in ideas about the purposes of universities, the debates about global public goods have been somewhat overshadowed by the growing marketised and economistic privatised discourse, albeit sometimes dressed up in a language of social justice. For example, in the UK and particularly in England there has come to be an acknowledgement of the strong Eurocentric dimension to the development of the increasingly economistic policies on lifelong learning. Key documents produced by the European Union (EU) and the Organisation for Economic Co-operation and Development (OECD) have framed much of the conceptualisation of lifelong learning policy globally (Preece, 2006;

---

[3] See for example http://www.hefce.ac.uk/widen/ – for current policy and funding steers

Warren and Webb, 2007: 6). Utilitarian lifelong learning has been promoted by policy texts across Europe, Australasia, Canada and Japan (Field, 2006; Warren and Webb, 2007). More optimistically, Marginson (2007c: 316) suggests that the public/private relationship to goodness is 'a positive sum, one can augment the other'. This leads me to ask whether there are spaces where individuals and institutions might position-take rather than be positioned, in order to engage in a debate about the criteria for developing global public good in globalised higher education. We might usefully draw on Lawler's (2005) conception of internationalism and the 'good' state, which is one that is committed to moral purposes beyond itself.

To develop these ideas further the next section of the chapter will argue that rather than taking existing audit measures and league table statistics as adequate indicators of a '*good university*', we need to remember that 'if historical ideas about the functions of universities are to be drawn on as resources for thinking and acting, they must be talked about in a language which challenges the language of managerialism.' (McLean, 2006: 50). Similarly, Montesinos *et al.* (2008) take up this concern and argue that there should be a new dimension to university rankings based on university mission. They explore the implications of going beyond teaching and research by considering the introduction of measurements and benchmarks to rank university contributions to a third mission, or Services to Society, which they argue has at least three dimensions: a non-profit social approach; an entrepreneurial focus and an innovative approximation. Arguably, this would require changing the competition to include activities that demonstrated how a university could do 'good' for different communities drawn from the public at large rather prioritising measures that only valorise being recognised as 'good' by one's like minded peers.

The 'good university' and community engagement in the past

University missions have undergone significant changes since their inception. The first wave of expansion in the late nineteenth century saw the ancient universities that had focused on religion and philosophy led by the clergy to educate a male elite being outstripped by institutions concerned to extend to a wider audience understanding of the scientific disciplines and professions associated with the growing industrial economies. But

Community engagement and the idea of a 'good university'

not all scholars embraced the new more utilitarian education. John Henry Newman's lectures, written whilst he was Rector of the Catholic University of Ireland in the 1850s and published under the title of 'The Idea of a University', presented a different form of liberalism. This acknowledged the value of useful knowledge, yet considered that the main purpose of a university education was to be the pursuit of

> *Liberal or Philosophical Knowledge . . . that it has a very tangible, real, and sufficient end, though the end cannot be divided from that knowledge itself. Knowledge is capable of being its own end. Such is the constitution of the human mind, that any kind of knowledge, if it be really such, is its own reward.* (Newman, 1858, reprinted 2007, 102–3).

A little earlier in the nineteenth century in Europe, a different brand of liberalism was being played out in debates about the purpose of universities. The Humboldtian idea of a university, associated with the founding of the University of Berlin in 1810, and influenced by a Kantian conception of liberalism is based on the notion of the Categorical Imperative. This categorical notion of goodness, which is about doing what is right for the right reason, rather than based on consequentialist or utilitarian decisions, became an influential underpinning of the Humboldtian university. Within this model university education was based on the unity of teaching and research and the search for truth combined with a desire to live a correct life (Bertilsson, 1992). Whilst such conceptualisations may have continued to inform debates about the role of universities, the state and their funding (Frflich, Coate, Mignot-Gerard and Knill, 2010), my purpose in reflecting back on these nineteenth century discussions is to consider what we can learn from the conceptualisations of 'public good' and universities from these two key thinkers. I am concerned to understand the extent to which the expansion of university education in the nineteenth century was part of a liberal movement for self actualisation and the search for the 'correct life' or was part of a process associated with the growth of new social groups and the formation of new professional social classes who were to steer the economic and social transformations of industrialisation.

The origins of many of the world's most well regarded universities, as measured by the good or top university league tables, lie in the nineteenth century struggles to widen participation in civil society and establish participatory democracies in distinct or emerging nation states.

Civic support was a significant factor in the establishment and initial missions of the Victorian civic universities in England and their counterparts in Canada, Australia and New Zealand and in the legislation for the land grant universities and colleges of the United States (Casey, 2006, McDowell, 2001; Watson, 2003). Today, these origins still resonate in the missions of some of these institutions. For example, in the United States, Land Grant universities established by federal law in the late nineteenth century still enshrine the rights to education for working people and a tripartite purpose of teaching, research and public service (McDowell, 2001). The historical foundational imperative to provide public benefit continues to reach beyond the foundational legal obligation argues Ostrander (2004), whose study of civic engagement in five institutions in the United States identified the importance of this historic factor in civic engagement today.

In Canada, Australia and New Zealand, where Marginson (2007) argues that universities in so-called 'Westminster' countries are aligned through their similarities (to the UK) in governance and the role of the central government steer, they share similarities in their social histories and fraught relationships and settlements with their indigenous populations, especially in relation to access to education. Similarly, in Europe, during the nineteenth century and early twentieth century, struggles were also taking place between, on the one hand, communities promoting the educational, political and social aspirations of the working class, women, and those concerned with fostering new national identities and, on the other, the traditional intellectuals and ancient university communities (Steele, 2007). This early struggle for access to lifelong learning inspired developments in Northern and Western Europe, and motivated Grundtvig's call for folk high schools and a Nordic university for 'a new historical, universal science, encompassing the whole of life' (Steele, 2007 citing a quote from Henningsen, 1993: 290).

Arguably therefore, what we might now call lifelong learning provided the seed-bed for the modern university system. Yet this seed-bed was formed out of an alliance of different interests, particularly in the UK. It contained elements of tension and discord out of which has come the mass higher education system we know today with its concerns about access, widening participation and social justice. In other words, we can trace back to that period the debates about who should have access to the universities, about what knowledge is important and what are the purposes of learning. Essentially this was a concern with who should have access to a public good, the new scientific and cultural knowledge that accompanied and enabled industrialisation and the growth of modern capitalism.

Taking the University of Sheffield as a case in point, it was awarded a Royal Charter in 1905 after the coming together of three local institutions: the Sheffield School of Medicine, Firth College and the Sheffield Technical School. Unpacking the interests and purposes of the three original constituent organisations of the University is revealing. The first of these institutions was set up to teach science subjects to medical students. By the late nineteenth century it had merged with Firth College. This originated in the Cambridge University Extension Movement, a scheme designed to bring university teaching to the large towns and cities of England. Skilled artisans, shop-keepers and other working people, both women and men were the main students. The success of these part-time evening courses led Mark Firth, a local steel manufacturer, to establish the College in 1879 as a centre for teaching Arts and Science subjects 'for the moral, social and intellectual elevation of the masses, as well as of the middle and upper classes' (cited in Mathers, 2005). Further fund raising by the local community established the Sheffield Technical School in 1884 to address the need for better technical training of the men responsible for running the industries of Sheffield, particularly steelmaking.

Looking back we can imagine the three institutions reflected three distinct constituencies in the struggle to establish what Habermas (1989) called the 'public sphere', or what we might call civil society. It is an essential component of our modern societal structures, because it is enables the formation of a separate political state, back then this meant a political state distinct from the monarchy and the church and underpinned by a market economy. Extending formal public education was critical to the formation of the public sphere, although not acknowledged by Habermas (Marginson, 2007b) and the struggle to widen educational access was hotly contested (Steele, 2007). There were two strands in this struggle: on the one hand, the activities of the largely middle class, professional and entrepreneurial groups seeking to spread the Enlightenment project of scientific understanding and rationality through their scientific societies; and on the other hand, the more working class mutual aid and co-operative self-help movements and nascent labour movements who wanted access to education and citizenship. These working class activists often used the same 'scientific rationalist' arguments (drawing on Marxism or religious nonconformism) to challenge the exclusionary effects of the bourgeois social policies that linked the right to vote and democratic representation to property ownership. I would add a third constituency in this struggle, that of women, both middle class and working class, who came together through the suffrage movement and trade union and co-operative movement campaigning for the right to vote, for access to skilled employment, trade union membership, and higher education. It was women from the *North of England Council for Promoting the Higher Education of Women* who first requested an extension lecture series in the north of England in 1867, a lecture series that was pivotal to the development of the northern civic universities (Mitchell, 2000). How the university positioned itself in relation to these different constituencies requires further empirical and historical analysis, however it is interesting to note that teaching and research in the three originating areas, medicine, engineering and adult education/lifelong learning continue to this day, arguably, ensuring that the university outcomes include both private and public goods, as well as, positional good within global league tables.

The 'good university' and community engagement in new times

Although I have argued so far that the dominance of university league tables and rankings has neglected wider conceptions of public good, increasingly there are alternative models or indicators that measure other outcomes. Arguably these are more in keeping with the categorical liberal purposes or alternatively the Galbraithian 'good society' liberalism outlined above. This is because they return to the historic missions of many of the nineteenth century state funded universities, albeit reformulated for new times. For example, in the United States the Community Engagement Classification (Carnegie Foundation for the Advancement of Teaching, 2008) has been developed. It is an elective classification designed to promote and develop standards to recognise those activities in institutional missions that are not included in other national data. The main focus is on capturing collaborations between institutions and their communities (local, regional, national or global) including curricular engagement and outreach and partnerships. The impact of this classification has grown significantly since the first listing in 2006 and extended its constituency well beyond the land grant universities so that in 2008, 120 institutions were successfully classified.

Similar developments are emerging in the UK, albeit less formally structured and extensive (UUK, 2007). In 2008 the Higher Education Funding Council for England funded a four year initiative for six higher education institutions from across the sector, to develop a co-ordinated approach to recognising, rewarding and building capacity for public engagement for the sector. And alongside this, twelve Russell Group Universities in the UK[4] in conjunction with The Corporate Citizenship Company (TCCC, 2004) have developed a Higher Education Community Engagement Model (HECEM) to provide a systematic tool for measuring community activities that are conducted over and above the university's core purposes of teaching and research. According to the HECEM User Guide the aims of this model are to develop data to inform strategic decisions, demonstrate value for money and for marketing and public relations purposes. Clearly, although the model is designed to 'capture' community activities (User Guide p1), the purposes behind this framework align well with a neoliberal marketised concept of the utility of the public goods produced by these activities, rather than a categorical notion of doing 'good' that is right for its own sake. This is hardly surprising given the initial argument of this chapter about the growth of neoliberalism and it suggests that conceptions of 'goodness' even in relation to community engagement may be informed by an audit and managerial culture. In this regard some caution and criticality is suggested in relation to these new indicators because they may be little different to those university league tables and rankings to which they are designed to add value. Whether or not these models constrain more inclusive approaches to lifelong learning because they set limits on the moral agency of universities and shape the ways their communities do 'good' things is a matter that can only be addressed through empirical work.

Yet, some universities deliberately connect their current activities in community engagement with those early forms of civic and community engagement that helped establish what Habermas called the public sphere. The scholarship of this community engagement has at its core a recognition that one of the purposes of a liberal higher education is to develop active citizens who are able to participate in the democratic

---

[4] The Russell Group is a collaboration of 20 UK research-intensive universities to which entry for students is highly competitive and selective. The group formed in 1994 to represent their interests to government, business and industry and the wider public and more details can be found on their website www.russellgroup.ac.uk.

conversation of the country and society more widely (see for example, in the USA (Sandmann, 2008), Canada (Hall, 2009) and Australia (Winter et al., 2006)). In the USA, although many align the literature on community engagement with the missions of universities to do 'public good' as argued by John Dewey, by educating citizens for democratic listening (Garrison, 1990) and active civic participation, some practitioners question whether the current practice of community education service work is always benign (Bringle and Hatcher, 2000, Peterson, 2009). Similar continuity of a mission narrative can be observed in the UK. Traces of the history of university extension units are visible in the current widening participation, community outreach, engagement and volunteering practices of some institutions (Webb, 2010). Yet Duke (2008) suggests that for the most part many university extension departments have failed to adapt to changing institutional priorities to the extent that these current practices have largely by-passed the field of continuing education. Arguably one consequence of this disjuncture and recent reinvention of community engagement could be a loss of collective memory and understanding amongst practitioners and therefore possibly a shift in the 'public good' done by this rebadged form of community engagement. In the UK, community engagement is often linked to a social justice mission for universities encompassing widening access, outreach, and student mentoring and volunteering. Yet unless this approach questions the meritocratic and qualifications based selection policies that determine who can benefit from higher education, the engagement with communities becomes somewhat limited (Furlong and Cartmel, 2009). In other words, the argument used is that if pedagogies and community engagement practitioners do not question the inequalities of power between universities and the communities with which they work, rather than doing 'public good', they are more likely to be contributing to a deficit-based model of service and provision. Likewise, Watson (2007) asks how can we manage civic and community engagement when different communities want the universities to engage for different purposes. He suggests that governments want universities to develop human capital, communities want both human capital and cohesive capital and modern students and teachers increasingly want to develop creative capital.

Conclusion

Community engagement has joined the list of indicators used to measure the performance of universities in several countries worldwide. To date, the extent to which these measure have more in common with those other tools of audit, new public management and marketing and public relations than they have with a concept of public good, is still an open question. For some institutions the rationale for community engagement is closely linked with their historic missions and arguably does sit more easily with a notion of 'good' based on doing what is right, rather than doing what maximises the greatest rewards. Whilst for others, community engagement has become the new malleable term for new times that neatly and usefully updates and replaces that slippery and now old and often exclusionary term, lifelong learning (Burke and Jackson, 2007; Field, 2006). To ascertain whether or not the turn towards communities in the discourses and practices of lifelong learning will further the project for social justice requires further empirical work, as this chapter has argued.

Nevertheless, the turn towards community engagement can be understood as a strategy of re-envisioning the mission of some universities and a countervailing activity to the globalising tendencies of differentiation, selectivity and exclusivity that mark the discussions of 'good' in market economies focused on league tables. However, institutions cannot escape completely the market expectations to be position-takers and to be positioned in all activities with which they engage. Thus utilitarian and instrumental notions of good are likely to pervade even those activities, such as community engagement, where institutions seek to link to a more categorical notion of good through doing the right thing to promote social justice. However well meaning are the strategies driven by those rediscovering their institutional missions and legacy narratives to be a 'good university', it is likely that there will be equally forceful internal and external pressures from the audit and accounting culture to identify the costs and benefits of such activities. Intervention in these debates requires not only the analysis derived from further empirical work, but also as this chapter has argued, it requires a critical and philosophical engagement with diverse liberal understandings of the concept of 'good'. Without this, institutional claims and position taking as a 'good university' should be treated with caution.

References

Barnett, R. (2003) *Beyond All Reason: Living With Ideology in the University*. Buckingham, UK: Society for Research into Higher Education and the Open University Press.

Berry, C. (1999) 'University league tables: artefacts and inconsistencies in individual rankings.' *Higher Education Review* 31: 2, 3–11.

Bertilsson, M. (1992) 'From university to comprehensive higher education: on the widening gap between "Lehre und Leben"', *Higher Education*, 24: 3, 333–49.

Boyer, E. L. (1996) 'The scholarship of engagement', *Journal of Public Service and Outreach*, 1: 1, 11–20.

Bringle R. G and Hatcher, J. A. (2000) 'Service Learning in Higher Education', *The Journal of Higher Education*, 71, 273–90.

Brown, P. and Hesketh, A. (2004) *The mismanagement of talent: employability and jobs in the knowledge economy*. Oxford: Oxford University Press.

Burke, P., and Jackson, S. (2007) *Reconceptualising lifelong learning, feminist interventions*. London: Routledge.

Carnegie Foundation for the Advancement of Teaching (2008) see http://classifications.carnegiefoundation.org/descriptions/community_engagement.php.

Casey, C. (2006) 'A Knowledge economy and a learning society: a comparative analysis of New Zealand and Australian Experiences', *Compare: A journal of comparative education*, 36: 3, 343–57.

TCCC – The Corporate Citizenship Company (2004) *Higher education community engagement model: final report and analysis*. London: The Corporate Citizenship Company and online http://www.leeds.ac.uk/ace/downloads/Higher%20education%20community%20engagement%20model%20final%20report1.pdf and see http://www2.warwick.ac.uk/about/community/communityhub/model/faq.

Deem, R., Hilyard, S. and Reed, M. (2007) *Knowledge, higher education, and the new managerialism: the changing management of UK universities*. Oxford: Oxford University Press.

Delanty, G. (2001) *2001 Challenging knowledge: the university in the knowledge society*. Buckingham: Open University Press.

Duke, C. (2008) 'Trapped in a local history: why did extramural fail to engage in an era of engagement?' *Adlib, Journal for Continuing Liberal Adult Education*, 36, 3–19.

Field, J. (2006) *Lifelong Learning and the new educational order*, 2nd edn. Stoke-on-Trent: Trentham Books.

Frflich, N., Coate, K., Mignot-Gerard, S. and Knill, C. (2010) 'Einheit von Forschung und Lehre: implications for state funding of universities', *Higher Education Policy*, 23: 2, 195–211.

Furlong, A., and Cartmel, F. (2009) *Higher education and social justice*, Maidenhead: McGraw-Hill Education, Open University Press.

Galbraith, J. K. (1996) *The Good Society*. New York: Mariner Books, Houghton Mifflin.

Garrison, J. W. (1990) 'Philosophy as (vocational) education', *Educational Theory*, 40: 3, 391–406.

Giroux, H. A. (2002) 'Neoliberalism, corporate culture, and the promise of higher education: the university as a democratic public sphere', *Harvard Education Review*, 72: 40, 425–64.

Hall, B. (2009) 'Higher education, community engagement and the public good: building the future of continuing education in Canada', *Canadian Journal of University Continuing Education*, 35: 1, 11–23.

Habermas, J (1989) *The structural transformation of the public sphere: an inquiry in the category of the bourgeois society*. Oxford: Polity.

Lawler, P. (2005) 'The good state in world politics: in praise of "classical internationalism",' *Review of International Studies*, 31: 3.

Levidow, L. (2002) 'Marketizing higher education: neoliberal strategies and counter-strategies', in Robins, K. and Webster, F. (eds), *The virtual university? Knowledge, markets and management*, 227–48. Oxford: Oxford University Press.

Lingard, B., Rowelle, S. and Taylor, S. (2005) 'Globalising policy sociology in education: working Bourdieu', *Journal of Education Policy*, 20: 6, 759–77.

Marginson, S. (2004) 'Competition and markets in higher education: a 'glonacal' analysis', *Policy Futures in Education*, 2: 2, 175–244.

Marginson, S. (2007a) 'Global university rankings: implications in general and for Australia', *Journal of Higher Education Policy and Management*, 29: 2, 131–42.

Marginson, S. (2007b) 'University mission and identity for a post post-public era', *Higher Education Research and Development*, 26: 1, 117–31.

Marginson, S. (2007c) 'The public/private divide in higher education: A global revision', *Higher Education*, 53, 307–33.

Mathers, H. (2005) *Steel city scholars*. London: James and James.

McClean, M. (2006) *Pedagogy and the university: critical theory and practice*. London: Continuum.

McDowell, G. (2001) *Land grant universities and extension in the 21st century renegotiating or extending a social contract*. Iowa: Iowa State University Press.

Montesinos, P., Carot, J.M., Martinez, J-M. and Mora F. (2008) 'Third mission ranking for world class universities: beyond teaching', *Higher Education in Europe*, 33, 259–71.

Newman, J. H. (2007) *The idea of a university*, found in *The Newman reader: works of John Henry Newman*. The National Institute for Newman Studies http://www.newmanreader.org/works/idea/#titlepage.

Ostrander, S.A. (2004) 'Democracy, civic participation and the university: a comparative study of civic engagement on five campuses', *Nonprofit and Voluntary Sector Quarterly*, 33, 74–93.

Olssen, M and Peters, M. (2005) 'Neoliberalism, higher education and the knowledge economy: from the free market to knowledge capitalism', *Journal of Education Policy*, 20, 313–45.

Peterson, T. H. (2009) 'Engaged scholarship: reflections and research on the pedagogy of social change', *Teaching in Higher Education*, 14: 5, 541–52.

Preece, J. (2006) 'Beyond the learning society: the learning world?' *International Journal of Lifelong Education*, 25: 3, 307–20.

Proven D. and Abercromby, K. (2000) *University league tables and rankings: A critical analysis*. CHEMS paper no 30.

Sandmann, L. R. (2008) 'Conceptualisation of the scholarship of engagement in higher education: a strategic review 1996–2006', *Journal of Higher Education Outreach and Engagement*, 12, 91–9.

Slaughter, S. and Rhodes, G. (2005) *Academic capitalism and the new economy, markets states and higher education*. Baltimore: John Hopkins University Press.

Sheil, T. (2010) 'Moving beyond university rankings: developing a world class university system in Australia', *Australian University Review*, 52: 1, 69–76.

Steele, T. (2007) *Knowledge is power, the rise and fall of European popular education movements, 1848–1939*. Bern: Peter Lang.

Tight, M. (2000) 'Do league tables contribute to the development of a quality culture? football and higher education compared', *Higher Education Quarterly*, 0951–5224 54: 1, 22–42.

UUK – Universities UK (2007) *Universities: engaging with local communities* http://www.universitiesuk.ac.uk/Publications/Pages/Publication-262.aspx.

Watson, D. (2003) 'Universities and civic engagement; a critique and a prospectus', Keynote address for the 2nd Biennial 'Inside-Out' conference on the civic role of universities – Charting Uncertainty: Capital, Community and Citizenship, University of Brighton.

Watson, D. (2007) *Managing civic and community engagement*. Maidenhead: McGraw-Hill, Open University Press.

Warren, S. and Webb, S. (2007) 'Challenging lifelong learning policy discourse: where is structure in agency in narrative-based research', *Studies in the Education of Adults* 39: 1, 5–21.

Williams, R. (2008) 'Methodology, meaning and usefulness of rankings', paper for *AFR Higher Education Conference*, Sydney, 14–16 March 2008.

Webb, S. (2010) 'A university for the people', *Adults Learning*, February, 2010, 21: 6, 10–13.

Sustaining communities: Conclusion

SUE JACKSON

The four chapters in this section have been concerned with ways in which social justice can be built and sustained through lifelong learning; and how lifelong learning is developed and sustained through communities and community engagement. Sustainability affects us all in differing ways and in this section the authors argue that more holistic understandings of lifelong learning are needed in order to develop sustainable communities and social justice.

The authors have pointed to communities as ways to help develop alternative frames of reference. Those alternative frames include more holistic and contextualised understandings of learning (Chapters One and Two); creative approaches to learning, including images, sounds and storytelling (Chapter Two); critical pedagogies of place (Chapters One and Two); and challenges to taken-for-granted beliefs and assumptions (Chapters Three and Four). The authors in this section (as in other sections) have described significant and unacceptable inequalities, which can be reproduced by formal education.

They have engaged with several of the themes highlighted in the introduction to this book, including neoliberalism (Chapters One and Four), globalisation (Chapter Four) and postcolonialism (Chapter Three), and literacy and language (Chapters Two and Four). These are themes which will be continued in Section Two to explore learning, working and social justice.

PART TWO

LEARNING AND WORKING

Learning and working: Introduction

SUE JACKSON

The three chapters in Section Two, the central section, consider some of the themes which are key throughout the volume. In particular, they consider the ways in which lifelong learning has become ever more firmly linked to economic participation through the employment market and the development of skills and training, whilst apparently also being located within a rhetoric of social justice. The authors of these chapters are interested in definitions and conceptualisations both of learning and of working, and the connections between the two. All three chapters, in their different ways, are concerned with ways in which such definitions and connections lead to constructions of disadvantage.

The globalisation of neoliberal concerns with individualism, participation and discourses of 'choice' has been a significant driver in the development of lifelong learning for participation in knowledge economies (Webb, Brine and Jackson, 2006). However, as Jacky Brine has demonstrated, within a knowledge economy there are high-skilled knowledge learners identified as those who know, and low-skilled knowledge learners, identified not just as those who do not, but also as those who are both at risk and the risk (Brine, 2006; see also Chapter Five).

Neoliberal discourses about working in a globalised knowledge economy state that workers are expected to be active lifelong learners, engaged in a cycle of (re-)training and (up-)skilling in order to quickly respond to changing economic demands. However, there remains little recognition that workers (and apparent non-workers) are constructed through gender, social class, 'race' and more, issues raised in each of the chapters in this section. Many occupations remain dominated by women or by men, and through differences of social class, ethnicity, sexual preference, and so forth. This has particular consequences and favoured solutions:

> Since it has tended to be women who have been channelled into lower-paid, lower status employment, schemes to de-segregate the workforce along gender lines have concentrated on encouraging women into non-traditional occupations, mainly through specific training programmes that target women and prepare them for workplaces dominated by men (Potter and Hill, 2009: 133).

However, such preparations for the workforce assumes that it is marginalised groups who are the 'problem', rather than the structures and definitions of 'work' and 'skills'. Who has access to higher level education, and who to training for lower level skills, is embedded in wider social relations and inequalities, and becomes enmeshed with constructions of learning and working (Burke and Jackson, 2007: 29) and of intersectionality.

In considering the reproduction of class, gender, and racial relations of inequality, Joan Acker (2006) uses the analytical tool of 'inequality regimes' to understand the creation of inequalities in work organisations, the 'interlocked practices and processes that result in continuing inequalities in all work organisations' (2006: 441). This is something which all three authors explore in this section. However, whilst Brine and Weedon and Riddell do so through examining training, skills and un/employment in the workplace, Willa Liu examines informal learning in the homeplace, arguing for definitions of work and of lifelong learning to be extended to include home work which, she maintains, is multi-dimensional and requires a wide range of skills and labour, including emotional labour. The authors of all three chapters demonstrate how the current economic recession brings more socially and educationally diverse disadvantages with intensified divisions of labour.

In Chapter Five Jacky Brine presents a gendered and classed analysis of what lifelong learning means for those who experience prolonged unemployment or 'economic inactivity'. In particular, she is interested in welfare-to-work policies that have, at their core, 'basic education' and 'training' programmes. She argues that policies focused on 'the unemployed' continue to essentialise them as 'low-level' learners, beyond the 'knowledge economy'. They are, she says, individualised and pathologised, in a culture of blame around their lack of formal employment and their presumed lack of qualifications. She demonstrates how discourses of 'the deserving and undeserving poor' become infused with the dominant discourses of social justice. Brine outlines the addition of a new category of 'economically inactive' people, including lone parents (primarily mothers) and people with disabilities and/or receiving sickness benefits. Her chapter is located at the interface of active labour market policies, welfare reforms and lifelong learning that impact directly on what are arguably the most vulnerable members of society. Brine underpins her discussion with theories of social justice, including those related to the distribution of resources and to constructions of disadvantage, and concludes that in the current economic climate 'the new unemployed', the new recipients of state benefits, will be more socially and educationally diverse and will further challenge existing policies.

Chapter Six moves from the broader (primarily EU/UK) focus of Chapter Five, to a specific focus on Scotland which has broader implications. Elisabet Weedon and Sheila Riddell explore how the concepts of social justice and inclusion are understood in lifelong learning in Scotland, and what tensions and contradictions are apparent. In doing so, they draw on empirical research funded by the European Union to outline what the experiences of adult returners to education reveal in relation to the application of social justice principles in practice. Like Jacky Brine in the previous chapter, they demonstrate that whilst learners with higher level qualifications have access to a wide range of learning opportunities, leading to portable qualifications, learners with low levels of initial education are often compelled to engage in a particular type of lifelong learning and to take courses which are unlikely to have a major impact in raising their earning potential. Weedon and Riddell draw on Levitas's model of social inclusion and exclusion policy discourses, to show that the model most apparent in lifelong learning strategies, economic strategies and poverty strategies is that of social integrationist discourse, which stresses a route out of poverty that is through engagement with the labour market. Like Jacky Brine, they conclude that lifelong learning as currently conceptualised tends to widen, rather than narrow the gap between the most and least socially advantaged and suggest that far more radical policies based on principles of redistribution and recognition (see also introduction to this book) are required in order to make lifelong learning transformative.

In the final chapter of this section, Lichun Willa Liu moves from learning for work to informal learning through unpaid work in the home which, she argues, remains largely undervalued and unexplored. She shows how definitions of work are gendered as well as classed and racialised, with dominant discourses about learning and working taking a market-oriented, economic-driven approach. This focuses mainly on formal training for paid work, ignoring the homeplace and unpaid household work as sites of and for learning, and paying scant attention to gender, class and 'race'. Her chapter is based on her empirical research with Chinese immigrants living in Canada, exploring their lifelong learning experiences through unpaid household work and demonstrating how immigration intersects with gender and ethnicity in influencing the gender division of labour in housework and carework. Willa Liu states that exploring the gendered nature of household work helps address social injustice and gender inequality in immigrant families, and in the larger society. By exploring unpaid work and the knowledge and skills involved in it, immigrant women are empowered to sustain themselves, their family and community in a transnational context. Whilst in Chapter Four Sue Webb was interested in the 'good university', in this chapter Willa Liu writes about the 'good citizen', calling for the learning essential for new immigrants to be made visible. She concludes that learning for immigrants is not only lifelong, it is also lifewide, and that informal learning for and through unpaid household work is one of the most important ways for new immigrants to acquire knowledge and skills in order to adapt to changes after immigration and to participate in the social, cultural and economic activities in their new home country.

References

Acker, J (2006) 'Inequality regimes gender, class, and race in organisations', *Gender and Society*, 20: 4, 441–64.

Burke, P. and Jackson, S. (2007) *Reconceptualising lifelong learning: Feminist interventions*. London: RoutledgeFalmer.

Brine, J (2006) 'Lifelong learning and the knowledge economy: those that know and those that do not', *British Educational Research Journal*, 32: 5, 649–65.

Potter, M. and Hill, M. (2009) 'Women into non-traditional sectors: addressing gender segregation in the Northern Ireland workplace', *Journal of Vocational Education and Training*, 61: 2, 133–50.

Webb, S., Brine, J. and Jackson, S. (2006) 'Foundation degrees and the knowledge economy', *Journal of Vocational Education and Training*: Special issue on Gender matters. *Perspectives on women, work and training*, 58: 4, 563–76.

CHAPTER FIVE

Welfare to work: Training, benefits, un/employment and social justice

JACKY BRINE

Introduction

This chapter explores a specific aspect of lifelong learning: of 'skills and training', of lifelong learning linked to economic participation through the employment market – or more accurately, to the underbelly of the employment market, to the 'unemployed', and most recently to those identified as 'economically inactive'. I focus here on 'lifelong learners' who through their prolonged unemployment or 'economic inactivity' are given 'opportunities' to participate in training and basic skills programmes. This chapter is located at the interface of active labour market policies, welfare reforms and lifelong learning that impact directly on what are arguably the most vulnerable members of society – those with chronic illness or disabilities. This discussion is underpinned by theories of social justice, particularly those related to distribution of resources and constructions of disadvantage (Levitas, 1998; Lister, 2001; Young, 1990).

Based on an analysis of UK/England policy documents published between 2006 and 2010 I detail the emergent discourse by which the 'economically inactive' are moved from a 'deserving' position regarding state benefits to one of 'undeserving', to join 'the unemployed' in a regulatory relationship with the state and an obligatory engagement with 'employment programmes': low-level vocational training, basic skills and, possibly, skills for self-employment or worker cooperatives.

There are three key points to note about this discursive broadening of 'the undeserving'. First, it builds on a similar construction of 'the unemployed', continuing a discourse that can, at least in England, be traced back to the Poor Laws of the mid nineteenth century (Thompson, 1963). Second, both the construction of the unemployed and the economically inactive are linked to dominant discursive shifts within the European Union (Brine, 2002; Dieckhoff, 2007). Third, the UK (England) policies are part of international neoliberal welfare reforms found also in the US (Daguerre, 2007), Australia (ACOSS, 2007), New Zealand (Perry and Maloney, 2008) and Canada (Evans, 2007). Grappling with the cost of welfare the state constructs a discourse of individual 'responsibility' (Beck and Beck-Gernsheim, 2002) and 'conditionality' through which welfare 'rights' are contested and systematically undermined (Dwyer, 2004). Across the states of the European Union, Australia, Canada, the United States and New Zealand differing political parties make very similar neoliberal responses towards those people not active within the formal labour market. This paper was written during the last six months of the UK Labour Government and was finalised as the new Liberal–Conservative coalition government took office.

This cycle of 2006–10 texts repositioning the economically inactive is the latest development in government welfare-labour-market policy that began in the aftermath of the oil crisis in the 1970s. The 1970s were also the time of the UK's entry to what was then commonly described as the 'Common Market', now the European Union (EU). Significantly, this gave the UK access to a major source of funding for training programmes aimed at the unemployed across the EU, the European Social Fund (ESF). As I have argued elsewhere (Brine, 1999) the significance of the ESF is not simply financial (as important as that is), it also defines the policy frame for member state policies and practices. An analysis of the policies of the North American Free Trade Agreement (NAFTA), the Organisation of Southeast Asian Nations (ASEAN) and Asia–Pacific Economic Co-operation (APEC), traced the common intertwining of lifelong learning with active labour market and welfare policies. Subsequent analyses of ESF policies (Brine, 2002) provided a deeper understanding of the European context for UK policies and further considered the significance of lifelong learning within it (see also Peppin, 2007).

The current ESF programme for 2007–13 (CEC, 2006) was published in 2006, the same year as the UK government's welfare Green Paper (DWP, 2006). The 2007–13 ESF programme has two primary objectives: first, convergence, where additional funds are targeted onto areas of particular need, for instance, within England, Cornwall and the Isles of Scilly; second, regional competitiveness and *employment*, where attention is focused on individual persons and on the development and modernisation of educational structures and systems across all educational levels. The ESF programme links to three other major European policies: the *Lisbon Strategy* (CEC, 2000), the *Employment Strategy* (EES) (CEC, 1999a) and the *Education and Training 2010 Work Programme* (CEC, 2008) which expresses the key EU target of 80 per cent employment. The *Lisbon Strategy* requires a policy response from each member state government. The UK's fundamental declaration of this aspirant 80 per cent employment is found in the Treasury's *UK National Reform Plan* of 2007. Indeed the full title of the 2007 UK Plan clearly confirms its relationship to the Lisbon Strategy: *Lisbon Strategy for jobs and growth: UK national reform plan: update on progress* (HMT, 2007). As will be shown in the analysis of the 2006–2010 texts there are repeated justificatory references to the '80 per cent employment' target – but no reference to the EU's Lisbon Strategy.

From within this wider EU policy context the current ESF 'work programme' identified three education and training policy areas. First, to improve the level of basic competences – that is 'the competences needed in order to live and work in the knowledge-based society'. Second, to make 'lifelong learning a reality for all', which includes increasing participation in adult education. Third, is to increase the quality and attractiveness of vocational education and training including increasing participation of older workers and of low skilled people and disadvantaged groups.

There is, within the ESF, repeated references to aspects of lifelong learning and social justice, both clearly linked to that of economic growth, for example through reference to 'lifelong vocational training' (CEC, 2006: 12). But, at the same time, both are also linked to a pervasive discourse of political stability, of control, which is nevertheless expressed through the language of social justice. The ESF Regulation states that it should 'focus, in particular, on ... reinforcing the social inclusion of disadvantaged people, combating discrimination, *encouraging economically inactive persons to enter the labour market a*nd promoting partnerships for reform' (p. 12; emphasis added). This is the current EU (ESF) policy context for the UK documents discussed below.

Constructing 'the economically inactive' and their learning needs

In this section of the chapter I present an analysis of the 2006–2010 sequence of 'welfare to work' policies focused on the economically inactive and incorporating 'basic education' and 'training' programmes. The early documents were developed and published in a rather different economic, social and political context to that which exists during the writing and publication of this chapter – 2009–2011. At the beginning of the policy sequence, 2006, employment was high, the labour market buoyant and the Labour government, as well as opposition parties, wished to reduce the costs of welfare, most particularly through the reconfiguration/reconstruction of those people identified as 'economically inactive': lone parents, people with disabilities and/or with long-term illness. In May 2010 a Liberal–Conservative coalition government took office against a backdrop of deep economic gloom and almost global language of 'cuts', restraint and predicted high job loss: as the election took place, the Euro crashed in Greece and people rioted, there were fears of this spreading to Spain and Portugal, and all three major UK parties spoke in general but threatening terms of deep economic cuts and hard times to come.

The sequence of 'welfare-to-work' papers between 2006 and 2009 is:

2006 (January) Department for Work and Pensions (DWP), Green Paper: *The new deal for welfare: empowering people to work*;
2007 (March) DWP, The Freud Report: *Reducing dependency, increasing opportunity: options for the future of welfare to work*. (Commissioned report);
2007 (May) Welfare Reform Act;
2007 (December) DWP, *Ready for work: full employment in our generation*;
2008 (October) DWP, *Opportunity for all: indicators update 2007*;
2008 (July) DWP, Green Paper: *No-one written off: reforming welfare to reward responsibility*;
[2008 (October) DWP, Employment Support Allowance into force]
2008 (2 December) DWP, The Gregg Report: *Realising potential: a vision for personalised conditionality and support* (Commissioned report);
2008 (10 December) DWP, White Paper: *Raising expectations and increasing support: reforming welfare for the future*;
2009 (introduced January) Welfare Reform Bill;
2009 DWP The Social Security Flexible New Deal Regulations.

There are two initial points to be made from these texts produced by the Department for Work and Pensions (DWP). The first is to note their two commissioned reports, one from the city financier David Freud (2007), and the other from Paul Gregg, a professor of economics (2008). Freud and Gregg are neither elected politicians nor professional civil servants (administration), but 'independent' advisors. Their reports come with an apparent political 'objectivity' that enables the government to both quote and endorse that which they find positive and to reject and distance themselves from that which they do not. As the following analysis indicates, both the Freud and Gregg reports are pivotal in provoking policy direction, in tuning policy processes and in conceptually underpinning the discourse, as well as providing 'expert' 'objective' justification of the government's own policy texts. The second point is to note the rhetoric of opportunity and social justice which is clearly in tension with the practices of control. The texts privilege 'individual responsibility' and benefit 'conditionality' rather than opportunity and justice. They construct a non-deserving 'claimant' controlled through regulatory processes that emerge from and enact the discourse – the practices of the policy.

These two points, identifiable from the titles of texts, are developed through the following chronological narrative of the construction of the 'economically inactive' subject, the education and training to be offered them and the emergent concept of conditionality. A chronological approach clearly illustrates the process by which this major shift in policy is developed through a multi-department series of Green and White Papers, commissioned reports and legislation. Within the UK legislative process, Green Papers are consultative documents; White Papers detail the government's decisions and legislative intentions. The subsequent Bill is presented to Parliament and if successful becomes an Act of Parliament. The analysis of this sequence of texts shows the reconstruction of the economically inactive from 'deserving' of state benefit to 'undeserving'; it also shows the significance of this particular strand of lifelong learning which, barely tangible/visible in the early documents, emerges in 2009 as a key disciplinary technology of state control and regulation.

Green Paper: the new deal for welfare: empowering people to work (DWP, 2006)

Published in January 2006, before the economic recession that began in the autumn of 2008, this Green Paper from the DWP outlined the objectives for the Welfare Reform Act of 2007; its aims mirrored those of the EU's Lisbon Strategy (CEC, 2000):

- *reach 80 per cent employment of all people of working age;*
- *reduce numbers claiming incapacity benefit by 1 million (incapacity benefit is a regular payment made by the government to those below state pension age who are unable to work due to long term illness or disability);*
- *help 300,000 lone parents back into work;*
- *increase the number of older workers, aged 50 or more, in work by 1 million.*

Although this paper identified and targeted those later described as 'economically inactive', it used this term rarely, and only in relation to 'older' workers, those approaching or following retirement. It referred to the principle of 'conditionality', but provided no explicit definition of what this meant, other than to state that 'as support is increased, so will the level of conditionality for claimants . . .' adding that 'those with the most severe health conditions and disabilities will receive the new benefit without any conditionality' (p. 6). It did not mention 'sanctions' other than directly in relation to benefit fraud.

The Green Paper made many references to the role education and training would play in helping 'economically inactive' people back into work: 'education, skills and training policies aimed at creating an adaptable, flexible and productive workforce' (p. 15). An apparent individualised tailored approach expressed through 'reaching full potential', 'tailored' provision and 'the particular needs of harder-to-help client groups' (p. 74), culminated not in opportunity and enhanced learning, but in the aim to 'ensure universal entitlement to free basic skills training and free tuition towards a first level 2 qualification' (p. 78). The Green Paper introduced ill-defined key concepts and, focused on the economically inactive and signalled the importance of education and training programmes, but only as basic skills up to level 2, thereby linking the economically inactive with basic/low educational needs.

The Freud Report (2007)

The Freud report, commissioned by the DWP in December 2006 was published in March 2007. Freud's brief was to 'make policy recommendations on how the Government can build on its success in using policies such as the New Deal to continue to *reduce inactivity* and in-work poverty, and meet the Government's 80 per cent employment aspiration' (Freud, 2007: 1; Grover, 2007). Providing context and policy continuity Freud referenced the earlier Treasury-commissioned Leitch review of the UK skills base:

> *Around 50 per cent of those with no qualifications are out of work. As the global economy changes, the employment opportunities of those lacking a platform of skills will fall still further. The millions of adults lacking functional literacy and numeracy skills risk becoming a lost generation, increasingly cut off from labour market opportunity. Equipping disadvantaged groups with a platform of skills, including literacy and numeracy, will be increasingly essential to improving their employment opportunities* (Leitch, 2006: 118).

Leitch recommended increased individualised opportunities for the 'least advantaged' defined as the 'low skilled'. Freud now shifted attention away from 'the unemployed' towards the 3.1 million people 'on long-term dependence overall' claiming that over 95 per cent of long-term dependent people were on 'inactive' benefits: 2.3 million on incapacity benefit [for the sick and disabled] and 600,000 lone parents on [means tested] income support (p. 4). Freud reiterated Leitch's claim that 35 per cent of the working age population do not have the equivalent of a good school-leaving qualification, 4.6 million have no qualification at all, 5 million working age people lack functional literacy and 7 million lack functional numeracy (Freud, 2007: 25). Freud, concerned with the costs of benefits, made only a few references to education or training (other than in the comparative chapters) and none to lifelong learning.

As in the Green Paper, Freud repeatedly referred to the government's 80 per cent employment aspiration yet similarly made no reference to its origin in the EU Lisbon Strategy. Nevertheless, to achieve this 80 per cent participation, he argued that the government would need to target its welfare strategy at tackling *all* of the inactive groups (p. 5) including those on Incapacity Benefit, thereby moving 300,000 lone parents, 1 million older people and 1 million of those on Incapacity Benefit into work. This document clearly constructed the economically inactive as a further large category of people dependent on state benefit.

The significance of Freud is his reference first to the earlier Treasury-commissioned Leitch Report, and most particularly to Leitch's claim regarding the basic and vocational skills deficit; second, to the oft-declared justificatory 80 per cent participation target; and third, his recommendation that many 'economically inactive' people be moved off incapacity benefit and into work. Significantly, this dual categorisation of the unemployed and the economically inactive is at this point boundaried and distinct.

Welfare Reform Act (2007)

The detail of the Welfare Reform Act was outlined in the DWP Green Paper *The new deal for welfare* (DWP, 2006) discussed above. The main point here is the further construction of the 'economically inactive' person. Like 'the unemployed' they are seen as more likely to live in social housing – a shorthand strongly classed descriptor (Hanley, 2007), and to have low education. Thus the education proposed within the Act is synonymous with basic skills and work related training up to level 2, and may be delivered either through the newly created *Jobcentre Plus* or their contracted-out external training providers. There is no mention at all of a more liberal education, nor of lifelong learning. Significantly, the Act has blurred Freud's earlier classificatory boundaries between the unemployed and the economically inactive, and in doing so further constructs 'the inactive' as no longer deserving of unconditional state benefit. The Act confirmed Freud's recommendation to reduce the number claiming incapacity benefit by 1 million; 'helping' 300,000 lone parents back into work; and increasing the number of older workers (aged 50 or over) in work by 1 million.

Ready for work: full employment in our generation (DWP, 2007)

Following the Act, this document published at the end of 2007 set out the steps the government would take to reach the long term goals of an 80 per cent employment rate. Its stated aim was 'to move people from being spectators on the margins – passive recipients of benefits – to become active participants – seeking work, improving their skills, and getting on' (www.dwp.gov.uk 7 January 2010).

There were no references to lifelong learning within this paper, and the term 'education' used only in relation to young people, either through the extension of the leaving age or as part of the NEET descriptor – not in education, employment or training. There is no mention of education in relation to older people, only training and basic skills, as in access to training, pre-employment training, employability focused training, or the

Jobcentre Plus' 'employability skills programme' ('rolled-out' during 2007), which included basic skills. The employability programme aimed to 'improve literacy, numeracy and language skills, and prepare for work with an employability qualification' (p. 30) – the government support for 'getting on'. This paper allowed for restrictions on study hours to be removed to allow people receiving benefits to 'study full time for up to eight weeks on employability focused training' (p. 31). This post-Act clarification defined a functional model of education; a model that forms the conceptual and structural basis for the subsequent Flexible New Deal regulations of 2009.

Green Paper: No one written off: reforming welfare to reward responsibility (DWP, 2008)

Published in July 2008, this Green Paper started a consultation that closed in October, and led to the welfare reform White Paper (December 2008). The City financier David Freud again made a key invited contribution to this paper which further strengthened the construction of the 'economically inactive' as lacking in skills: 'a lack of skills should no longer mean that people simply remain on benefit ... *Legislative powers* [will] require those who need it to undertake training to help them get into work' (p. 12 emphasis added). 'Inactivity' (and the resultant need for state benefit) is removed from a medically defined condition of disability or chronic illness: 'inactivity' is constructed as a personal deficit linked to 'choice', and 'effort', and lack of skill: the individual can, with the aid of personal advisors and employment training programmes, put this right – that is, come off benefit. There are repeated references to 'training', to 'tougher sanctions' (p. 13) and a sub-classification of 'the inactive' into a smaller group of the seriously disabled and ill who are entitled to state benefit – the deserving; and a larger group, redefined as active, no longer deserving of state benefit.

The Gregg Report: Realising potential: a vision for personalised conditionality and support (2008)

At the same time as the Green Paper was published (July 2008) Paul Gregg, a professor of economics, was commissioned to undertake 'a wide ranging review of conditionality, to look at how more people can be helped off benefits and into work' (p. 10). This was published a few months later (December 2008). Between July and December 2008 (between commissioning and reporting), the economy 'collapsed', marking a financial, welfare and employment watershed separating the early development of policy from 2006 to 2008 from the implementation through 2009–2011. Gregg acknowledged that the 'economic situation had considerably worsened' which, he argued, made his proposals 'even more important' (p. 19) – he ignored the fact that it made employment more difficult.

The concept of 'conditionality' – introduced in the 2006 Green Paper *New deal for welfare* – is that 'entitlement to benefits should be dependent on satisfying certain conditions' (p. 10) and be accompanied by a closely defined structure of sanctions. Gregg considered the 'conditionality regimes' that currently applied to unemployed people: a compulsory focus on job search, a 'requirement' 'to actively seek and be available for work', and compulsory attendance at 'work-focused interviews' with the Jobcentre. He wrote that this regime be extended from 'the unemployed' to the majority of lone parents and to those with 'health problems or disabilities'; only lone parents caring for children aged less than 12 months, or people seriously ill or seriously disabled would be exempt. This, he said, would drastically cut the numbers of people on unconditional state benefit, and would 'bring a wider range of claimants than ever before into a system of personalised conditionality' (p. 7) meaning that '*virtually everyone* claiming benefits and not in work should':

- *be required to engage in activity that will help them to move towards, and then into employment;*
- *have an advisor with whom they will be able to plan and agree a route back to work;*
- *be obliged to act on the steps that they agree will help them;*
- *have a clear understanding of the expectations placed upon them (and why) and what the consequences are for failing to meet these; and*
- *be able to access a wider range of personalised support on the basis of need not what benefit they are on.* (p. 7)

The language of compulsion is clear; a 'sanctions' regime of 'tighter rules', 'early warning systems' and 'fixed fines' accompany this 'vision' of conditionality, centred primarily around the required attendance at interview, where 'a stronger approach based around *mandatory* activity' will be established for 'repeat offenders', (p. 8 emphasis added) 'those found to be playing the system' (p. 15). Whereas the 2006 Green Paper gave reassurance that the most severely ill or disabled would continue to receive benefit without conditionality being placed on them, Gregg's report made it clear that conditionality would in fact apply to 'virtually everyone claiming benefit'.

From within this regime of personalised conditionality Gregg, like the July Green Paper, identified three broad groups in which classification would be determined primarily by 'a more individualised and sophisticated assessment of distance from the labour market' (p. 13): a 'work-ready' group, a 'progression to work' group, and a 'no conditionality' group. The work-ready group would join the current Jobseekers category with its emphasis on active job seeking, training courses and availability for work. Lone parents (and partners) with older children will be defined as 'work-ready', along with many of those with 'less serious' health conditions or disabilities.

The 'progression to work' group: lone parents and partners where the youngest child is aged between one and seven, and people with long term health problems or 'less serious' disabilities are also moved from the deserving to the undeserving category; brought into the framework of conditionality Gregg stated they should:

- *attend work-focused interview with an advisor at appropriate points;*
- *design and agree an action plan that outlines steps towards work;*
- *undertake work-related activity to support their own route back towards work, with progress monitored through Jobcentre Plus work-focused interviews (WFI);*
- *follow short, focused, advisor directions when required (p. 50).*

Gregg also recommended that the 'progression to work' group be 'required to undertake some work-related activity between WFIs for as long as the WFI regime remains in place' (p. 51). He defined this work-related activity (as in the 2007 Welfare Reform Act) as anything agreed that will enable them to stabilise their own, or their family, situation; manage their health for work; look for work; improve their skills for work, or prepare for full-time employment. The stated example of improving skills for work is that of 'undertaking a basic skills programme or attending a Jobcentre Plus or external training programme' (p. 51), and along the same lines, preparation for full-time work may include 'preparation for self-employment'.

Finally, those left in the no-conditionality group would include only those with serious disabilities or ill health, as well as lone parents and partners whose youngest child was less than 12 months old. These are the only people still seen as 'deserving' of state benefit.

The classification into these three categories is critical – a decision made solely by the individual (non-medical) personal advisor of Jobcentre Plus. The classification of health-related ability to work is no longer a decision of the medical profession. Gregg defined the main instrument of conditionality as the monthly or two-monthly work-focused interview within which the Jobcentre personal advisor would have all decision-making powers regarding the claimant and their agreed 'individualised' programme – a critical point which I return to below. Despite emphasising the individualised and sophisticated assessment of individuals Gregg argued that the classification of individuals should be 'on the basis of general characteristics, e.g. lone parenthood and age of youngest child' (p. 14).

The consistent emphasis on basic and low level skills continued throughout the report, for instance, Gregg recommended 'relatively cheap but effective support such as help completing an electronic CV or with online job applications in the first six months of unemployment' (p. 80); a 'skills health check' that included basic literacy and numeracy (p. 92). The assumption, like that towards the unemployed, is that people who are ill or disabled, or lone parents, only have *basic* educational needs. Conversely, only those with low education, or as quoted earlier, living in social housing, become long-term ill, disabled or solely responsible for their child/children. These classed assumptions are fundamental to the re/construction and pathologisation of the 'undeserving' recipient of state benefit.

White Paper: Raising expectations and increasing support: reforming welfare for the future (DWP, 2008c)

On the 10 December 2008, one week after the publication of the Gregg Report, the Government's White Paper was published. The consultation for the Green Paper, *No one written off*, published in July 2008, closed at the end of October.

As stated earlier, this process of welfare reform began at a time of high employment and relative economic stability. The White Paper, like Gregg, acknowledged the 'substantial change' in the economic climate, that 'times are tough' and 'many families [are] struggling to make ends meet'

(p. 9) but concluded that although 'some people have argued that now is not the time to press ahead with welfare reform' (p. 10) the government 'believe the opposite is true', indeed 'the current economic climate means we must step up both the support we offer to people on benefits and the expectations of them to get themselves *prepared* for work' (p. 10, emphasis added). This represents a shift from 'moving *into* work' to being '*prepared for* work', a shift that mirrors an earlier discursive shift from employment to employability (Brine, 2002).

The White Paper accepted Gregg's definitions of the three groups and his vision of conditionality attached to them (pp. 13–14): the 'work-ready', the 'progression to work', and the 'no conditionality', and pointed out that 'the vast majority of people in receipt of the Employment and Support Allowance (ESA), lone parents and partners with younger children' will be in the progression to work group, and only those with very young children (under 12 months), careers and the most disabled people should be in the 'no conditionality' group (p. 13).

Incapacity Benefit for new claimants was replaced (April 2009) by the Employment and Support Allowance (ESA) to be fully in place by 2013, and reviewed 'to ensure that only those who are *genuinely not capable of work* are on this benefit' (para 32, p. 15). Only those in Gregg's 'no conditionality' category will receive it, Jobseekers benefit is the clear default position. The clarification of the 'no conditionality' category with their *genuine* incapacity for work simultaneously constructs the other, all others, as not being genuine, of deceit and fraud. At the same time the government planned to abolish 'income support', a means-tested allowance paid by the state to those on very low income. This means that apart from the remaining small category of 'no conditionality' people supported through the ESA, the state benefit for all others will be the Jobseekers Allowance which is tied to mandatory attendance for interview with the personal advisor, an agreed programme of activity, and mandatory attendance on the education and training work programme. Jobseekers' Allowance, linked now to the Flexible New Deal (para 40, p16) discussed below, would be 'modified' to suit 'the broader range of people (lone parents, ill, disabled) who will be claiming it'. There is a policy lineage here back to one of the very early welfare-to-work policies, the 'W2' programme of the US state of Wisconsin where people 'were paid less than the state minimum wage for working up to 30 hours a week on community service' (Brine, 1999: 147).

Accepting the earlier recommendation of Freud, Jobcentre Plus would operate as the single public organisation processing initial benefit claims and job search activities for all. As recommended by Gregg, Jobcentre Plus personal advisers will be given 'greater flexibility' to 'tailor the support they offer to individual's needs and circumstances' (p. 12) – that is, as suggested by Gregg, the individual personal adviser would make the classification decision. Government legislation would 'allow advisers to decide what activity is appropriate for someone where an individual is not addressing their barriers to work'.

Most significantly, the White Paper accepted Gregg's 'sanctions' and stated that the government would legislate to

> *make the sanctions regime within Jobseeker's Allowance clearer and more consistent and introduce a new sanction that will affect benefit entitlement after a first benefit fraud offence'* including *'supplementing financial penalties with* mandatory full-time activity *for those repeatedly not meeting their obligations.* (para 41, p. 16).

The emphasis throughout the White Paper is on 'conditionality', on regulatory and disciplinary techniques of 'preparedness'. Earlier references to training and basic skills are now replaced by the cipher-like 'Flexible New Deal' (FND) which, competitively contracted out to the private and voluntary sector, would provide 'employment programmes that include basic education and training'; and would require all 'clients' to go through a four-week, full-time activity programme. In this way 'education', lifelong learning, is firmly, visibly, and explicitly, tied into the conditionality of welfare reform.

Welfare Reform Bill (2009)

Less than two years after the Welfare Reform Act of 2007, shortly after the economic crisis that began in autumn 2008, the Bill to reform the Welfare Reform Act of 2007 was introduced to Parliament (January 2009). This Bill consolidated and legislated for the recommendations developed since the Welfare Reform Act of 2007. It abolished Income Support, moved all claimants on to either Jobseekers' Allowance (if 'well'), or Employment and Support Allowance (if 'sick'); introduced a regime of 'benefit sanctions' for non-attendance at Jobcentres, required 'job search by partners of benefit claimants', introduced work-focused interviews for those aged over 60 and, for those who are 'sick', required 'work-related activity in return for receipt of Employment and Support Allowance' (http://services.parliament.uk/bills/2008-09/welfarereform.html). As recommended by Gregg and detailed in the White Paper (DWP, 2008c), the Bill also introduced a regime of benefit sanctions for non-attendance at Jobcentres or work-programmes (including their education and training provision). Thus, for both the 'ready for work' and the 'progression to work' groups, the Bill required work-related activity in return for benefit. Unlike the rhetoric of opportunity expressed within the titles of the Green and White Papers, the language of the Bill is punitive and regulatory.

Flexible New Deal Regulations (DWP, 2009)

The Flexible New Deal (FND), an employment programme linked to the Jobseeker's Allowance Regulation of 1996, replaced earlier New Deal programmes. The first phase of FND was introduced to some parts of England in October 2009, with the second phase in 2010. The Jobcentre Plus would, for the first twelve months, be responsible for the new claimant and would place 'increasing requirements' upon them (House of Commons Standard Note, 17 March 2009: p. 1).

At the end of these twelve months, contracted providers in the private or voluntary sector would take over responsibility from Jobcentre Plus. In a rare acknowledgement within these documents, the Gregg Report drew attention to the need to 'fully explore the capacity of the European Social Fund' (p. 80) to deliver 'training and support', and 'where this does not deliver the needed help, [to explore] how *low-value* procurement can be used to deliver bespoke provision' (p. 80, emphasis added). Figure 1 shows that although the first three stages of FND will be provided by Jobcentre Plus, the fourth stage is contracted out to independent provider. Stage 1, the first three months, named 'self-help' provided a mandatory 'back to work' group session, assessment of skills and 'relatively light intervention from an adviser' whilst the claimant looked for work. During stage 2, the next three months, titled 'directed job search', the adviser 'helps' the individual to 'widen' their job search. The claimant would be required to attend six weekly meetings with Jobcentre Plus advisers. At six months the claimant enters 'the gateway' stage, (or earlier for the most disadvantaged jobseeker), with the increased 'thorough' level of support of an adviser who undertakes a full assessment of their needs and situation, and develops an 'action plan'.

Lifelong Learning and Social Justice

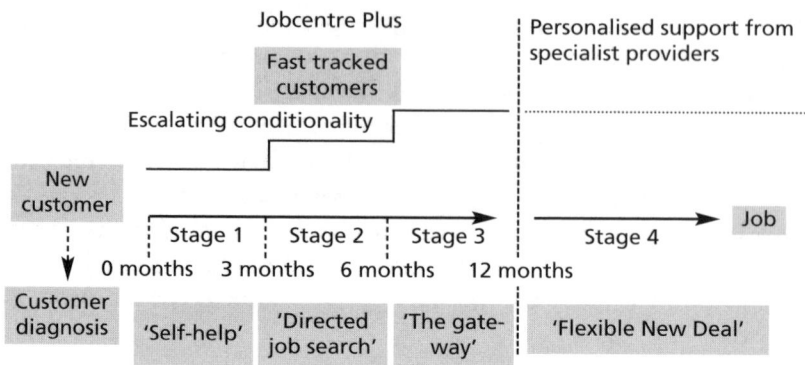

Figure 1: Jobcentre Plus and Flexible New Deal (House of Commons Standard Note, 17 March 2009: p. 2)

The aim is that the person would, during the first twelve months, find paid work. If still unemployed or 'inactive' then the person is passed on to the contracted-out provider for a further 12-to-18 month programme determined by that provider.

> *Participation . . . and compliance with the accompanying action plan will be* mandatory. *Failure to undertake any back-to-work activity arranged by the service provider would mean a referral to Jobcentre Plus to consider* benefit sanctions. (House of Commons Standard Note, p. 4; emphasis added)

There are no minimum hour requirements, but the provider must deliver at least four weeks of work experience to each claimant/customer during their first year on the programme. An internet search of provider programmes suggest, in addition to the obligatory 4 week work experience, a skeletal programme focused on self-employment, on job search, on identifying and overcoming 'barriers', and on developing skills and experience. Not only are these practices regulatory, they impinge on the person's 'time', an under-acknowledged (and under-theorised) component of social justice (Fitzpatrick, 2004).

Summary of policy texts

There are four key points to make following this analysis of the chronological development of the discursive construction of 'the economically inactive'. First, and most obvious, there is the shift in status from 'deserving of state benefit' to 'undeserving'. Second, this shift takes place, one document to the next, incrementally, building on the development of particular concepts and descriptive constructions of the 'inactive' subject. Third, and here it is worth recalling the ESF intention of 'making lifelong learning a reality for all', the restricted notion of lifelong learning emerges as a disciplinary technology that is interwoven with regular reporting to, and recording by, the personal advisor of Jobcentre Plus. Fourth, like 'the unemployed', the 'economically inactive' are constructed as 'low-level' learners, as beyond the 'knowledge economy': individualised and pathologised, blamed for their lack of formal employment, their presumed lack of qualifications (Beck and Beck-Gernsheim, 2001; Brine, 2006), and it seems for their illness or disability also.

Welfare, lifelong learning and social justice

This chapter has explored a specific aspect of lifelong learning, of skills and training for those not in the labour market, a mandatory requirement linked to state welfare benefits. Previously aimed at 'the unemployed' it is, across the EU and beyond, expanded to include 'the economically inactive' – the disabled, the long-term sick, and lone parents.

The policy texts and the detail of the process outlined in this chapter is country specific; the demise of the welfare state is widespread. The nation state has to be seen to be doing something to help people, unemployed and 'inactive' back into work; they would be criticised and blamed for doing nothing. The surface discourse of opportunity and responsibility speaks to this need. At the same time the state struggles to satisfy the demands of 'the market' in terms of fiscal, social and political stability – as for example during the UK election and the collapse of the Euro in Greece during Spring 2010. Most specifically the state has to reduce the economic deficit, and along with public services in general welfare benefits are an obvious target. Yet, the problem of a shrinking labour market remains the elephant within these policy texts – only ever addressed in terms of 'the needs' or 'the future needs'.

I have previously argued that beneath this surface discourse of opportunity, 'help' and individual responsibility, 'social welfare exists to maintain capitalism, or perhaps more crudely, to pacify and contain those that capitalism no longer needs' (Brine, 2001: 129). The state is not passive to global economic forces, they make choices, and they choose to cut welfare provision. Within the UK the Labour government's policy considered in this chapter will be seamlessly continued and strengthened by that of the incoming Liberal–Conservative coalition. Whilst accusing Labour of failure and employing the usual electoral discourse of change, they nevertheless continue, in both the Coalition Agreement (Liberal–Conservative Coalition, 2010) and the underpinning Conservative election manifesto (Conservative Party, 2010), to adopt the same concepts of conditionality and individual responsibility as Labour, similarly based on a single welfare-to-work programme.

The basic and vocational education element of the welfare-to-work programmes constructs a discursive tension between the general understanding of learning as opportunity, and its application here as mandatory requirement. The discourse of lifelong learning is often unproblematically associated with social justice, opportunity and individual fulfilment. In these texts there is no liberal education, no choice-based approach to lifelong learning. Indeed, in contrast to Labour's own welfare policies of the late 1990s (Prideaux, 2001), the very notion of 'lifelong learning' is absent. Yet for many people on these 'employment programmes', their only engagement with either formal or non-formal lifelong learning is through this often cyclical, basic skills provision and low-level vocational training: this is it: this is what 'lifelong learning' is.

As shown in the analysis of these documents there are, despite the superficial rhetoric of individualised needs and tailored programmes, an essentialising pathological assumption made regarding the educational needs of unemployed and economically inactive people: that is of *basic* needs (literacy, numeracy, IT), *social* skills and vocational training up to level 2. Furthermore, this state of low-education (Descy, 2002) is divorced from any critique of a compulsory education/schooling sector which, after eleven years, still apparently leaves so many people needing such low-level education. The texts now construct the economically inactive person as also someone who is low-educated and likely to live in social housing – that is, most likely 'working'-class. Such classed assumptions continue to echo a Victorian binary of the deserving and undeserving poor (Thompson, 1963; Daguerre, 2007), a construction in which, like those defined as the 'underclass', these people are seen as '*deliberately* living an alternative, threatening lifestyle in contradistinction to the functional norms of society as a whole' (Bagguley and Mann, 1992: 118). In its current incantation this construction draws on a powerful discursive mixture of the economic and the moral (Brine, 2001; Levitas, 1998), as well as that of opportunity and social justice (Young, 1990). The documents provide no evidence to support such a classed-educational reading of long-term illness, disability or lone-parenthood. The current economic recession brings with it a new, even more socially and educationally diverse, unemployed population that further challenge the classed-gendered assumptions and constructions of the welfare-to-work and related education/training programmes.

The perniciousness of this construction of the subject lies in the interweaving of assumptions of class, educational level and need, and 'entitlement' to state benefit. The underlying argument of the text is that only the working-class and the low-educated become unemployed, become long-term ill or disabled, and only the working-class choose, or become, 'lone' parents. This construction is a vital step in the pathologisation, the blame of the unemployed/inactive person and the shift of so many from 'deserving' to 'undeserving': an association of 'a lack of paid employment with individual failings' (Grover, 2007: 543), and a binary classification of the moral-employed and the unmoral-unemployed/inactive. As Prideaux (2001: 109) asks in his comparison of US and UK welfare reforms, how is it that one can then become the other?

The Jobcentre Plus personal advisor plays a vital role in this reclassification, for they are both pivotal to the system overall and to the individual claimant. It is the individual personal advisor who makes the critical classification of the ill and disabled and defines the programme for their return to work, including their 'individualised' programme of education/training. A study of Jobcentre Plus 'frontline workers' found that despite the emphasis on 'the customer':

> *customers are portrayed not so much as sovereigns, but as potential fraudsters, cheats and aggressors. They are subject to explicit admonitions and warnings and to various methods of surveillance and control.* (Rosenthal and Peccei, 2006: 663).

The study found that personal advisors classified and treated 'customers' differently: those seen as motivated and active were given information and training resources, whereas with those seen as 'recalcitrant', tactics of regulation and control were used, and with the more overtly recalcitrant, they used more direct practices of control, such as demanding more frequent attendance. With the third classification, the passively un-co-operative, the advisors emphasised 'identity work', enterprise, self-reliance and confidence building – a clear pathologisation of the claimant.

Alongside the surface (and highly contestable) discourse of opportunity, there is an equally superficial yet persistently dominant 'economic' discourse, that the 'employment programme' and its individualised/low-level education and training will increase their 'employability', or in the most recent terms, 'increase their *preparedness* for employment'. This 'preparedness', like the earlier concept of 'employability' is important as neither these policies, nor the 'preparedness' of individuals, create employment. Preparing oneself for work, the allure of paid employment, its association with inclusivity and morality, are the means of controlling the time and the activity of those receiving that benefit. Despite the recession, the dominance of this economic discourse remains, as shown most clearly in the key publications of 2008 (the Gregg Report and The White Paper), which both acknowledged the 'substantial change' in the economic climate, yet argued that rather than allow this to delay the welfare reforms, it was more important to 'press ahead' with them and that these people 'prepare' themselves for work (DWP, 2008c: 10).

To further understand this binary re/construction of people into 'un/deserving', 'low /educated' and 'un/moral' I return to Marx's (1849) concept of 'surplus population' and the 'reserve army of labour', which he argued, was necessary to the continued functioning and expansion of capitalism. I also return to Bauman's (1998) argument that, within the age of consumerism, these concepts no longer apply, for these people are those that society harshly discounts as no longer economically relevant to the growth of capitalism: 'the new poor are fully and truly useless and redundant, and thus become burdensome 'others' who have outstayed their welcome' (Bauman, 1998: 4–5). The (less severely) disabled and long-term sick (Grover and Piggott, 2005) must now be included within analyses of 'the unemployed' (Brine, 2001).

Among those not employed in the labour market, there is a rather fudgy continuum that includes both a possible reserve army of labour that could meet the needs of 'flexible' capitalisms, *and* towards the other end of the continuum, those that move in and out of government 'training' programmes with, for some, occasional very short-term low-paid work. There will be some (less severely) disabled and long-term ill people, and some lone parents, who will move into actual employment (Bambra et al., 2005; Descy, 2007). There will also be some who will move into the 'reserve army' end of the continuum. But there will be many more who will be stuck at the other end, lodged here between the 'reserve army' and the dwindling category of those 'deserving' of state benefit – the seriously ill, severely disabled and lone parents of children aged under 12 months. Now reconstructed as 'undeserving', the less-severely ill or disabled and lone parents of children over 12 months, are blamed for their position, required to engage in regular practices of reporting at the Jobcentre Plus and, despite the rhetoric of individualism, engage in low-level basic skills and job-search training, arguably devoid of any pedagogical notions of development, self-interest or fulfilment – or indeed of raising the knowledge/skills level for their subsequent employment in the much promoted 'knowledge economy'.

The level of provision, whilst offering basic skills and introductory level training to some who need it, narrows the expectation and aspiration of others, constructing a highly regulated and internalised sense of self. The inclusion of 'the economically inactive' into the category of 'employable and active' is a pathologising discursive shift that legitimates the introduction of disciplining technologies of control and regulation. Education and training, whilst providing the gloss of 'opportunity' are deeply entwined with regulatory practices – indeed they actually become the regulatory practice. Combined with demands for regular attendance they impact on, and demand, as for someone tagged for parole, the person's physical presence at a particular time and place. The accompanying threat of the loss of benefits will, as many in the field of disability studies have argued (see for example Grover and Piggott, 2005), cause stress and distress for those people who, previously medically recognised as long-term sick or with disabilities, are, through the decision of the Jobcentre Plus personal advisor deemed 'fit for work' and constructed as undeserving of state benefit. Despite an initially thin but rapidly vaporised veiling of a discourse of opportunity, of lifelong learning and of social justice, the welfare-to-work policies are, as this analysis has shown, its antithesis. They are, irrespective of the particular hue of the UK political party, and within the context of recession and predicted high unemployment, policies of social control and personal limitation.

References

ACOSS (Australian Council of Social Service) (2007) *The role of further education and training in welfare to work policies*. Strawberry Hills, NSW: ACOSS.

Bagguley P. and Mann, K. (1992) 'Idle thieving bastards? Scholarly representations of the underclass', *Work, Employment and Society*, 6: 1, 113–126.

Bambra, C. Hamilton, V. and Whitehead, M. (2005) 'Does "welfare-to-work" work? A systematic review of the effectiveness of the UK's welfare-to-work programmes for people with a disability or chronic illness', *Social Science and Medicine*, 60: 9, 1905–18.

Bauman, Z. (1998) *Work, consumerism and the new poor*. Buckingham: Open University Press.

Beck, U. and Beck-Gernsheim, E. (2001) *Individualization*. London: Sage.

Brine, J. (1999) *Under educating women: globalising inequality*. Buckingham: Open University Press.

Brine, J. (2001) 'Education, social exclusion and the supranational state', *International Journal of Inclusive Education*, 5: 2/3, 119–31.

Brine, J. (2002) *The European Social Fund and the EU: flexibility, growth, security*. London: Continuum.

Brine, J. (2006) 'Lifelong learning and the knowledge economy: those that know and those that do not – the discourse of the European Union', *British Educational Research Journal*, 32: 5, 649–66.

CEC (Commission for European Communities) (1999) *The 1999 Employment Guidelines: Council Resolution of 22 February 1999 (European Employment Strategy)*. Luxembourg: Office for Official Publications of the European Communities (OOPEC).

CEC (2000) Presidency conclusions: Lisbon European Council, 23 and 24 March 2000, (Lisbon Strategy), Luxembourg: OOPEC.

CEC (2006) Regulation (EC) No 1081/2006 of the European Parliament and of the Council of 5 July 2006 on the European Social Fund and repealing Regulation (EC) No 1784/1999, *Official Journal of the European Union*, L.210 31.7.2006: 12–18.

CEC (2008) *Education and Training 2010: main policy initiatives and outputs in education and training since the year 2000*. Brussels: Education and Culture: Lifelong Learning.

Daguerre, A. (2007) 'Active labour market policies and welfare reform: Europe and the US in comparative perspective', London: Palgrave Macmillan.

Descy, P. (2002) 'Combating labour market exclusion: does training work?', *European Journal of Vocational Training*, 41, 64–83.

Dieckhoff, M. (2007) 'Does it work? The effect of continuing training on labour market outcomes: a comparative study of Germany, Denmark and the United Kingdom', *European Sociological Review*, 23: 3, 295–308.

DCSF/DIUS (Department for Children, Schools and Families and Department for Innovation, Universities and Skills) (2008) *Raising expectations*

DfES (Department for Education and Skills) (2007) Green Paper: *Raising expectations: enabling the system to deliver*. London: DfES.

DWP (Department for Work and Pensions) (2006) Green Paper: *New deal for welfare: empowering people to work*. London: DWP.

DWP (2007) *Ready for work: full employment in our generation*. London: DWP.

DWP (2008a) *Opportunity for all: indicators update 2007*. London: DWP.

DWP (2008b) Green Paper: *No one written off: reforming welfare to reward responsibility*. London: DWP.

DWP (2008c) White Paper: *Raising expectations and increasing support: reforming welfare for the future*. London: DWP.

DWP (2009) *The Social Security Flexible New Deal regulations 2009* (CM 7566). London: DWP.

Dwyer, P. (2004) 'Creeping conditionality in the UK: from welfare rights to conditional entitlements?' *Canadian Journal of Sociology*, 29: 2, 265–87.

Esping-Andersen, G. (1996) 'After the golden age? Welfare state dilemmas in a global economy', in G. Esping-Andersen (ed.) *Welfare states in transition: national adaptations in global economics*. London: Sage.

Evans, P. (2007) '(Not) taking account of precarious employment: workfare policies and lone mothers in Ontario and the UK', *Social Policy and Administration*, 41: 1, 29–49.

Fitzpatrick, T. (2004) 'Time, social justice and UK welfare reform', *Economy and Society*, 33: 3, 335–58.

Freud, D. (2007) *The Freud Report: reducing dependency, increasing opportunity: options for the future of welfare to work*. London: DWP.

Gregg, P. (2008) *The Gregg Report: realising potential: a vision for personalised conditionality and support*. London: DWP.

Grover, C. (2007) 'The Freud Report on the future of welfare to work: some initial reflections', *Critical Social Policy*, 27: 4, 534–45.

Grover, C. and Piggott, L. (2005) 'Disabled people, the reserve army of labour and welfare reform', *Disability and Society*, 20: 7, 705–17.

Hanley, L. (2007) *Estates: an intimate history*. London: Granta.

HMT (Her Majesty's Treasury) (2007) *Lisbon Strategy for jobs and growth: UK national reform plan: update on progress*. London: Treasury.

House of Commons Standard Note (2009) *Flexible New Deal, (Standard Note SN/EP/4849)*. London: House of Commons Library.

Leitch, S. (2006) *Prosperity for all in the global economy – world class skills (final report)*. London: Her Majesty's Treasury.

Levitas, R. (1998) *The inclusive society? Social exclusion and New Labour*. London: Macmillan.

Liberal-Conservative Coalition (2010) www.guardian.co.uk/politics/2010/may/12/lib-dem-tory-deal-coalition.

Lister, R. (2001) 'Towards a citizens' welfare state: the 3+2 "R"s of welfare reform', *Theory, Culture and Society*, 18: 2–3, 91–111.

Marx, K. (1849) 'Wage-labour and capital', reproduced in D. McLellan (ed.) (1990), *Karl Marx: selected writings*. Oxford: Oxford University Press.

Peppin, L. (2007) 'The history of EU co-operation in the field of education and training: how lifelong learning became a strategic objective', *European Journal of Education*, 42: 1, 121–32.

Perry, G. and Maloney, T. (2008) 'Economic evaluation of the training opportunities programme in New Zealand', *Australian Journal of Labour Economics*, 11: 2, 163–85.

Prideaux, S. (2001) 'New Labour, old functionalism: the underlying contradictions of welfare reform in the US and the UK', *Social Policy and Administration*, 35: 1, 85–115.

Rosenthal, P. and Peccei, R. (2006) 'Consuming work: front-line workers and their customers in Jobcentre Plus', *International Journal of Public Sector Management*, 19: 7, 659–72.

Thompson, E. P. (1963) *The making of the English working class*. Harmondsworth: Penguin.

Welfare Reform Act (2007) London: HMSO.

Welfare Reform Bill (2009) London: HMSO.

Young, I. M. (1990) *Justice and the politics of difference*. Princeton New Jersey: Princeton University Press.

CHAPTER SIX

Social justice, inclusion and lifelong learning in Scotland: the experiences of adult learners

ELISABET WEEDON AND SHEILA RIDDELL

Introduction

Scotland sees itself as a country with a strong belief in education and lifelong learning. This is assumed to promote the creation of a strong democracy and a meritocratic social system (Devine, 1999). Many policy texts produced by the previous Labour and present Scottish Nationalist Party (SNP) administrations express commitment to the achievement of social justice. A recent policy document, *Skills for Scotland: a lifelong learning skills strategy* (Scottish Government, 2007a), identified, as one of its major aims, the achievement of equal access to and participation in skills and learning for everyone, including 'those trapped by persistent disadvantage' (Scottish Government, 2007a: 5) Some commentators, for example Scott and Mooney (2005) are somewhat sceptical of the imagery of Scotland as a collectivist and egalitarian society, but the strength of the rhetoric in Government publications, particularly those relating to lifelong learning, cannot be denied. The Scottish emphasis on lifelong learning has not occurred in a vacuum. It has been strongly influenced by changes in the global economy stressing the importance of the knowledge economy and developments within the European Union (EU). The Scottish lifelong learning strategy reflected the Lisbon Strategy which viewed learning and human capital development as the key economic well-being. Although social justice featured as an aspect of the policies developed at EU level, the dominant theme was the role of lifelong learning in economic and human capital development (Holford et al., 2008).

This chapter draws on the findings from an European Union Sixth Framework Project LLL2010 (www.lll2010.tlu.ee). It uses data from a questionnaire survey of adult returners to education and interviews with managers of lifelong learning provision, one government official from Learning Connections and one official from the Scottish Funding Council, a non-departmental public body. Policy rhetoric promotes learning and qualifications as a means to gainful employment which in turn is assumed to lead to social inclusion. The extent to which all learning provides relevant qualifications and lead to increased opportunities is the focus of this chapter. It explores what the experiences of adult learners reveal about social justice principles in practice, how learning contributes to the individual's social or human capital development and how this relates to social inclusion or exclusion. It also examines the views of the senior managers and managers on the role of education in relation to lifelong learning provision.

The next section provides a description of the methodology. This is followed by an overview of the role of lifelong learning in developing human and social capital and the extent to which this leads to social inclusion. It draws on Levitas's (2005) three-fold model of social inclusion and exclusion policy discourses (redistributionist, moral underclass and social integrationist). Scottish lifelong learning policy, including the views on policy by the senior managers, is then examined before turning to the findings from the survey and interviews with particular emphasis on learners with differing levels of previous qualifications.

The following questions are considered:

- How are the concepts of social justice and inclusion understood in lifelong learning policy in Scotland, and what tensions and contradictions are apparent?
- What do the experiences of adult returners to education and the views of education managers reveal in relation to the application of social justice principles in practice?
- If there are tensions and contradictions, what changes are necessary in order to ensure that the gaps between rhetoric and reality are reduced?

Methodology

The survey

The Scottish survey included 1021 adult learners stratified by ISCED levels of current study. Within the Scottish education system qualifications at ISCED level 2 are those that provide basic skills, ISCED level 3 encompass Standard and Higher grade qualifications, ISCED level 4 refers to Access to Higher Education courses and ISCED level 5 includes HNC/D, undergraduate and masters degrees. It was not feasible due to resource and time constraints to do a stratified postcode sample; instead we sampled according to institutions. The focus was on further education colleges but the sample included 1 pre-92 and 1 post-92 university, 1 HEI, 2 Community Learning and Development (CLD) local authority departments and 1 voluntary organisation. Scotland has 43 colleges which provide education from basic skills up to and including degree level. They are seen as making a substantial contribution to economic growth as they provide learners with vocational and transferable skills; in addition, they are considered effective in tackling poverty and disadvantage (Scottish Executive, 2006). They are thus seen as key players in the promotion of lifelong learning and social justice. Thirteen colleges were included based in the central belt, central Scotland and the north and north-west. Of the voluntary organisations included, one had learners throughout Scotland and one was based in a large city; the local authority learners were from the east of Scotland. Table 1 shows the location and number of learners at each level. As can be seen the majority came from further education colleges. An online version of the survey was used with some students studying online at ISCED level 5.

Table 1: Location and level of study of the learners.

ISCED level[a]	University/ HEI	FE Colleges	Voluntary organisation	Local Authority CLD	Total
2		37	29	5	71
3		277	17		294
4		292		9	301
5	125	230			355
Total	125	836	46	14	1021

[a] International Standard Classification of Education (ISCED) is an instrument for classifying educational programmes to allow cross-country comparison (OECD, 2004).

Qualifications were converted from Scottish/UK qualifications using the NEAC classification also used to convert qualifications in the National Adult Education Survey, 2005 for Eurostat.

Interviews with managers of lifelong learning

Six institutions/organisations were included in this project and a total of 46 people were interviewed as shown in table 2 below.

Individual interviews were carried out with all of these participants except the interview with the two managers from the urban CLD who were interviewed together. In each case the interview lasted from 45 minutes to 1.5 hours. Most of the interviews were carried out in the place of work of the person being interviewed. In addition to these interviews, one manager and one tutor working in prison education were interviewed. However, no prisoners were included in the survey of learners; the data from these two have therefore not been included here.

Review of literature and policy

Social inclusion and exclusion

Social inclusion and exclusion are terms that frequently feature in European social policy. In spite of their common usage there is no single agreed upon definition within the European community. Levitas, in her discussion of social inclusion and exclusion, suggests evidence for three different discourses in the UK (Levitas, 2005). The first one, redistribution discourse (RED) stresses the role of poverty in social exclusion, an individual or household living in poverty is considered at risk of social exclusion. Poverty is seen as relative and households with less than 60 per cent of the median household income are regarded as living in poverty. The solution advocated is redistribution of wealth and increases in social transfers to ensure inclusion. It emphasises material explanations in contrast to the second model which focuses on the moral underclass and dependency discourse (MUD). In this model, the excluded are portrayed as a culturally distinct underclass that has become dependent on benefits. According to this model, the poor are responsible for their exclusion because of their behaviour. A key focus is on the unemployed and unemployable, who are seen as lacking basic skills, the right role models, education or a culture

Table 2: Overview of institutions and participants.

Type of institution	No. of institutions	Total no Interviews	No of interviews
Colleges:	2	32	Principal: 1; Vice-principals: 3; Senior managers/managers: 19; Head of learner support: 2; Lecturers: 7.
University: pre-92	1	5	Registry/admissions/ widening participation (5)
Voluntary Organisation	1	2	Senior manager: 1; Work-based learning tutor organiser (1).
Local Authority Community and Learning Development (CLD)	2	3	CLD 1 semi-rural: Manager: 1 CLD 2 urban: Senior manager: 1 Manager of adult learning: 1
Government official Non-governmental public body (NDPB) official	–	2	Senior manager, Learning Connections[a] (LC) (1) Senior manager, Scottish Funding Council (SFC) (1)
Total	5	44	

[a] Learning Connections has two strands of work organised into two teams: Adult Literacies and Community Learning and Development. The latter (CLD) includes both learning and social development for individuals and groups within their own communities.

of work or all of these. Although lack of a culture of work features in MUD, it is the third model, the social integrationist discourse (SID), that stresses the role of the labour market in social integration. Paid work is seen as the key to achieving inclusion. Levitas emphasises that these models of discourses are ideal types and are not necessarily mutually exclusive; however, they do help in identifying the key aspects of any particular policy initiative. It could also be suggested that they weave in and out of the welfare and lifelong learning policies of European countries.

It is evident that within each of these discourses lifelong learning can potentially play a key role. If education is considered a social good then it could be argued, from the redistributionist position that social inclusion could be achieved if learning opportunities are opened up. The extent to which any learning is translated into improved life chances will be affected by the quality and status of the learning provided. Education could be considered as playing an important role within the cultural (MUD) discourse as it provides an opportunity for learning social norms and values, as well as the need to respect others. Finally, the social integrationist discourse, with its strong focus on labour market integration is likely to advocate learning as a means of developing the skills necessary to obtain and retain employment and also through upskilling and reskilling to deal with the demands of the knowledge society and/or threats of redundancy.

Lifelong learning

Education as a means of promoting social justice is not a recent phenomenon; for example, the Workers' Educational Association (WEA) was founded in 1903 to provide access to learning for those excluded from the formal education system. The terms 'lifelong education' and 'lifelong learning' emerged later; lifelong education in the 1960s fostered by organisations such as UNESCO drawing on humanist values and, in more human capital terms, OECD; and in the 1990s lifelong learning formed the basis for the Lisbon Strategy (Field, 2006). Although the Lisbon strategy purports to acknowledge all three aspects of lifelong learning: human capital, social capital and personal development, its critics still see it as too focused on human capital development (Holford et al., 2008)

Within the academic literature there has been considerable questioning of the term 'lifelong learning'. It has been described as a 'broad, imprecise and 'elastic' term' (Johnston, 2000, cited in Rogers, 2006: 125) and by Boshier as 'human resource development in drag' (Boshier, 1998:

4). Nonetheless, it is in widespread use and could be seen as replacing the term adult education. Field (2006) argues that the term is useful for a number of reasons; one of these is that it reflects changes in society that are evident in the ways that people nowadays acquire new skills and capacities. On the other hand, he also suggests that there is a danger that it becomes a mechanism for exclusion and social control. Field further notes that the discourse stresses individual agency and that learners are expected to take control of their own learning. Quality assured learning is also part of the new lifelong learning agenda which has led to the development of more accredited learning. Mills argues that what can be discerned is a marketisation of learning with a focus on employability (Mills, 2002). He suggests that the focus on the individual as a learner does not recognise learning as a social activity and limits learning to that which is useful for work. In addition, it does not recognise the role of social class in attitudes to learning. It fails to take into account that those with already high qualifications are most likely to engage with learning; those with no qualifications are least likely to do so. This is borne out by figures from the National Adult Learning Survey (NALS) 2005 Scotland Report (Ormston et al., 2007) which show that 85 per cent of those with SVQ level 5 (ISCED level 5) had taken part in taught learning in the 3 years preceding the survey. Of those with no qualifications (ISCED level 1–2) only 23 per cent had taken part in taught learning. This survey also showed that 82 per cent of those with parents who had a degree qualification were likely to engage in taught learning compared with only 63 per cent of those whose parents left school at 16. Clearly then, an emphasis on the individual in charge of his/her own learning may serve to exacerbate inequalities in education. The emphasis on individual agency and the fact that individuals have access to different levels of learning may lead to greater inequality in society. Hudson, exploring the relationship between inequality and the knowledge economy (Hudson, 2006), claims that development of the knowledge economy is likely to increase inequality as changes in employment patterns leads to differentials in income. This is due to the development of a highly skilled workforce serving the knowledge economy, a decline in skilled trades and an increase in unskilled labour. These concerns were also voiced by Hake in relation to the stress for autonomous learners who felt that this would 'sharpen the divisions between the socially included and excluded' (Hake, 1999: 67).

Lifelong learning policy in Scotland

This section overviews the lifelong learning strategies in Scotland and includes views from the senior managers in the Scottish Funding Council and Learning Connections. It focuses specifically on the extent to which human capital, social capital or personal development is evidenced in the strategy and what evidence there is for the different discourses identified by Levitas.

The first lifelong learning strategy published in 2003 identified lifelong learning as important in bringing benefits both to the individual and to society:

> *lifelong learning has an important and distinctive contribution to make to people's wellbeing, to a more inclusive society and to a vibrant and sustainable economy.* (Scottish Executive, 2003: 4).

This strategy built on the green paper *Opportunity Scotland* (Scottish Executive, 1998). It was published by a Labour administration and focused on post compulsory education and training and clearly reflected the EU Lisbon strategy. Although the aims included all aspects of lifelong learning, the measures used to evaluate the strategy tended to stress human capital development (Scottish Executive, 2005), and an emphasis on 'learning for work' has also been noted by others (see, e.g., Smith, 2008). In 2007 a new lifelong learning skill strategy was published – *Skills for Scotland: a lifelong learning skill strategy* (Scottish Government, 2007a). It had, as its title implies, a strong emphasis on skills development and employability and, in contrast with the policy of the previous Labour administration, it includes early years and compulsory education within the lifelong learning agenda. However, the inclusion of compulsory education reflects the aim to increase vocational education within the compulsory education system either through more vocational courses in secondary schools or through school–college links.

This shift in the government thinking towards greater emphasis on skills and human capital development was clearly welcomed by the funding council interviewee who felt there was a greater clarity of purpose in the new strategy:

> *[the skill strategy is] really quite distinctive from what was there before . . . a real sense of purpose and of trying to make sure that people aren't*

> *overlapping, aren't getting in each others' way but are also pulling in the same sort of direction* (Senior manager, SFC).

When asked whether it had a strong focus on human capital he agreed that it had but added that it was not just about development of human capital but also its utilisation, he explained:

> *I hadn't thought of it in those terms [human capital] actually . . . I'm not quite sure how I can answer that because the other bit of it which is new is the skills utilisation bit. So it's not just the building of the human capital. It's the use of the human capital. But it is . . . I mean that's what it, that's the two bits of it really . . .* (Senior manager SFC).

By way of contrast, the emphasis on human capital development was criticised by the Learning Connections interviewee, who generally viewed both the earlier lifelong learning strategy and the skills strategy critically. The key issue for him was the lack of appreciation of learning outside the formal setting and the overall focus on employability:

> *However, it doesn't for me acknowledge learning in life outside a learning institution and I think that is a massive gap . . . skills equals the chance to be employed* (Senior manager LC).

The LC manager emphasised the need for blurring boundaries between institutions and encouraging learning in a range of settings. He also commented on the inequalities within our society:

> *We are on the back of 15 to 20 years of greed that was spotted by the original 7: 84 principle, you know the wealth owned by 7 per cent of people . . . I think that's probably worse now, it's just shocking, and our society should never allow that . . . So therefore I said that needs addressed, it is too simple to say that we need redistribution of wealth I think, not on the Marxist/ socialist idea, the access to contentment at the bottom line should be easier to develop* (Senior manager LC).

Unsurprisingly given their different roles, the positions of these two managers clearly differ, highlighting potential tensions within the government. The most recent lifelong learning skills strategy and the senior manager from the SFC strongly emphasise the importance of education and learning that equips the individual for the labour market, reflecting the SID discourse. This contrasts with LC senior manager who sees learning as having much wider benefits, and also stressed the more difficult to measure aspects of learning such as increased confidence. Although he does not advocate redistribution of wealth, he is more closely aligned to the discourse of redistribution. With a budget of around £1.7billion, it could be argued that SFC is likely to have a greater impact on practice than Learning Connections, responsible for community learning and development and adult literacy and numeracy, but relying on local authorities for its budget, which is not ring-fenced.

This overview of policy indicates a strong emphasis on the human capital aspect of lifelong learning within policy discourse and also in terms of funding for lifelong learning. The following section examines the motivations and experiences of adult learners with particular emphasis on differences between those with high and low levels of previous qualifications. Chi-square tests have been used to test for statistically significant differences. Where a significant finding is reported this is at $p< 0.05$ or below.

Findings from the learners and managers in institutions

Characteristics of the learners

The majority of respondents (73 per cent) were women and most were born between 1960 and 1989 which meant they were aged between 18 and 47. There were more, older learners doing basic skills courses. Most, over 90 per cent, considered themselves to be either Scottish or British and the majority spoke English as their first language. Of those that responded, 70 per cent were not doing another course and had not been involved in another course over the past 12 months. About 22 per cent had done one other course but few learners had done more than one other course. The programmes of study were mainly in the area of education, social science and health and welfare as is shown in the table below. These are traditionally 'female' subjects and this is reflected in the composition of the sample.

Examining the data according to previous level of qualification, it can be seen from figure 1 that 8 per cent of learners in our survey stated they had no previous formal qualification, 66 per cent with ISCED level 3 and

Table 2: Courses undertaken by learners in the survey.

Programme of study	Frequency	Percentage
General programmes	76	7.4
Other: includes engineering and services	66	6.5
Teacher training and education	199	19.5
Humanities, languages and arts	91	8.9
Social sciences, business and law	239	23.4
Science, mathematics and computing	88	8.6
Health and welfare	262	25.7
Total	1021	100.0

26 per cent with ISCED level 5. There are more learners aged 41 and over who had no previous formal qualification (11 per cent). In 2007, 14 per cent of the working age population in Scotland was recorded as having no qualification (http://www.sns.gov.uk/AnRep/AreaTree.asp); however, the randomised sample of learners and non-learners in the NALS survey (Ormston et al., 2007) included around 9 per cent of people who had no previous qualification. In contrast to national statistics our sample contained a higher proportion among those over 41 who had a degree. This is likely to be due to the fact that the Annual Population Survey (based on the Labour Force Survey) draws on both non-learners and learners and excludes those in formal full-time education, our survey focused specifically on adult learners in formal education. As our sample included only learners it would be expected to have a lower percentage of those with no previous qualifications and higher percentage of those with higher qualification. The former is because those with no qualifications are least likely to engage with any form of learning.

Learners with no previous formal qualifications were significantly more likely to be male and over 41 years; however, 7 per cent fell into the youngest age group. There was, as would be expected a difference between the different groups in terms of parents' educational background; those with no previous formal qualification had parents with no or low levels of qualifications. There was limited data on fathers' backgrounds, especially from those with no formal education. More than half stated that they did not know or preferred not to disclose, compared to 30 per cent of those at ISCED level 5. This group of learners were significantly more likely not to have been married; it was the case for half

Figure 1: Learners' previous level of qualification of total survey sample.

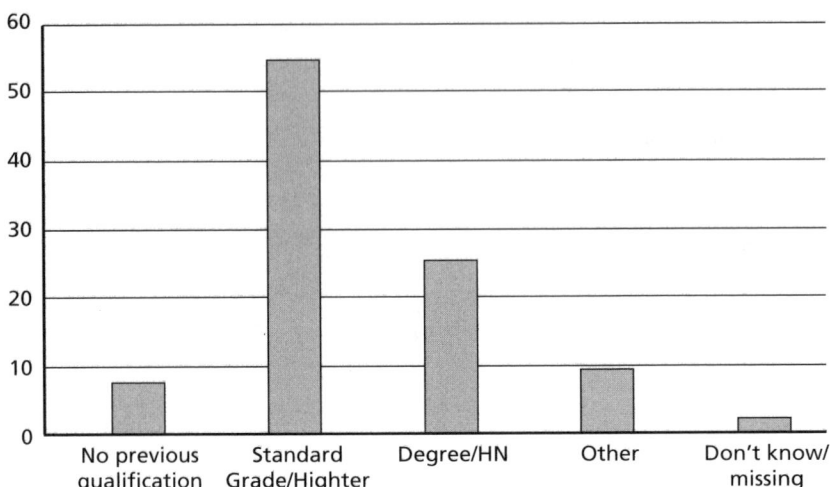

of the group compared to 43 per cent of ISCED level 3 and 28 per cent of ISCED level 5 learners.

The majority were located in further education with just over quarter in voluntary organisations/CLD. These latter types of institutions cater mainly for adult learners with either no formal qualification or ISCED level 3, especially those undertaking basic level courses. General programmes such as literacy and numeracy, computer use followed by social sciences and health and welfare were their main courses of study. Only 14 per cent from this group were in employment compared to 40 per cent of those at ISCED level 5.

The main reason for leaving school/their initial education for just under half of this group was to start working, and a similar proportion of those with ISCED level 3 qualifications also cited this reason, compared to only just over a quarter of those with ISCED level 5 qualifications. This group were considerably more likely to state that a dislike of the learning environment or personal/emotional problem had led them to leave. There is a strong contrast with those who had ISCED level 5 qualifications as their main reason for leaving was that they had achieved the qualification they required. Those with formal qualifications were also likely to have reengaged with learning, even if they had abandoned the course and, whilst the majority of all learners were only doing the current course, those with higher previous qualifications were significantly more likely to be doing more than one course.

Attitudes to learning and education were probed with nine statements on a Likert scale and attitudes were positive for all groups. There were few differences between the learners according to previous level of qualification, the main exception that learners with no previous experience were more likely to view learning as something for those with little else to do.

In terms of main motivation, learners with no previous formal qualification were significantly more likely to be learning for personal rather than job related reasons than other learners. The difference was greatest between this group and those with ISCED level 5 qualifications. However, a significant proportion (43 per cent) cited job related reasons as well as personal reasons, as per the following quote – added by one of the respondents with no previous formal qualifications:

to learn to read and write, hoping to get a job (female, 44, Literacy course)

ISCED level 5 learners were most likely to say that their reason for learning was that this was a job requirement; since they were most likely to be in employment. In this group, 40 per cent were employed compared to 14 per cent amongst those with no previous formal qualifications. Whilst the majority cited personal reasons, in a second question nearly 70 per cent of those with no previous qualification also stated they wanted to get a job; however, this varied according to learning provider. Those studying in FE who had no previous formal qualification were considerably more likely to state job reasons than those in voluntary/local authority provision.

Participants' motivations for undertaking the course were probed using eighteen statements on a five-point Likert scale, based on the Education Participation Scale (Boshier, 1991). These were classified according to whether they were externally enforced or autonomous motivations and further divided into four types: social control, human capital, social capital and personal fulfilment. Examples of statements and their classifications are:

- *'To learn more about a subject that interests me'* (autonomous/personal fulfilment).
- *'Because my employer required me to'* (externally enforced/social control).

- *'To do my job better'* (externally enforced/human capital).
- *'To start my own business'* (autonomous/human capital).
- *'To contribute more to my community'* (autonomous/social capital.

It was found that learners with no previous qualification were significantly more likely to be influenced by social motives for learning. Participating in group activities and meeting new people was particularly important for these learners, especially so if they were learning in a voluntary/local authority setting. Learners with no formal qualifications were also significantly more likely to have been advised to do the course by someone else and to be doing it to avoid redundancy or as a requirement of claiming benefit and this was particularly the case for those in a voluntary/local authority setting. Numbers were small and should therefore be treated with caution but it does seem that different types of learning providers attract a different profile of learners even in terms of those with no previous qualifications. Admittedly, the voluntary organisations catered specifically for adult learners; however, further education colleges also claim to cater for all ages and stages of learning.

The survey also considered other aspects such as the teaching and learning process using a set of fifteen statements on a five point Likert scale. These focused on three main areas:

- Relationships between learners, e.g. 'the course provides opportun-ities for making new friends.
- Learners' engagement in the learning process, e.g. 'students can select assignments that are of personal interest to them'.
- Teacher support and organisation of the course, e.g. 'the teacher makes every effort to help the student succeed'.

There were a number of statistically significant differences between learners with no previous qualifications and the other two levels of qualifications. They were more likely to say that the course offered opportunities to make new friends, that students on the course enjoyed it and that students enjoyed working together. Once again, those learning in voluntary/local authority organisations were most likely to stress these aspects.

In terms of the overall organisation of the course it was those with no previous formal qualification who were most positive and, again those in voluntary/local authority organisations were more positive than those in further education; however it was students on ISCED level 5 and in HE who felt that coursework was focused on essential activities. Learners with no previous formal qualifications were most likely to experience a flexible curriculum as they were more likely to be able to question course requirements and select assignments that are of personal interest, with those in voluntary/local authority organisations most likely to say so. On the other hand, this group of learners was also most likely to say that the teacher insisted on them doing things her/his way.

The data on motivation for learning and the experiences of the learning process suggest that learners with no previous formal qualifications value the social aspect of learning and that this need was satisfied by their course. They felt well supported by tutors who offered a flexible and learner centred curriculum. The data also indicate that this is particularly so for learners in voluntary/local authority organisations. It is interesting to note that Tett *et al.* found similar institutional differences in terms of learners' satisfaction with the teaching and learning experience (Tett *et al.*, 2006). Their evaluation focused specifically on literacy and numeracy provision and included both quantitative and qualitative data, whilst our research included other basic skills such as ICT.

Finally, more than 80 per cent of the learners were confident in their ability to complete the course, those with no formal qualification were slightly less confident but this difference was not statistically significant. There was little difference between the different levels of qualification groups in relation to support from family and friends; learners with no previous qualifications were slightly less likely to cite support from family and friends but this was not statistically significant. This group was significantly less likely to be involved with social activities such as recreation/leisure pursuits, voluntary organisation or church; however, there was no difference in participation in cultural activities such as music, cinema or sport. They were significantly less likely than the other groups, especially those with degree level qualifications, to be involved in political activities.

Overall then, the suggestion is that those most at risk of exclusion, learners with no previous qualifications, were strongly motivated by the social aspects of learning and that those with the highest qualifications were more likely to be motivated by human capital aspects of learning. Our interview data with managers and tutors in educational institutions and organisations indicated the following:

- A strengthening emphasis on employability and learning for work.
- An increasing stress on engaging young people in learning, especially those at risk of exclusion.
- Widening participation measures within the elite university at risk.

The shift towards employability and learning for work was noted by one of the college lecturers who highlighted differences in earlier attitudes to education and current ones. In his view, the Government has shifted its focus in recent years towards developing a skills base that is applicable to the employers and this has been felt by the college:

> *There is a bigger emphasis coming through now for skills, the government appears to be aligning itself to the skills issues. I think gone are the days where you bring people in and just put them on a course for the sake of it. Now it is, do they have the skills to get work and is the education and training good enough to get a job and prosper* (Lecturer, College A).

It was also clear that the colleges were strongly affected by the steer from the funding council as can be seen from this comment by a college senior manager:

> *We are advised by, but not led by, the government. I think there is a respect there that says we know what the agenda is and we know what to anticipate, they say that they want to see us addressing access and inclusion and they want us to respond to the skills agenda, how we do it is up to us* (Vice Principal, College A).

The employability agenda was also evident in Community Learning and Development and the voluntary organisation. The manager from the voluntary organisation noted a shift in their learning provision which was driven by ability (or lack of it) to access funding:

> *But the actual numbers of students over five years is about stationary...And that's because funding for community learning has declined... whilst project funding in the workplace has increased... so there's been a decline in community learning and a growth in workplace education* (Voluntary organisation manager).

The focus on young people can be seen in the implementation of the new 'Curriculum for Excellence' currently being implemented in schools. It aims to provide a curriculum for those aged 3 to 18 which will 'enable each child or young person to be a successful learner, a confident individual, a responsible citizen and an effective contributor' (http://www.ltscotland.org.uk/curriculumforexcellence/. According the Executive Director in College A this is seen as *'a fundamental key driver to the future development of the college and the education sector as a whole'*. The Government is trying to promote colleges as a link between school and university and by pushing policies such as those for the MCMC (More Choices More Chances) group, it hopes that more young people will go to college instead of dropping out of the education system.

It may be that this drive towards skills for younger people will have an impact on the availability of college places for mature learners. At the time of writing, there is only one Scottish college where the 18 and under year group is in majority; however, there has been a steady increase in the younger student population. Across the whole college sector, this group accounted for 28 per cent of the student population in 2003, the proportion in this age group increased to 36 per cent in 2007–08. Current funding priorities focus on younger learners, the colleges are capped in terms of numbers that they can admit which would suggest the current policies may lead to fewer opportunities for older learners.

The short term focus for the Government is on the role that colleges can play in the current recession, and the Government uses phrases such as *'re-training, re-generation, supporting the unemployed, apprenticeships for young people'*. Colleges are viewed as central to educational policy and the Scottish economy. A lecturer in one of the colleges described colleges as *'the glue in the middle of the school and HE sectors and it is about that transition and flow'*. The colleges were also described by the funding council manager as excellent at widening participation and as offering a route to higher education for non-traditional students. He acknowledged, though that this route was most likely to be through a post-92 university and that elite universities were unlikely, at least in immediate future, to increase access for socially disadvantaged students. This was also the view of those within the elite university involved with widening participation measures. They offered some interesting examples of innovative practice but in overall terms the intake of those from lower socioeconomic backgrounds had decreased rather than increased.

Managers in organisations working most closely with socially disadvantaged groups, highlighted funding as problematic and likely to have a considerable impact on provision. One of the managers noted that her work had focused on making efficiency savings and her colleague added that adult education was at risk due to an increased emphasis on young people. The manager of the semi-rural CLD noted that funding for adult literacy and numeracy was likely to suffer due to the changes in funding regime. A further area that was highlighted by the CLD managers was the lack of effective transition arrangements for learners wishing to move to a higher level. This was stressed in particular for vulnerable learners who may require support beyond that which a college or a university could offer. As can be seen from the survey findings, learners in voluntary and CLD settings were the most satisfied in terms of learning and teaching. This suggests that the concerns of the managers are valid and would warrant attention.

Summary and conclusion

Three questions were posed at the start of the chapter, and these will now be considered. The first question aimed to consider how the concepts of social justice and inclusion were understood in Scottish lifelong learning policy and what contradictions there might be within the policy. Since the new SNP administration took over in May 2007 the overarching aim has been to promote sustainable economic growth. This is set out in the Government Economic Strategy (Scottish Government, 2007b) which stresses the need to create a wealthier and fairer, smarter, healthier, safer and stronger and greener Scottish society. In terms of equity this strategy states that it intends to:

- provide the opportunities – and incentives – for all to contribute to Scotland's sustainable economic growth;
- accord greater priority to achieving a more balanced growth across Scotland, to give all across Scotland the chance to succeed; and
- promote economic growth and environmental quality and responsib - ility as mutually advancing.

Clearly the focus is on labour market participation; more specific policy which sets out the intentions for tackling poverty – *Achieving our Potential* (Scottish Government, 2008), sees participation in the labour market as the main way of tackling income inequality.

The aims of the economic strategy are evident in current lifelong learning policy, especially the most recent skill strategy, which has a strong focus on human capital development. As discussed above, this focus on human capital is endorsed by the senior manager at the Scottish Funding Council but viewed as negative by the senior manager in Learning Connections, suggesting possible tensions within the government in terms of priorities. It has also been argued above, these two have differing amount of power in terms of influencing practice due to the funding arrangements. Learning provided through local authority CLD has a strong focus on those that are 'hard to reach' and for providing learning that develops the individual and the community. It uses the social practice model of teaching and values soft outcome such as an increase in learner confidence as much as accredited learning. All of this is potentially at risk due to the current emphasis on skills development.

In terms of Levitas' three discourses, the one most apparent, both in lifelong learning strategies, the economic strategy and the poverty strategy is Social Integrationist Discourse (SID). All these documents stress that the route out of poverty is through engagement with the labour market. Measures proposed to tackle poverty include ensuring access work with reasonable pay and removing barriers to employment, e.g. through accessible and affordable child care. However, if the policy was to lead to an actual reduction in poverty through this route it could be argued that lifelong learning has the potential for redistribution (RED). There is no evidence for a MUD discourse within Scottish policy as the government stresses its role in assisting the most vulnerable.

The second question sought to examine what the experiences of adult returners to education and the views of education managers revealed in relation to the application of social justice principles in practice. The survey data suggest a clear distinction between those learners who are now engaging with learning but had no formal previous qualifications and those with previous qualifications, especially those with degree or sub-degree level qualifications. Learners with higher level qualifications have access to a wide range of learning opportunities, leading to portable qualifications which increase their human capital. They are also critical of learning which does not fully meet their needs. By way of contrast, learners with low levels of initial education are more often compelled to engage in lifelong learning and take courses which are unlikely to have a major impact in raising their earning potential. They value the social capital which they gain from the courses they undertake possibly because they were less likely than the other groups to engage in other social activities. However, their social capital tended to be of the bonding rather than bridging variety as it was not clear whether their engagement with learning was leading on from the basic courses to higher levels of learning. As argued earlier, there is potential for learning to have a redistributionist role if it provides access to qualifications that will enhance labour market participation. There seemed little evidence from our learners with no formal qualification, that they were gaining the skills that would allow them access to better paid jobs. In addition, the data from the interviews with managers highlighted the lack of effective transition mechanisms, suggesting that participation in these kind of courses would not automatically translate into better labour market prospects. However, what is of importance was that these courses engaged with learners who are, as a group, reluctant to participate in learning and that they were providing valuable opportunities in relation to developing new social networks and a potential for progression.

The third question focused on tensions and contradictions and what changes might be necessary in order to bridge the gap between rhetoric and reality. In terms of policy there is some tension between a social integrationist discourse and a redistributionist one; learning is seen as a mechanism for ensuring labour market participation (SID) but provision of education is also seen as potentially allowing for a redistribution of wealth if those currently excluded from the labour market participate in learning and thereby enhance their qualifications. However, in practice, our survey and other research has shown that those already well qualified are more likely to engage in learning that will further promote their opportunities in the labour market. In contrast, learners with no previous qualifications are less likely to gain portable qualifications and, even if they engage in the labour market, are likely to end up in work with low pay. If the redistributionist potential of learning was to be promoted there would need to be a recognition that the social aspect of learning is valued by those with low level of qualifications but that this needs to be built upon by providing more effective transitions routes. However, at present, lifelong learning and its emphasis on human capital tends to widen, rather than narrow the gap between the most and least socially advantaged.

References

Boshier, R. (1991) 'Psychometric properties of the alternative from the Education Participation Scale', *Adult Education Quarterly*, 41, 150–67.
Boshier, R. (1998) 'Edgar Faure after 25 years: down but not out', in J.

Holford, P. Jarvis and C. Griffin (eds) *International perspectives on lifelong learning*. London, Kogan Page.

Devine, T. M. (1999) *The Scottish nation 1700–2000?* (London: Allen Lane).

Faure, E., Herrera, F., Kadoura, A-R, Lpes, H., Petrovski, A.V., Rahenma, M. and Ward, F.C. (1972) *Learning to be: the world of education today and tomorrow*. Paris: UNESCO.

Field, J. (2006) *Lifelong learning and the new educational order*. Stoke on Trent, Trentham Books.

Hake, B. J. (1999) 'Lifelong learning policies in the European Union: developments and issues', *Compare*, 29: 1, 53–69.

Holford, J., Riddell, S, Weedon, E., Litjens, J. and Hannan, G. (2008) *Patterns of lifelong learning: policy and practice in an expanding Europe*. Wien: Lit Verlag.

Hudson, J. (2006) 'Inequality and the knowledge economy: running to stand still'? *Social Policy and Society*, 5: 2, 207–22.

Levitas, R. (2005) *The inclusive society? Social exclusion and New Labour*, 2nd edn. Basingstoke: Macmillan.

Mills, V. (2002) 'Employability, globalisation and lifelong learning – a Scottish perspective', *International Journal of Lifelong Education*, 21: 4, 347–56.

Ormston, R., Dobbie, F., Cleghorn, N. with Davidson, A. (2007) *National adult learning survey (NALS) Scotland report*. Scottish Executive, 2007.

Rogers, A. (2006) 'Escaping the slums or changing the slums? Lifelong learning and social transformation', *International Journal of Lifelong Education*, 25: 2, 125–37.

Scott, G. and Mooney, G. (2005) 'Conclusion: Social policy in Scotland: imagining a different future?' in G. Mooney and G. Scott (eds) *Exploring social policy in the 'new' Scotland* Bristol: Policy Press.

Scottish Executive (2003) *Life through learning: learning through life*. Edinburgh, Scottish Executive.

Scottish Executive (2005) *Lifelong Learning Statistics, 2005*. Edinburgh, Scottish Executive.

Scottish Executive (2006) *Review of Scotland's colleges: unlocking opportunity, the difference Scotland's colleges make to learners, the economy and wider society*. Edinburgh: Scottish Executive.

Scottish Government (2007a) *Skills for Scotland: a lifelong skills strategy*. Edinburgh: Scottish Government.

Scottish Government (2007b) *The Government economic strategy*. Edinburgh: Scottish Government.

Scottish Government (2008) *Achieving our potential: a framework to tackle poverty and income inequality in Scotland*. Edinburgh: Scottish Government.

Scottish Office (1998) *Opportunity Scotland: a paper on lifelong learning*. Edinburgh: HMSO.

Smith, I. (2008) 'Educational provision: an overview', in: T. G. K. Bryce and W. M. Humes (eds) *Scottish education, 3rd edition: beyond devolution*. Edinburgh: Edinburgh University Press.

Tett, L., Hall, S., Maclachlan, K., Thorpe, G, Edwards, V. and Garside, L. (2006) *Evaluation of the Scottish literacy and numeracy (ALN) strategy*. Edinburgh: Scottish Executive.

CHAPTER SEVEN

Learning to be a good citizen: Informal learning through unpaid household work among recent Chinese immigrants in Canada

LICHUN WILLA LIU

Introduction

Every year, about a quarter million of immigrants came to Canada, and most of them settle in three major Canadian cities: Toronto, Vancouver and Montreal. According to the 2006 Census, Canada is home to over 200 ethnic communities, and 19.8 per cent of its total population was born outside of the country (Statistics Canada, 2008). The Chinese community, with a population of over 1.3 million, is the largest visible minority group in the country, and immigrants from Mainland China make up the largest proportion (14.6 per cent) of all immigrants to Canada in the past decade (Citizenship and Immigration Canada, 2009). Between 2001 and 2006, 63,900 newcomers from Mainland Chinese (14.3 per cent of the total) settled in Toronto – the largest and most culturally diverse city in Canada (Statistics Canada, 2007).

Immigrants not only play a key role in the economic development in Canada, the growing immigrant population also enriches the Canadian society with its cultural and ethnic diversity. Learning to adapt to changes and to integrate in the multicultural Canadian society poses both challenges and opportunities for new immigrants. However, so far most studies on immigrant integration in Canada have focused on immigrants' economic performances and formal education/training for participation in the Canadian labour market, limited research has been done on their unpaid household activities, and informal learning in the homeplace.

Unpaid household work, especially routine housework, such as feeding the family and caring for children, is crucial to the social reproduction of labour and the maintenance of the society. This chapter emphasises the importance of 'learning for life' through our lifeworld (Collins, 1998: 21; Welton, 1998; Williamson, 1998) by focusing on informal learning involved in unpaid household work.

Unlike other chapters in this section, which examined public activities and spaces, this chapter explores lifelong learning, especially informal learning through the private arena of the home and the often hidden world of unpaid household work, with the focus on new Chinese immigrants, especially immigrant women in Canada. Based on data from a Canadian Survey on Work and Lifelong Learning (2004),[1] individual interviews, a focus group and a discussion group with the Chinese immigrants in Toronto, Canada, this chapter examines three aspects of household work: food work, childcare and eldercare, and the informal learning the Chinese immigrants undertook in order to cope with the changes in each of these household tasks. This chapter takes a gender perspective in exploring how immigration interacts with gender, class and ethnicity in influencing the gender division of labour in housework and carework as well as the learning involved in each of those unpaid activities. By making visible the changes in household work, this chapter intends to make visible lifelong learning involved in it, which is crucial for new immigrants to sustain their family and community and to promote gender equality between women and men.

My study on Chinese immigrants, household work and lifelong learning intends to bridge the gaps in these three groups of literature, as the boundaries between them seem to have rarely been crossed. Despite a voluminous literature on housework, much of the research focuses on white middle-class women and the gendered division of household labour, and the power relations between women and men. There is limited research on household work among immigrant families, especially Chinese immigrant families. In the past two decades, lifelong learning has become one of the fastest growing subfields in adult education and is increasingly taken as synonymous with formal training for paid employment. As a consequence, learning in the homeplace, especially informal

---

[1] Special thanks to Doug Hart for helping me get data from the WALL Survey database.

learning through and for household work remains largely unexplored. By integrating Chinese immigrants, household work and lifelong learning, and by focusing on gender and its intersections with race and class, this chapter explores social justice and lifelong learning for new immigrant women, specifically Chinese women in Canada. This chapter argues that household work in a transnational context is an important site to promote social justice, both locally and globally and that lifelong learning through unpaid work is an important means for the new immigrants to sustain the community in which they live their lives.

The literature: household work, lifelong learning and Chinese immigrants

Studies on housework have pointed to a unanimous view that unpaid household work is a highly gendered activity, with women performing the bulk of it, regardless of family types, women's employment rates, racial, ethnic or national backgrounds (Baxter, 2005; Beaujot et al., 2000; Coltrane and Ishii-Kuntz, 1992; Demo and Acock, 1993; Man, 1997; Marshall, 1995; Ng and Ramirez, 1981; Orbuch and Eyster, 1997; Pessar, 1995; South and Spitze, 1994; Zuo and Bian, 2001). Studies on unpaid food work and caregiving reveal a similar gendered pattern (Armstrong and Armstrong, 2002; Beagan, Chapman, Sylva and Bassett, 2008; Zukewich, 2002). Despite a voluminous literature on the gendered nature of domestic labour, there is no consensus as to what housework is (Coverman, 1983; Davidoff, 1976; DeVault, 1991; Mederer, 1993). Many researchers tend to treat housework as a given or understand it as a commonsense concept. Many empirical studies have focused mainly on some low-skilled, repetitive tasks, ignoring other but less visible tasks, such as meal planning or emotional support. In many cases, carework, especially eldercare, is treated separately and is not included in housework literature (see Eichler and Albanese, 2007 for a critical review of empirical studies on housework).

When it was first introduced in a UNESCO report in the early 1970s, the concept of lifelong learning was defined as 'learning to know, learning to do, learning to live together and learning to be' (Faure et al., 1972, cited in Delors et al., 1998: 37). It was perceived as an approach to promote some of the democratic goals of the United Nations such as equal educational conditions/opportunities and improved quality of life for people all over the world, as it emphasises self-realisation, personal development, and rights. However, in the past two decades, the dominant discourse of lifelong learning has been closely tied with the human capital theory that focuses on formal education for economic benefits (Blackmore, 2006; Schugurensky, 2007). With the globalisation of the world economy, lifelong learning has become a condition or a strategy enthusiastically promoted by governments in the developed countries and by international organisations such as the European Union (EU) and the Organisation for Economic Co-operation and Development (OECD), to enhance the economic competitiveness of their workforce in a globalised economy and for individual citizens to secure their employability in a global marketplace of opportunities (Edwards, 2000).

Feminist scholars have criticised the dominant discourse of lifelong learning for its genderless, classless and raceless agenda (Leathwood and Francis, 2006), and for its market-oriented, economic-driven approach which focuses mainly on formal training for paid work, ignoring the homeplace and unpaid household work as learning sites (Eichler, 2005; Gouthro, 1998, 2005; Liu, 2007a). A recent survey notes that informal learning, though most widespread, remains largely undervalued and unexplored (Livingstone and Scholtz, 2006). This is especially the case with informal learning for/through unpaid household work (Eichler *et al.*, 2010; Liu, 2007b).

Chinese immigrants have been in Canada for over 150 years. However, compared to the relatively long history and large population (1.3 million) of the Chinese in Canada, research on this group of immigrants is fairly recent. Of the limited research on Chinese immigrants, the focus is usually on the discriminatory Canadian immigration policies such as the 'head tax' imposed onto the early Chinese immigrants to Canada (Chan, 1983; Knowles, 1997; Li, 1998, 2003a; Taylor, 1991), and the labour market barriers that recent Chinese immigrants encountered in their new home country (Han, 2007; Li, 2003b; Zhu, 2005; Zong, 2004). Chinese immigrant women were either absent or remained minimal in many of those studies. While a few studies explored the struggles of early Chinese women (Nipp, 1986; Poy, 2003), there is a slowly growing literature on recent Chinese immigrant women to Canada, examining the new challenges that the recent professional women faced with in navigating the Canadian labour market (Man, 2004; Ng, Man, Shan and Liu, 2007; Shan, 2009a and b), and in their housework and childcare responsibilities (Man, 1997; Liu, 2009a and b; Salaff and Greve, 2004; Waters, 2002).

Guided by a new definition of household work, which includes both housework and carework, and which is 'the sum of physical, mental, emotional, and spiritual activities performed for one's own or for someone else's household and that maintains the daily life of those one has responsibility for' (Eichler and Albanese, 2004: 248), this chapter explores informal learning involved in the various dimensions of three aspects of household work: food work, which includes food preparation, cooking and grocery shopping; childcare, which includes childcare and parenting; and eldercare in a transnational context.[2] This chapter concludes by arguing that learning among the new Chinese immigrants is not only lifelong, but also lifewide, and that unpaid household work is an important site to acquire new knowledge and skills necessary to successful adaptation to the changed social, cultural and economic situations and to become a responsible and qualified citizen in their new home country.

Methods

Data used in this chapter were collected as part of a large research network on The Changing Nature of Work and Lifelong Learning funded by the Social Sciences and Humanities Research Council of Canada. This network was composed of a large national survey and 12 case study projects.[3] Quantitative data were drawn from the 2004 Canadian Work in Lifelong Learning Survey (WALL), which was the largest and one of the first surveys in North America to examine both paid and unpaid work, formal and informal learning extensively in relation to job, household work, volunteer work, and general interests. This survey involved 9,063 Canadian adults over age 18, of whom 5,121 were women (56 per cent) and 3,942 were men (44 per cent). Based on their self reports, the majority of the people were white (86 per cent), and 14 per cent, non-white. 80 per cent of the participants were Canadian-born and 20 per cent were immigrants to Canada. There were 183 people in the survey who reported Chinese origin (2 per cent), of whom 115 (1.3 per cent) were immigrants from mainland China, Hong Kong or Taiwan (Livingstone, 2005).

This chapter examines the weekly hours and participation rates of

---

[2] Some of the research findings in this chapter have been presented at related conferences and publications.
[3] For further information about the WALL project and its sub-projects, please see the network website: www.wallnetwork.ca.

informal learning involved in household work and general interests-related activities among the Chinese immigrants in the WALL survey. Qualitative data includes individual interviews, a focus group and a discussion group, which were collected as part of the WALL case study project on Household Work and Lifelong Learning. I conducted 20 individual interviews and facilitated a focus group and a discussion group with Chinese immigrants who had resided in Canada within five years prior to their participation in this research and were living in the Greater Toronto Area at the time of participation in my research. Of the 20 people I interviewed, 14 were women and six men, most of whom were married (90 per cent) and have children between ages of about one and 25 (70 per cent). All the participants in the focus and discussion groups are married women and have one or two children. All the participants had university/college degrees and held professional jobs before immigration, but very few of them were able to find a job equivalent to their education or training.

I interviewed more women than men because housework literature indicates that women still do two-thirds of all household work despite their increased participation in the labour force. I chose new immigrants within five years of residence in Canada because the literature on lifelong learning suggests that major life transitions lead to significant learning. Therefore, for the new immigrants, the first five years of immigration is crucial in terms of learning to adjust to a new life in a physically as well as socioculturally different environment.

In the following sections, I will turn to my research findings from the 2004 Canadian Survey on Work and Lifelong Learning (WALL) and from the individual and group interviews.

Household work and informal learning in the WALL Survey

This section focuses on the WALL survey data on household work-related informal learning among Chinese immigrants. The results are presented in the following two tables. Here, informal learning refers to 'any activity involving the pursuit of understanding, knowledge or skill which occurs without the presence of externally imposed curricular criteria' (Livingstone, 2001). For accuracy purposes, figures presented in this chapter are weighted by age, gender, formal education and region to match population parameters.

Table 1 indicates that, compared to their female counterparts, Chinese immigrant males reported slightly higher involvement in household work-related informal learning (87 per cent for men versus 81 per cent for women), and devoted nearly double the time to learning household work (close to 6 hours for men versus 3.6 hours for women). This finding suggests that Chinese immigrant males may have experienced more changes in their household responsibilities than Chinese women and that they may face a greater need to learn in order to cope with the changes after immigration. In contrast, women were slightly more involved in general interests-related learning (93 per cent for women versus 85 per cent for men), but the average hours women and men devoted to general interests-related learning were more or less similar (3.5 hours for women and 3.7 hours for men).

Table 1: Participation rates (per cent) and average weekly hours on informal learning by sex among the Chinese immigrants.

Sex	Household work [%]	Hours	General Interests [%]	Hours
Male	87	5.9	85	3.7
Female	81	3.6	93	3.5
Total number	105		106	

Sources: WALL Survey, 2004.
Note: 1. Household work in this table includes housework, childcare/ parenting and eldercare.
2. The total number in this table refers to the number of people who reported informal learning on household work and general interests.

Table 2 shows that over half of the Chinese immigrant women (53 per cent) were involved in learning about cooking while only a third of the males (33 per cent) gave such a report. In contrast, over a fifth of the Chinese immigrant males reported learning about childcare (21 per cent) and eldercare (23 per cent), which was surprisingly higher than the rates reported by their female counterparts (17 per cent for childcare and 14 per cent for eldercare respectively), even though the overall involvement of the Chinese immigrants in learning about childcare and eldercare is much lower than the average participation rates of informal learning (averaging 34 per cent for childcare and 25 per cent for eldercare) among other participants in the Survey. The low participation rates of informal learning partly suggests that Chinese immigrant women, who have always been the major caregivers in their families, may have experienced less change than their male counterparts, thus were less likely to need to learn what they have already been doing – childcare and eldercare.

Table 2 Participation rates (per cent) in informal learning on cooking, childcare and eldercare by sex among the Chinese immigrants

Sex	Cooking [%]	Childcare [%]	Eldercare [%]
Male	33	21	23
Female	53	17	14
Total Number	112	112	113

Sources: WALL Survey, 2004.
Note: The total number in this table refers to the number of people who reported informal learning on the specified activities.

Based on the findings from the 2004 WALL Survey, it seems that Chinese immigrant males experienced more changes than their female counterparts in household work, especially in childcare and eldercare. In the next section, I will turn to qualitative data from interviews, the focus group and the discussion group with the Chinese immigrants, and examine how household work has changed for the new Chinese immigrants, and whether there is a gender difference in what they do and what they learn in food work, childcare and eldercare.

Findings from interviews, the focus and discussion groups

Learning to cope with changes in food work

Although all the respondents in this study were well-educated professionals before immigration, most of them were doing non-professional jobs at the time of interviews. Some of them were unemployed and others were reschooling or retraining themselves in a field different from their previous profession at a Canadian university or college. As a result, nearly all the people I interviewed, male and female, married and single, reported a sudden decline of family/personal income and a dramatic increase of their food-related household work upon their arrival in Canada. Nearly all the women talked about spending more time than before on food preparation, especially of staple food such as steamed bread, noodles and dumplings, which they used to buy in China. This is partly because they did not know where to get these foods, but more frequently because they could not afford to buy them. 'I do all the cooking now because that's a good way to save money,' said Juan, a 40-year-old woman who was previously a college professor but now a salesclerk in a supermarket. Yun, a 46-year-old woman who was an engineer before immigration, but now a daycare assistant, gave a similar account, detailing some of the reasons for her increased food work:

> *In China, I used to buy many foodstuffs in our cafeteria, like the steamed bread, it is very cheap: 5 big buns for just 1 yuan.*[4] *So, why bother making them yourself? There is more housework here because I want to save money. I have to make the bread by myself. I have to mix the flour, wait for it to rise, knead the dough ... It is very time-consuming.*[5]

Apart from the need to reduce food expenses, preparing the right kind of ethnic food constitutes another, and perhaps the most important, reason for their new routines. Ying, a woman in her mid-40s, a paediatrician by profession but a lab technician in Canada said, 'Cooking Chinese dishes (food) is not easy here. It is very time-consuming. But I must cook by myself. I must cook Chinese food. Otherwise, I will lose weight.' Mei, a woman close to her 50, a gynaecologist before immigration, also said, 'I hate cooking, the mess, the smell ... But I have to learn to do it. Otherwise, I will starve.' Lisha, a lone mother with a 11-year-old boy, who used to be responsible for all the household work in her family in China, said that she did not see much change in her household responsibilities except that she had to cook every meal and cook more food each time, as she had to pack lunch boxes for herself and her son. Jie, a computer engineer, and a lone mother with a three-year-old son, cited another reason for her increased food work. '*In China, the company provides lunch. But here I have to cook and bring lunch every day. That's a challenge.*' For many of the women, doing more cooking is a strategy that they learned to cope with their changed social and economic situations in the host country: to save money, to stay healthy, to have their own ethnic food, as well as to adapt to the new living and workplace arrangements in Canada.

---

[4] *Yuan* is a unit of Chinese currency. One *yuan* consists of 100 *fen*. Currently 1 *yuan* equals to about 0.15 Canadian dollars.
[5] For clarity purposes, quotes from interviews conducted in English were slightly edited in grammar.

For Juan, Lishan and Jie, the three lone mothers in my interviews, increased household responsibilities were not only associated with their deteriorated economic situations, but also with their living-alone situation in Canada. Unable to find professional jobs in Canada, all three women's husbands returned to China shortly after landing, leaving them alone here to raise the children: taking sole responsibility for all the household work, including childcare, while supporting themselves and their children with low-paid, sometimes physically demanding jobs.

Of the six Chinese males I interviewed, five of them reported that they are more involved in food work in their family than before. Zhong, a man in his early 40s, previously a chemical engineer, but now a physical labourer in a factory said he did more housework, especially more cooking than before because his wife, previously a nurse, got exhausted after a long-day work on an assembly line in an auto factory. Liang, a young man in his early 30s, said that he did 90 percent of all the housework in his household, because his wife was pregnant and working full-time while he had just started going back to school at the time of interview. Guang, the only single young man in my interviews who used to live with his parents before immigration, reported that he became thinner the first year in Canada because he did not know how to cook and had to eat the same kinds of tasteless food for days before he had something else for a change. For Guang, learning the basic cooking skills is essential for his survival after immigration. *'When I first cooked rice, I failed many times, as I didn't know how much water it needs.'* Guang said, *'So I tried, tried and tried. And eventually I succeeded.'* For Liang, much of his food-related learning was revolved on providing healthy food for his pregnant wife and her foetus. *'I read books, and learned something about pregnancy, how to take care about pregnant wife, and how to take care of the kid in the future.'*

For many of the new Chinese immigrants who never or rarely cooked before coming to Canada, they started with staple Chinese food, such as rice, noodles and steamed bread. For instance, Zhong said that, through his involvement in food work, he learned from his wife how to cook noodles – his favourite food. In addition, he also learned meal planning (e.g. what to cook, how to cook, and where to buy), and time management so that he had enough time for cooking, job searching and helping his daughter with her school work. Nearly all the women in the interviews talked about learning new food and new ways of cooking. Many women also incorporate western-style or other ethnic food such as pizza, sandwiches and sushi in their diet. For example, Fang said she learned to eat raw salads because they are good for health. Jie learned to make sandwiches for lunch as they do not take much time to prepare nor do they require heating. Hua talked about relearning how to make steamed bread, which she used to buy in China. Hong, a young mother with a one-year-old son, learned to cook healthy food for her son, but simple, fast food for herself and the other adult members of her family, as she had to juggle her household responsibilities and her busy school studies. However, as a young mother without much English, Hong claimed that the foods she learned to cook are all Chinese.

To accommodate the changes in the Canadian kitchen, such as the lack of a power fan to pump out of the smoke, several women talked about modifying or changing their traditional ways of cooking. Fang, a 58-year-old woman who was a college professor in China, but a housewife in Canada, talked about a number of adaptations she has made in her new cooking practices in Canada:

> *I've changed a lot in my ways of cooking. I eat more salad, as it does not require cooking. I learned to steam fish. I used to enjoy fried fish. Now I eat steamed fish. When I cook green vegetables, I dip them in boiling water first and then dress them with sauce. If I stir-fry them, I will pour a little water first, then oil, before I put the vegetables in the pan, so that it won't produce too much smoke. It's good for health, and also improves the living environment at home.*

Several women talked about learning to use the oven to bake or roast their food, as the oven is not a common kitchen appliance in China. Fang said she experimented with the oven in cooking different kinds of food: making cakes, baking bread, roasting chicken and yams as well as for reheating food. Xinyan, a living-in caregiver at the time of interview, talked about experimenting with different sauces and spices to marinate chicken and beef before roasting them in the oven.

All the participants in my study reported changes in grocery shopping. 'In China, I did grocery shopping every day because it (the food) was more fresh.' Juan said, 'Now I do grocery shopping once a week or every two weeks.' Many women said that grocery shopping in China was more frequent but much easier, as there are grocery stores or markets within walking distance or can be reached easily by bicycle. In Canada, grocery shopping becomes less frequent but more difficult as most of the large supermarkets are located in the suburbs and most of them did not have a car to get there. Thus, for new Chinese immigrants, finding the closest Chinese supermarket and arranging for a car pool for grocery shopping were among the first things they had to learn upon their arrival. To adapt to the changes, they learned to make weekly meal plans ahead of time, where to buy and what to shop for the food items they need for the week. To cut their food expenses, many also learned to read flyers for food on sale and by purchasing food at different supermarkets. Xinyan, a young woman who was working as a living-in caregiver at the time of interview, called her shopping activities 'learning from experience.' She said, 'At first, I didn't know the places well, and just shopped at the store near-by. Now I know every place, and by reading their flyers, I learned to compare the prices, and shop at the place where food is the cheapest, where something is better [of good quality]. This is all learned from experience.'

Zhong and Fang reported prioritising their limited family resources as a strategy to cutting down the monthly expenses in his family. *'Except for the essential stuffs for life, we almost buy nothing else.'* Zhong said. *'We seldom buy bread, or get food from a restaurant. We always cook by ourselves, and make everything from scratch.'* Zhong talked about learning from his neighbours and co-workers where to shop for cheap groceries:

> *Most of the time we buy from the Chinese food market, like Dazhonghua, because everything is fresh, and the prices are reasonable. But we also buy food from Food Basics. We buy rice and flours from Food Basics. And we buy some meat and flour and milk from No Frills. We have to learn to be a smarter buyer, smart shopper.*

In addition, Zhong also revealed how he uses food as a way to communicate with his co-workers:

> *I found that in the workplace, it is easier for the smokers to make new friends than for the non-smokers. I think Chinese food is my 'cigarette'. Although I don't smoke cigarettes, I 'smoke' Chinese food. We exchange food with co-workers from Europe, from Africa. Food is my medium . . . It gives me more knowledge about food, more topics, and more channels to communicate with my co-workers. It helps me to get along with my co-workers.*

For Zhong, food embodies both practical and symbolic meanings. When he cooks for his family, he feels like he is showing care and support for his wife. When he shares his food with his co-workers, he is expressing his friendship to people he worked with.

Learning childcare and parenting the Canadian way

Most of the Chinese parents with young children in the interviews reported a dramatic increase in childcare-related household work, largely due to a sudden decline in family income and lack of social support for childcare that they used to enjoy in their home country. Far away from their extended families who used to lend a hand in childcare, many of these parents find it a huge challenge balancing their paid work and unpaid childcare responsibilities. Ping, mother of a 9-year-old son, who used to be a university professor and administrator before immigration, recalled her childcare experiences when she first arrived in Canada.

> *The first half-year was the most difficult. Just coming from China, you know, you suddenly found – too much housework! ... At first, I wasn't used to it at all that my son was with me all the time, wherever I went, because here children under 12 are not allowed to be left home alone. Besides, he went to kindergarten for only two hours, only from 9: 30 to 11: 30 in the morning, then I had to pick him up. So every day, the child was around, and I had to cook three meals a day ... I felt so tired spending so much time cooking, doing grocery shopping, taking care of the child.*

Increased childcare responsibility is also reported by male parents with young children. Ming, who claimed having never done any housework before immigration, reported a sudden increase of workload in childcare when his son was born three years ago:

When we had the baby, I was still studying at [name] University. So, every day after studying for more than 12 hours, I still had to spare time to take care of my son and my wife because (in Chinese) she was in birth confinement.[6] I did everything, cooking, changing the baby's diapers ... You know, in China when you have a baby, you can always find someone, like parents, relatives, to come over to help, right? You need not worry

---

[6] According to traditional Chinese medical beliefs, it is not good for a woman's health if she does physical labour right after she gives birth. So a 30-day confinement is observed in order to avoid heavy physical labour, cold food and cold water.

about anything. You can also hire people to take care of your baby. But here we cannot. Our finances do not allow us to have more people to come over to help [us] . . .

According to Ming, attending to his baby son's needs such as preparing baby food, washing the diapers, and sometimes interpreting the baby's needs from his crying are both physically demanding and emotionally challenging.

To cope with the increased workload in childcare, the new Chinese immigrants used different strategies to accommodate their increased childcare responsibilities and their work/school schedules. For example, Hong, a young mother of a one-year-old son, mobilised her social network transnationally for childcare. In order to resume her studies after giving birth, Hong brought her mother-in-law from China to help look after her baby son. Tao, a woman in the focus group, and a doctor of Traditional Chinese Medicine, sent her five-year-old daughter back to China to be taken care of by the grandparents, shortly before she started a training programme in nursing at a community college.

However, not all parents with young children can afford transnational grand-parenting. Lilian, a woman in the focus group, said that she found a solution to after-school childcare for her pre-teen son by co-operating with her neighbours in the same apartment building:

> *My son came home at 3: 30 in the afternoon, but my husband and I, we finish our work or study at five or six o'clock, so nobody will take care of my son for us. So, we discussed this problem with our neighbours. And now, my husband or I pick up my son, and my neighbour's son, every other day. And my neighbours, they pick up my son and their son every other day. So, we share the work. My husband and I also share the duty . . .*

When asked about what they have learned in parenting, almost all the Chinese parents talking about various efforts and strategies they learned in adjusting to the Canadian ways of parenting. Ping, mother of a 10-year-old son, said that she learned new rules about childcare in Canada. *'I learned from my LINC[7] class, from daycare, from my kid's school teacher, that it is against the law to leave children under 12 alone at home'* Ping said,

---

[7] The Language Instruction for Newcomers to Canada (LINC) is a government-funded Programme that provides free basic French and English language training to adult permanent residents in Canada.

'If my son makes a mistake or does something wrong, I can only talk to him about it. I cannot scold or spank him.' Juan, a lone mother of a 15-year-old daughter, talked about learning to be less authoritarian when helping her daughter with her school work:

> Before, in China, I always ordered my daughter to do this, to do that. Now I can no longer do it. I have to talk with her, discuss with her. Even with her homework, if she doesn't like me to read it, I cannot do so. I have to ask her for permission.

On the one hand, Juan said she learned to compromise when in conflicts with her daughter and less interfering as to who she should go out with. On the other hand, Juan also learned to reject her husband's constant request through his daily long-distant 'instructions' from China, pushing her to urge their daughter to focus more on her study, to go to bed earlier, and to do less internet chatting with friends, etc.

Like many newcomer families who immigrated to Canada for the sake of their children (Anisef, Kilbride, Ochocka and Janzen, 2001: 27), many Chinese immigrants in my study cited children's future education as one of the main reasons for immigration to Canada, usually at the expense of their own career development. Zhong, father of a 15-year-old daughter, said he paid a lot of attention to his daughter's education. *'My daughter's future means everything to us. That's our main purpose of immigrating to Canada,'* said Zhong. To help his daughter excel at school, Zhong made it part of his daily routine checking with her on her school life and helped her with her school work. By reading books, by talking with her schoolteachers and by talking with other students' parents, Zhong learned how the Canadian school system works, and how to help his daughter choose courses and to give her proper advice regarding her study. Meanwhile, Zhong said that his learning benefited not only his daughter but himself as well, as it helped him understand the Canadian culture, improved his relationship with his daughter, and gave him the opportunity to get to know her friends and her teachers.

Zhong's engagement in his daughter's school work is not unique, as Chinese immigrant parents' great involvement in their children's education has been well documented in literature (Chao, 1994; Chen, Dong and Zhou, 1997; Liu *et al.*, 2005). Like Zhong, Yong, a father with a 12-year-old son, was also actively involved in his son's education after immigration. However, Yong soon noticed that his efforts were no longer appreciated nor his advice well followed by his son. Yong compared the changes and adjustment he made in his parenting practices:

> *In China, you ask the kids to follow you. But here you need to understand them in order to let them follow you . . . That's a big adjustment, trying to understand the children. In the Chinese way, you don't care if they understand or not. If you think it is good for them, you just do it and believe they will understand you in time, in the future. But here you have to understand them, and then they will try to understand you.*

Instead of focusing on imparting academic knowledge to his son, Yong said he now pays more attention to developing his son's learning skills and to training him to be an independent learner. When I asked him how he learned to understand and communicate with his son, Yong brushed away the idea of learning:

> *I wouldn't say it's learning, it's just changing. This community, this society changed you, not that you want to learn, but naturally they changed you. You have no way to avoid this change because you are living here.*

But after some thoughts, Yong added, 'I learned from my work, from friends, neighbours, from my son himself, and from the school. I attended almost every school meeting, like orientations, parent sessions.' Yong continued. 'I know, this is a new place, you need to understand how the school works. So I tried to get all the information. You need to learn. Yeah, I think that's what you mean by learning.'

Both Zhong and Yong's stories suggest that successful adaptation in parenting practices after immigration involves enormous efforts on the parents' side in understanding their children's needs, and in learning adequate knowledge of the Canadian school system as well as the Canadian cultural values on child education.

Despite their efforts in learning new ways of parenting, many more Chinese immigrant parents express their ambivalence, anxiety and frustration for not knowing the 'right' way of disciplining their children or handling conflicts with their children in a 'proper' manner in the new social context. *'Children behave differently here,'* said Wei, a woman in the focus group and mother of a 10 year-old son. *'In China, children must obey their parents. Here, he thinks we are equal and refuses to listen.'* For Tao, another woman in the focus group, getting her daughter of

Grade 2 to watch less TV and do her homework on time was a big headache, as children get out of school very early in the afternoon and have a lot of free time at home after school. Great concern for their children's future education was also reported by Liang, a would-be-father, and by Ming, father of a three-year-old son. In addition to his searching for new business opportunities in order to save enough money to buy RESP[8] for his son, Ming also revealed how the birth of his son changed his attitudes towards life and his responsibility as a father: *'Before I had the baby, I did everything for fun. But now, I need to think about the future, I need to care about the family.'* Meanwhile, Ming felt ambivalent about how to discipline children properly in the Canadian context. *'What am I supposed to do if he misbehaves, without using physical disciplining?'* asked Ming. *'What if he smokes and even uses drug when he reaches his teens? How can I educate him? What if you cannot persuade him or make him listen?'* The worries Ming expressed in his questions were not unfounded. During the past few years I was in Canada, I have learned from the local media several cases in which the Chinese parents were charged with child abuse due to lack of knowledge about Canadian ways of parenting (see Mu Ran, 2006).

Many Chinese women indicated that lack of proficiency in English poses a big challenge to their role as parents, a big barrier for them to help their children with their studies, to access information on public childcare services and government support for low-income parents. For example, Hong, mother of a one-year-old son, said that she relies on the Chinese language media, such as books, magazines, and the internet, for information on childrearing. For a few women, inadequate English was detrimental to their self-esteem and to their image as a 'qualified parent.' *'My son doesn't want me to show up in his school because he thinks I can't speak good English, and can't communicate with his teachers.'* Lisha, mother with an 11-year-old son, said sadly. Similarly, Yun, a senior engineer prior to immigration but now a daycare assistant, felt extremely upset for losing the respect from her son because of her poor English:

> *In China, whenever I helped my son solve a difficult math problem, he would say, 'Mom, you are wonderful.' Now he would say, 'Mom, your English is not*

---

[8] Registered Education Savings Plans (RESP) is a special savings plan for education subsidized by the government in Canada.

> *good, you are not good at this, you are not good at that.'* In his eyes, I am not able to do anything. There is nothing good about me now (bitter laugh).

Thus, for those women, learning English is not merely to improve their job opportunities, but also to boost their self-esteem or to provide the support that their children need in their school work and in integrating into the Canadian culture. *'That's why I go back to school,'* said Ping, who was taking courses at a community College. *'It is not only to learn a new skill for paid work. It is also to improve my English language skills so that I can continue to care for my son's school work as he grows.'*

Learning new ways of eldercare in a transnational context

Chinese culture emphasises filial piety (*xiao*) that requires young children to obey their parents and adult children to support their elderly parents, both physically and financially (Zhan, 2004). Traditionally, eldercare, an essential part of filial piety, was primarily carried out by women, daughters-in-law in particular, with sons as the ultimate financial providers (Zhan and Montgomery, 2003). However, due to Canadian immigration policies, all the Chinese respondents in my interviews came to Canada only with their nuclear families, leaving their elderly parents in their home country. As a result, many new immigrants find that eldercare takes on a new form, as much of the physical tasks of eldercare have diminished. Instead, transnational emotional care of the elderly, usually conducted in a virtual manner – through long-distance phone calls or emails – were reported by nearly all the respondents in the interviews and the focus group. Mei's experience in transnational eldercare well illustrates this point. During the two or three years prior to the interview, Mei had travelled back and forth several times between Canada and China, first to take care of her seriously ill mother, and later her sick father with lung cancer. In addition, she also keeps an eye on her father's condition through regular telephone calls back home:

> *I often call my brother and ask him about my father's condition. I made arrangements for his surgeries, and checked on the medicines they used on him and the treatment they gave him. I flew back immediately whenever I learned that his condition was getting worse. That's why I kept going back to China in the past few years, at least once a year.*

For Mei, transnational elder care involved physical, mental, and emotional efforts. According to Mei, part of her weekly routine phone calls to China also includes instructions to the live-in caregivers looking after her sick father and her widowed mother-in-law about the housework tasks they need to complete during that week.

Indeed, for many of the new immigrants, calling their aged parents regularly, usually once a week, to check on their living and health conditions is an important part of their emotion work for their elderly, a way to fulfil their filial piety in a transnational context. Ying, a woman in her mid-40s and a medical doctor before immigration, talked about calling her mother every week as she had heart disease. *'In China, I took (physical) care of my mother. But here I can't. But I am worried about her. My niece is looking after my mother now. If my mother has a problem, I will call her right away.'* Ming, a man in his late 30s described how he provided emotional support for his aged father:

My father is old. He is living with my sister in Shanghai. He is old and has got some mental illness. Every time I call, I will talk to him. That makes him feel very happy. I always try to encourage him to do exercise to keep healthy. [I'd say] 'If you cannot keep healthy, you cannot come to visit me in Canada.' That's the way I encourage him to keep doing exercise and to overcome his illness.

As eldercare becomes more emotional than physical, what many new immigrants learned is more related to *how* they provided emotional support rather than on *what* they actually did for their parents. For example, many respondents talked about learning to find better ways to call their parents, such as where to get cheaper phone cards, which cards have better voice quality, and which software is easier to use to make phone calls through the internet as well as how to combine different means of communication in order to cut down the costs. Many respondents said they called their parents regularly because it is much cheaper to do so from Canada than from China. Guang, a young computer engineer, living alone and unemployed here in Canada, talked about sending text messages to his parents' cell phone through the internet everyday in order to keep his parents free from worrying about him.

Gender, identities, and household work-related learning

Consistent with the voluminous body of literature on household work, the research revealed that despite their universal employment in their home country and dramatic changes in paid work after immigration, the Chinese women continued to shoulder the bulk of household responsibilities in food work, childcare and eldercare, and the tasks they do were more likely to be on-going, time-consuming and less flexible (such as preparing staple food, attending to their children's daily needs). While Chinese males also talked about increased workload in cooking and childcare, their involvement in such work is selective, and exceptional, usually done under special circumstances, for example, when their wives were out at work, became pregnant or gave birth.

This research reveals that for some of the women, immigration led to an intensified gender division of household work, an exacerbation of women's dependence and subordination to men and a reversion of traditional gender roles as wives and mothers, due to the loss of professional jobs after immigration. Furthermore, whenever there is a conflict between paid and unpaid work, women tend to sacrifice their career for their family responsibilities (as in the case of Mei and Fang), whereas men were more likely to sacrifice their family life for their career (as in the case of the three lone mothers in the interviews).

Inconsistent with the WALL Survey, in which Chinese immigrant males showed slightly higher involvement in learning childcare and eldercare, Chinese immigrant women in the interviews, however, showed an equally high if not higher involvement in both childcare and eldercare. Although both women and men reported increase in food work and childcare, women were more involved in learning the more time-consuming, less visible tasks of food preparation, and feeding the children, while men were more involved in learning to cook their favourite food, and in learning new ways to help their children with their school work. However, there is almost no gender differences in what women and men learn in terms of eldercare, given the absence of their elders in their new home country.

Conclusion

By examining learning involved in a variety of household activities, from the routine tasks of cooking and childcare, to the less visible tasks of meal planning, budgeting and financial management, to organisational and management skills, this chapter has demonstrated that household work and the related learning is multi-dimensional: physical, mental, and emotional. By exploring the new beliefs and practices the Chinese immigrants learned in food work, in childcare and eldercare, this chapter provides ample evidence that learning is both lifelong and lifewide – in the private home, and through unpaid tasks and activities. This chapter also demonstrated that unlike job-oriented learning, household work-related learning is informal, self-directed, and experiential – learning by doing. But some of the learning, be it intentional or unintentional, voluntary or involuntary, is transformative in that it changed the new immigrants' views of family, about paid and unpaid work, about who they are and what the meaning of life is.

This chapter argues that household work allocation is embedded in complex social relations and that doing household work is more than simple physical labour. It highlights the fact that gender ideologies and gender identities are fluid and socially constructed, and that gender roles are learned, performed and reinforced.

In conclusion, reconceptualising household work expands the dimensions of research on household work, and helps make visible the value and worth of unpaid work among the professional Chinese immigrant women, who undervalued unpaid work due to an over-emphasis of paid work in their home country. By exploring the content and the ways of lifelong learning involved in unpaid household work, this chapter argues that household work is an important site where new immigrants learn to sustain their own community, and to promote social justice, both locally and globally Similarly, by expanding the scope of lifelong learning to include the home and unpaid household activities the chapter helps raise the awareness among the new immigrants the importance of informal learning to successful settlement and adaptability to the new culture and society. Finally, by exploring unpaid work and the knowledge and skills involved it, it aims to empower immigrant women in sustaining their family and community in a transnational context finding meaningful ways to become citizens in their new homeland.

References

Anisef, P., Kilbride, K. M., Ochocka, J., and Janzen, R. (2001) *Study on parenting issues of newcomer families in Ontario*. Toronto: Joint Centre of Excellence for Research on Immigration and Settlement and Centre for Research and Education in Human Services.

Armstrong, P., and Armstrong, H. (2002) 'Thinking it through: women, work and caring in the new millennium', *Canadian Woman Studies*, 21/22: 4, 44–50.

Baxter, J. (2005) 'To marry or not to marry: marital status and the household division of labor', *Journal of Family Issues*, 26: 3), 300–21.

Beagan, B., Chapman, G., Sylva, A. D., and Bassett, B. (2008) '"It's just easier for me to do it": rationalizing the family division of foodwork', *Sociology [U.K.]*, *42* (4), 653–71.

Beaujot, R., Haddad, T., and McFarlane, S. (2000) 'Time constraints and relative resources as determinants of the sexual division of domestic work', *Canadian Journal of Sociology*, 25: 1, 61–82.

Blackmore, J. (2006) 'Unprotected participation in lifelong learning and the politics of hope', in C. Leathwood and B. Francis (eds), *Gender and lifelong Learning: Critical feminist engagements*, 9–26. London: Routledge.

Chan, A. (1983) *Gold mountain: the Chinese in the New World*. Vancouver: New Star Books.

Chao, R. K. (1994) 'Beyond parenting control and authoritarian parenting style: Understanding Chinese parenting through the cultural notion of training', *Child Development*, 65, 1111–19.

Chen, X., Dong, Q. and Zhou, H. (1997) 'Authoritative and authoritarian parenting practices and social and school performance in Chinese children', *International Journal of Behavioral Development*, 21: 4, 855–74.

Citizenship and Immigration Canada (2009) *Facts and Figures 2008 Immigration Overview: Permanent and Temporary Residents*. http://www.cic.gc.ca/english/pdf/research-stats/facts2008.pdf .

Coltrane, S. and Ishii-Kuntz, M. (1992) 'Men's housework: a life course perspective', *Journal of Marriage and the Family*, 54: 1, 43–57.

Coverman, S. (1983) 'Gender, domestic labor time, and wage inequality', *American Sociological Review*, 48, 623–37.

Davidoff, L. (1976) 'The rationalization of housework', in D. L. Barker and S. Allen (eds), *Dependence and exploitation in work and marriage*, 121–51. London: Croom Helm.

Delors, J. et al. (1998) *Learning: the treasure within: Report to UNESCO of the International Commission on education for the twenty-first century*.

Demo, D. H. and Acock, A. C. (1993) 'Family diversity and the division of domestic labour: how much have things really changed?' *Family Relations*, 42, 323–31.

DeVault, M. L. (1991) *Feeding the family: the social organisation of caring as gendered work*. Chicago: University of Chicago Press.

Edwards, R. (2000) 'Lifelong learning, lifelong learning, lifelong learning:

a recurrent education?' in J. Field and M. Leicester (eds), *Lifelong Learning Across the Lifespan*, 3–11. London: Routledge Falmer.

Eichler, M. (2005) 'The other half (or more) of the story: unpaid household and care work and lifelong learning', in N. Bascia, A. Cumming, A. Batnow, K. Leithwood and D. Livingston (eds), *International Handbook of Educational Policy*, 1–17. Manchester: Page Express.

Eichler, M., and Albanese, P. (2007) 'What is household work? A critique of assumptions underlying empirical studies of housework and an alternative approach', *Canadian Journal of Sociology*, 32: 2, 227–58.

Eichler, M., Albanese, P., Ferguson, S., Hyndman, N., Liu, L. W. and Matthews, A. (2010) *More than it seems: learning through household work*. Toronto Women's Press.

Faure, E., Herrara, F., Kaddoura, A.-R., Lopes, H., Petrovsky, A., Rahnema, M. et al. (1972) *Learning To Be*. Paris: Harrap/UNESCO.

Gouthro, P. (1998) 'Lifelong learning and the homeplace', unpublished PhD Dissertation, Dalhousie University, Halifax, Nova Scotia.

Gouthro, P. (2005) 'A critical feminist analysis of the homeplace as learning site: expanding the discourse of lifelong learning to consider adult women learners', *International Journal of Lifelong Education*, 24: 1, 5–19.

Han, H. (2007) 'Language, religion and immigrant settlement: An ethnography', unpublished PhD dissertation, University of Toronto, Toronto.

Knowles, V. (1997) *Strangers at our gates: Canadian immigration and immigration policy, 1540–1997*. Toronto: Dundurn Press.

Leathwood, C. and Francis, B. (eds) (2006) *Gender and lifelong learning: critical feminist engagements*. New York: Routledge.

Li, P. S. (1998) *The Chinese in Canada* (2nd edn). Toronto: Oxford University Press.

Li, P. S. (2003a) 'Chinese diaspora in occidental societies: Canada and Europe', in D. Hoerder, C. Harzig and A. Shubert (eds), *The historical practice of diversity: transcultural interactions from the early modern Mediterranean to the postcolonial world*, 134–51. New York: Berghahn Books.

Li, P. S. (2003b) 'Understanding economic performance of immigrants', *Canadian Issues*, 25–26.

Liu, L. (2007a) 'New home, new learning: Chinese immigrants and unpaid housework and carework', in D. W. Livingstone, K. Mirchandani and P. S. Sawchuk (eds), *The future of lifelong learning and work:*

critical perspectives, 190–97. Rotterdam: Sense Publishers.

Liu, L. (2007b) 'Unveiling the invisible learning from unpaid household work: Chinese immigrants' perspective', *The Canadian Journal for the Study of Adult Education*, 20: 2, 25–40.

Liu, L. (2009a) 'Double transitions, double learning: Chinese immigrants and childrearing', Paper presented at the 28th annual conference of the Canadian Association for the Study of Adult Education (CASAE), in association with the Congress of the Social Sciences and Humanities, Ottawa, Canada, May 25–27.

Liu, L. (2009b) 'Transnational elder care and kin maintenance: Chinese immigrants and informal learning on emotion work', Paper presented at the World Congress of Anthropological and Ethnological Sciences (IUAES), July 27–31.

Liu, M., Chen, X., Rubin, K. H., Zheng, S., Cui, L., Li, D. et al. (2005) 'Autonomy- vs. connectedness-oriented parenting behaviours in Chinese and Canadian mothers', *International Journal of Behavioral Development*, 29: 6, 489–95.

Livingstone, D. (2001) 'Adults' informal learning: definitions, findings, gaps and future research', *NALL Working Paper #21-2001*. Also available at: http://www.oise.utoronto.ca/depts/sese/csew/nall/res/21adultsifnormallearning.htm .

Livingstone, D.W. (2005) *WALL Code Book: National Survey of Work and Lifelong Learning* Toronto: Centre for the Study of Education and Work, Ontario Institute for Studies in Education, University of Toronto.

Livingstone, D.W. and Scholtz, A. (2006) *Work and Lifelong Learning in Canada: Basic Findings of the 2004 WALL Survey*. Toronto: Ontario Institute for Studies in Education. http://www.wallnetwork.ca .

Man, G. (1997) 'Women's work is never done: social organisation of work and the experience of women in middle-class Hong Kong Chinese immigrant families in Canada', *Advances in Gender Research*, 2, 183–226.

Man, G. (2004) 'Gender, work and migration: deskilling Chinese immig-rant women in Canada', *Women's Studies International Forum*, 27, 135–48.

Marshall, K. (1993/1995) 'Dual earners: who's responsible for house-work?' *Canadian Social Trends, Cat 11-008E*(Spring/Winter), 11–14.

Mederer, H. J. (1993) 'Division of labor in two-earner homes: Task accomplishment versus household management as critical variables in perceptions about family work', *Journal of Marriage and the Family*, 55: 1, 133–45.

Mu Ran (2006,) 'Who can take your child away?' (in Chinese). November 14. http://info.51.ca/news/canada/2006/11/14/23329.shtml,

Ng, R. and Ramirez, J. (1981) *Immigrant housewives in Canada*. Toronto: Immigrant Women's Centre.

Ng, R., Man, G., Shan, H. and Liu, W. (2007) Learning to be good citizens: informal learning and the labour market experiences of professional Chinese immigrant women. Toronto: CERIS – The Ontario Metropolis Centre.

Nipp, D. (1986) '"But women did come": Working Chinese women in the interwar years', in J. Burnet (ed.), *Looking into my sisters' eyes: An exploration in women's history*, 179–94. Toronto: The Multicultural History Society of Ontario.

Orbuch, T. L. and Eyster, S. L. (1997) ,Division of household labor among black couples and white couples', *Social Forces*, 76, 301–32.

Pessar, P. R. (1995) 'On the homefront and in the workplace: integrating immigrant women into feminist discourse', *Anthropological Quarterly*, 68: 1, 37–47.

Poy, V. (2003) 'Calling Canada home: Canadian law and immigrant Chinese women from south China and Hong Kong, 1860—1990', unpublished PhD thesis, University of Toronto, Toronto.

Salaff, J. W., Greve, A., and Chen, X. (2004) 'Motherhood shifts when Chinese families relocate: Chinese women's education work in Canada', paper presented at the Workshop on the Lives of Asian Mothers: Negotiating Work Challenges and Family Commitments.

Schugurensky, D. (2007) 'The learning society in Canada and the US', in M. Kuhn (ed.), *New Society Models for a New Millennium. The learning society in Europe and beyond*, 295–334. New York: Peter Lang.

Shan, H. (2009) 'Practices on the periphery: highly educated Chinese immigrant women negotiating occupational settlement in Canada', *Canadian Journal for the Studies of Adult Education*, 21: 2, 1–17

Shan, H. (2009) 'Shaping the re-training and re-education experiences of immigrant women: The credential and certificate regime in Canada', *International Journal of Lifelong Education*, 28: 3, 353–69.

South, S. J. and Spitze, G. (1994) 'Housework in marital and nonmarital households', *American Sociological Review*, 59: 3, 327–47.

Statistics Canada. (2007) Immigration in Canada: A Portrait of the Foreign-born Population, 2006 Census: Portraits of major metropolitan centres: Toronto: Canada's major immigrant gateway. Catalogue no. 97-557-XIE200600. http://www12.statcan.ca/census-recensement/2006/as-sa/97-557/pdf/97-557-XIE2006001.pdf .

Statistics Canada. (2008) Ethnic Origin (247), Single and Multiple Ethnic Origin Responses (3) and Sex (3) for the Population of Canada, Provinces, Territories, Census Metropolitan Areas and Census Agglomerations, 2006 Census – 20 per cent Sample Data (table). 2006 Census of Population. Statistics Canada catalogue no. 97-562-XCB2006006. Ottawa. http://www12.statcan.ca/english/census06/data/topics/Print.cfm?PID=92333&GID=837928&D1=0&D2=0&D3=0&D4=0&D5=0&D6=0 .

Taylor, K. W. (1991) 'Racism in Canadian immigration policy', *Canadian Ethnic Studies, XXIII*: 1, 1–20.

Waters, J. L. (2002) 'Flexible families? 'Astronaut' households and the experiences of lone mothers in Vancouver, British Columbia', *Social and Cultural Geography*, 3: 2, 117–34.

Zhan, H. J. (2004) 'Socialization or social structure: investigating predictors of attitudes toward filial responsibility among Chinese urban youth from one- and multiple-child families', *International Journal of Aging and Human Development*, 59: 2, 105–24.

Zhan, H. J. and Montgomery, R. J. V. (2003) 'Gender and elder care in China: the influence of filial piety and structural constraints', *Gender Society*, 17, 209–29.

Zhu, H. (2005) 'Capital transformation and immigrant integration: Chinese independent immigrants' language and social practices in Canada', unpublished Ph.D. dissertation, University of Toronto, Canada.

Zong, L. (2004) 'International transference of human capital and occupational attainment of recent Chinese professional immigrants in Canada', *PCERII Working Paper Series, Working Paper No. WP03-04*.

Zukewich, N. (2002) 'Using time use data to measure and value unpaid caregiving work', Unpublished Master of Arts in Canadian Studies, Carleton University.

Zuo, J., and Bian, Y. (2001) 'Gender resources, division of housework and perceived fairness: A case in urban China', *Journal of Marriage and the Family*, 63, 1122–33.

Learning and working: Conclusion

SUE JACKSON

The three chapters in this section demonstrate a critique of ways in which social justice for adult learners is debated in lifelong learning policies, arguing that as currently conceptualised, lifelong learning is more likely to widen social inequalities. They show how lifelong learning has become ever more firmly linked to economic participation through the employment market and the development of skills and training (Chapters Five and Six), further embedding differences of gender, class and race (Chapters Five and Seven) and argue for new definitions of work and lifelong learning which include learning and working in the home (Chapter Seven).

All three chapters have explored meanings of social inclusion and exclusion, a global language of cuts and restraints, and of the 'deserving' and 'undeserving' poor, considering what this means for the poorest in society. They have shown how these global discourses have led to intensified divisions of labour, including gendered divisions, leading to an exacerbation of dependence and – especially for migrants (Chapter Seven) – loss of professional work.

The authors have examined working and learning through policy and through practice (Chapters Five and Six), and through engaging with intersectionalities of disadvantage (Chapters Five and Seven). Intersectionalities of gender, class, 'race' and more will be central themes in the third and final section of this book, which turns to questions of learner identities and social justice.

PART THREE

IDENTITIES

Identities: Introduction

SUE JACKSON

Although the theme of the final section of the book, identities, has been a thread through Sections one and two, it is in Section three that the chapters engage explicitly with explorations of lifelong learning, social justice and identities. As the chapter authors demonstrate, and key to the development of, and engagement with, lifelong learning, identities are neither fixed nor stable, but are multiple, fragmented and move through and beyond fixed positions. They are located in the intersections of gender, social class, 'race' and more (Brah and Phoenix, 2004), as well as the intersections of mental wellbeing and mental illness (Chapter Eleven), and of constructions of learner and non-learner (Chapter Ten). As Olivia Sagan (Chapter Eleven) shows, identity is also performance. Vicki Carpenter (Chapter Nine) demonstrates that although the performance of identity and the transformations this can bring may lead to disequilibrium, it is nevertheless an important aspect of the learning process. It can result in new ways of seeing, alternate world views, and new forms solidarities, allowing learners (and teachers) to share both identities and (local and global) worlds.

Several of the authors are interested in identities of spaces and places developed through the local and the global, and through the resulting imagined communities (Anderson, 2004). In Chapter Eight, Nataly Tcherepashenets and Lisa Snyder argue that renewal of identity is closely connected with the changing notion of place, with globalisation challenging the stability that can be associated both with geographical place and with apparently fixed identities. They demonstrate how this is particularly important to the identities that immigrants bring with them to new homelands (Jackson, 2010a) and explore the ways in which such identities can be shared through inter-cultural communication in the classroom (Holmes, 2010). As Helen Aberton (Chapter Ten) demonstrates, such inter-cultural communication also works within and across socio-material practices and constructions of learning in which people in the 'knowledge society' are defined either as learners or non-learners, as educable subjects or as 'other'.

Stuart Hall (2000) conceptualises identity as a continual process of becoming through identifications – through discursive spaces including those of colonialism and postcolonialism and empire:

> *Precisely because identities are constructed within, not outside, discourse, we need to understand them as produced in specific historical and institutional sites within specific discursive formations and practices, by specific enunciative strategies. Moreover, they emerge within the play of specific modulations of power, and thus are more the product of the marking of difference and exclusion . . . Above all . . . identities are constructed through, not outside, difference* (Hall, 2000: 17).

The authors in this section are interested in such constructions, and in the connections and disconnections between 'I' and the 'other'. For example, in Chapter Eleven Olivia Sagan powerfully demonstrates the re/negotiations of spaces of the self between 'I' and 'other', and Nataly Tcherepashenets and Lisa Snyder (Chapter Eight) argue that globalisation brings about challenges to the relationship between 'I' and the 'other'. The authors of these chapters are interested in the transformations to identities that come about through those relationships, and the critical learning that comes about in localised/globalised societies (Jackson, 2010b). In Chapter Ten, Helen Aberton demonstrates the role of everyday informal learning through local/global communities that contributes to challenging dominant constructions of learning that places some learner identities as lacking. In Chapter Eight, Nataly Tcherepashenets and Lisa Snyder clearly demonstrate the changing perceptions that develop through accessing and sharing knowledge, bringing critical understandings of diverse (and often marginalised) histories and cultures.

Chapter Eight argues that globalisation brings challenges which lead to transformations of identities, with students and teachers equally engaged in deepening their knowledge both about themselves and the (globalised) social world in which they live. Drawing on empirical studies, Nataly Tcherepashenets and Lisa Snyder show how for students 'transformation' can come about through formal learning processes whilst for teachers change can be facilitated through engaging with their students. Their respondents – both students and teachers – have come to see how individual identities, including their own, are formed at least partially by collective dialogues. Tcherepashenets and Snyder show how students and teachers confronted and, on several occasions, overcame limitations of their previously developed views and practices. They illustrate the developing learners' ability to question and critique existent conceptions, fostering learners' critical thinking on social justice. This enhances understanding of how the relationship between social justice, diversity, democracy and globalisation are at the core of lifelong learning. The authors conclude that in an era of globalisation, the fulfilment of social justice more than ever depends on fostering cosmopolitan citizenship and enhancing solidarity, developing an ability to interconnect with people of different backgrounds, and making it possible for them to participate in intercultural dialogue on equal terms.

Chapter Nine is written from the perspective of a teacher. Vicki Carpenter states clearly from the outset that as the writer of the chapter, she is placed firmly within the text, with the chapter exploring her own pedagogic practices, and how she has strived to transform them. She shows how these practices exist alongside the changes brought about by neoliberal policies which have impacted on the way teaching is carried out, including in a climate that demands more, larger and more crowded classrooms and a myriad of pressures on teacher time, including competition, administration and publication. Carpenter demonstrates how, as a lecturer with a commitment to social justice, she grapples with the impact of structural changes, and what they mean for her, her values and her work, as well as for her learners. Her chapter draws on two pedagogical contexts: a postgraduate class of students who are also teachers; and a critical action research project. In exploring these pedagogical contexts, Carpenter shows how her identity, and the values of social justice she holds close in claiming her identity, influence her practices. There are risks, she argues, in teaching differently but there are also exciting opportunities involved in changing accustomed practices, both for students and teachers.

In Chapter Ten Helen Aberton moves from the formal classrooms of universities to consider women's informal learning. Her chapter challenges constructed learner identities such as reluctant or resistant learners, showing that these constructs are limited and limiting, and arguing for a need to look at 'learning' differently. Instead, there needs to be greater recognition of the many ways in which people participate in everyday living and learning, trying new ventures and experiences. It is these practices, argues Aberton, through which many lifelong learners identify: practices through which they develop and maintain a sense of self and place. Lifelong learners, who may not necessarily self-identify *as* learners, need affirmation, confirmation and validation of their pursuit of interests and practices located in their social worlds. In this chapter, Aberton suggests an alternative framing to the conventional ways in which she argues that informal learning and identity formation is most often researched and understood. In doing so, she draws on her empirical research of women's informal learning in voluntary community organisations in an Australian rural town. This approach, she argues, has provided a window on emergent learning in practices often too mundane to be noticed, allowing the possibility that adult identity formation and learning can and does effectively take place without formal pedagogical interventions.

The final chapter of the section, and therefore also of the book, moves into two under-researched and little recognised arenas: mental illness and love, It does so through drawing on an empirical longitudinal study of a group of chronically mentally ill learners of basic literacy, which it locates in a broader social critique. Olivia Sagan's chapter draws on data gathered from two heterosexual partners with literacy levels below the national average who both wished to learn to write more creatively about their lives. She powerfully demonstrates how, in wanting to learn to write 'I love you', the female partner seemed to fall into gaps in thinking about love, learning, gender and sanity. As Sagan argues, within neoliberal educational policies of upskilling, dispassionate and unemotional encounters of education leave little or no toleration either for 'love' or for expressions of a lifelong love of learning. By splitting emotion from policy, the aims of education for social equity and of welfare for wellbeing are being severely undermined. Sagan concludes that welfare and education provision fall far short, with narratives being constructed through a language of responsibility rather than choice, leading to a consequential loss of the autobiographical 'I' for those who lack privilege. Sagan ends her chapter with a warning that 'such an 'I', prized achievement that it has become, and much sought-after accomplishment of a postmodern fragmented self, is a privilege; one not yet on the radar of those for whom making it through to tomorrow is achievement enough'.

References

Anderson, B. (2006) *Imagined Communities*. London: Verso.

Brah, A. and Phoenix, A. (2004) 'Ain't I a woman? Revisiting Intersectionality', *Journal of International Women's Studies* 5: 3, 75–86.

Hall, S. (2000), 'Who needs "identity"?' in du Gay, P., Evans, J. and Redman P. (eds), *Identity: a reader*. London: Sage.

Holmes, P. (2010) 'Negotiating differences in learning and intercultural communication: ethnic Chinese students in a New Zealand University', *Business Communication Quarterly*, 67: 3, 294–307.

Jackson, S. (2010a) 'Learning through social spaces: migrant women and lifelong learning in post-colonial London', *International Journal of Lifelong Education* – Special issue: *Lifelong Education in the Age of Transnational Migration*, 29: 2, 237–54.

Jackson, S. (2010b), 'Lifelong learning in a globalised world: politics, power and pedagogic practices', Keynote lecture, Asian Conference on Education, Osaka, December 3.

CHAPTER EIGHT

Transformations: Lifelong learners in the era of globalisation

NATALY TCHEREPASHENETS WITH LISA SNYDER

Globalisation and the quest for the renewal of identity

Identity has been one of the most debated concepts in both the history of human thought and the field of education. Two themes stand out in these discussions: identity and its relation to place and the link between 'I' and 'the other.' We contend that in the era of globalisation, which challenges inside/outside opposition and an association of the local with the national, these themes become firmly intertwined, making a renewal of identity a desired open-ended process, where self-invention and self-discovery coexist. Life-long learning plays a key role in this process, the important element of which is the development of cosmopolitan outlooks and sensibilities, indispensable, in our view, for the success of globalisation and for the life of democracy in the contemporary world, with its historically cherished values of tolerance, solidarity and social justice.[1]

The renewal of identity is closely connected with the changing notion of place. Globalisation challenges stability associated with both geographical place and identity. In contrast to the place-identity-relations

---

[1] The development of cosmopolitan position of identity is often viewed as a threat to 'cultural identity.' John Tomlinson defines 'cultural identity' as 'a collective treasures of local communities,' as an 'existential possession, an inheritance, a benefit of traditional long dwelling, of continuity with the past' (161)

continuum, typical for anthropological place of modernity; a 'non-place' of contemporaneity is equivalent to 'passage' (de Certea, 1998: 156), whose archetype is a travel space (Augé, 1995: 85). This change has several implications for the formation of identity. On the one hand, the trope of mobility, central to globalisation, weakens the ties of culture to place, making it impossible to map traditional anthropological notions of community or identity on to locality. As George Marcus observes, identity 'is produced simultaneously in many different locales. One's identity where one lives is only one social context and perhaps not the most important one in which it is shaped' (1992: 315). It can be further argued that identity can be then conceptualised in performative terms in parallel to what Benedict Anderson defines as a nation; an enacted space within which we try on roles and relationships of belonging and foreignness. These dynamics on the other hand, as Zygmunt Bauman perceptively notices, brings the renewed emphasis on the 'territorial principle' (1998: 67). Bauman views globalisation and reterritorialisation as two complementary processes, which exemplify two forces in action 'yearning for individual freedom of self-creation and the equally strong desire for security' (2008: 19).

The operation of these forces, we suggest, is driven by the constant reconfiguring of the relationships between the self and the other, which always have been at the core of identity formation and renewal, and which globalisation arguably makes more intensive, dynamic and unpredictable. As the Russian philosopher, Mikhail Bakhtin suggests, the architectonics of being has three fundamental elements, around which all values of actual life and culture are arranged.: 'I, the other, and I-for-the-other' (1993: 54). He affirms that life that ignores these relationships, falls away from responsibility or answerability and cannot have a philosophy. Emphasising the importance of transition from abstract models to the empirical world of action, Bakhtin underscores singularity and uniqueness of each particular action, performed answerably or responsibly by the particular individual in a particular time and in a particular place. Each of these actions either explicitly or implicitly exemplifies interaction, which is essential for the identity formation that is for bringing an individual to 'Being' in a responsible and answerable way. Jay Lemke's approach to identity intriguingly coincides with Bakhtin's view, when the North American educator asserts that a construction of identity is a combination of prior patterns of interaction with others, as well as uniqueness of the moment (Lemke, 2004). Socialisation is also at the core of Claude Dubar's concept of identity, which the French sociologist views as a 'result simultaneously stable and provisional, individual and collective, subjective and objective, biographical and structured, of diverse processes of socialisation which at the same time construct the individuals and define the institutions' (1991: 113).[2] The Canadian educator, Bonny Norton points out the need to develop a conception of identity 'that is understood with reference to larger, and frequently inequitable, social structures, which are reproduced in day-to-day interactions' (2000: 5). Furthering these approaches, we suggest that on-going transformation of relationships at all levels, which globalisation celebrates, makes the definition of identity a particularly challenging task. Instead, globalisation allows one to view identity as a 'work in progress,' a creation 'on the move' and in the need of continuous renewal. We contend that this renewal is largely shaped by both the apparent geographic, cultural, and economic flexibility, which globalisation brings, and the reaction to it: the growing sense and even fear of insecurity.

Life-long learning, which emphasises a development of cosmopolitan outlooks and sensibilities, can be both a constructive response to this reaction and an approach, instrumental for the facilitation of identity renewal, indispensable for the empowerment of individuals in the era of globalisation.[3] There are at least two major challenges for educators in fulfilling of this task: global racism, which opens the door to the paralyzing power of stereotypes and prejudice, and consumerism, which leads to political apathy and prospering ignorance.[4] Both challenges impede globalisation, and undermine the very foundation of democracy as a structure based on active participation of its citizens in public deliberations and discussions, where everybody has a right to intervene and question the naturalisation of order.

The overcoming of these challenges implies a transformation of the perception of the world order, the change, or at least a questioning of

---

[2] Translated by Zygmunt Bauman in Does ethics have a chance in a world of consumers? pp. 18–19

[3] Cosmopolitan position (cosmopolitanism) is based upon the assumption (premise) that 'every human shares, or should share, equal status as a 'citizen of the world' '(Houk 'Cosmopolitanism'); it entails the 'recognition, acceptance and eager exploration of diversity.' (Hollinger, 84)

[4] According to Walter Mignolo, '[T]he racial structure with which the imperial and colonial differences have been historically founded ... is the major impediment today to thinking seriously of global citizenship.'

the 'common sense,' in which happiness becomes synonymous to accumulation and well-being is measured by the ability to purchase goods and services. Life-long learning can and should facilitate this transformation effectively. In his influential theory of transformation, Jack Mezirow (2000) distinguishes the fostering of critical reflection on assumptions, which learners and others have as a key element in perspective transformation. He suggests this reflection is important for the adult development, and therefore for adult education. Mezirow suggests that transformative learning may lead to a fuller realisation of human capabilities. One may add that perspective transformation is closely linked to the renewal of identity, where self-invention, the fundamental elements of which are fantasy and innovation, and self-discovery, which implies deepening understanding of oneself and the unravelling of the potential, which was not evident before, coexist. Lifelong learning opens broad opportunities for both perspective transformation and identity renewal in formal and informal settings.[5] Drawing on the university, and especially on the case of humanities, the North American educator Walter Mignolo (2006) suggests two complimentary ways for educators to facilitate perspective transformation and foster identity renewal in the era of globalisation: (1) critique of the increasing dominance of corporate values within the university; (2) bringing to the curriculum epistemic and political projects from historical agents, experiences and memories that were disqualified as epistemic subjects. Similarly, pointing out 'the growing pressure to make needs of business and industry into the primary goals of the educational system,' as the right wing response to the current economic crisis, Michael Apple emphasises that 'keeping alive in the minds of the people the collective memory of the struggle for equality, for personal rights in *all* the institutions of our society,' is one of the most significant tasks for educators to accomplish (original emphasis, 2000: 40). We view this task as linked to the reaching across the boundaries that separate oneself and one's group ('kind') from the other and 'the other's group ('kind'),' to the development of cosmopolitan identity position, and to recognition of the essential humanity of others.

As we will further demonstrate, this can be achieved via engaging learners' in debates on controversial topics, the interest to which can be stimulated through the research via 'non-educational' websites, which

---

[5] We will follow Sue Jackson's definition of informal learning as 'the unstructured learning which most of us do on a daily basis' (237)

may appeal to students' emotions, as well as by the encouraging of learning through social spaces and building of 'relational capital.'[6] These activities can be instrumental for the purpose of dismantling of global racism through the questioning and reconsidering of the self/other dichotomy, exercising critical thinking and fostering learners' to take responsibility for their views and their lives, as active, responsive and creative individuals in consumerist age. The discussion of two transformative experiences later in this chapter will allow us to demonstrate that lifelong learning allows students and educators alike to test their own beliefs and attitudes, to enter in a dialogue with oneself and 'the other,' and to open themselves to the life-changing experiences. We believe that these steps are at the core of education in global citizenship, intrinsic for the empowerment of individuals in a contemporary democratic society.

Foreign language education and the renewal of identity

Language learning opens multiple opportunities for self-examination, identity renewal and for the exploration of the phenomenon of 'foreignness,' inherently bound to the education in democracy and citizenship. Our goal has been to make these opportunities available to adult students who enrolled in the online courses Introductory Spanish: Language and Culture or Spanish for Health Care Professionals. Most of these students enrolled in foreign language courses to satisfy a general education requirement, which is mandated by the State University of New York. In our view, in addition to the development of four basic skills associated with language acquisition, such as speaking, writing, reading, and listening, it is our responsibility as educators in world languages to foster cross- national and cross-cultural understanding and acceptance. One of the activities, which we designed in order to achieve this goal, focused on the examining of the issue of immigration. This activity allowed students to question/reassert their previous views about immigrants, to become engaged in national political debate on this topic, as well as to explore complex relationships between this debate and the international phenomenon of globalisation.

Immigration has been one of the most widely debated issues in the United States from its birth and it continues to be 'a heated matter' in

---

[6] Jackson defines 'relational capital as 'the development of relational understanding of different realities of knowing and experiencing sometimes competing worlds' (251)

media and press today. The dramatic increase in the number of undocumented aliens, to some 12 million illegal immigrants, according to the Pew Hispanic Center, their presence and their possible competition for scarce jobs are sources of ongoing political and ethnic controversy and tension. The signing of the Arizona Law of Immigration by the governor Jen Brewer in April 2010, which makes the failure to carry immigration papers a state crime and gives police officers the right to detain under 'the lawful stop' anyone suspected of being in the country illegally, exemplifies this tension and controversy par excellence.[7]

The enactment of this law can be also seen as a voice in the continuing struggle to define America's cultural understandings of itself. This voice seeks to define and virulently defend the borders of identity: American citizen or other, or a certain type of American citizen or other; views that correspond to an understanding of the concept of 'nation,' which is tied to an imagined reading of what defines America and Americanism. Thus one can ask, are we White Christians of English and Scots-Irish stock? Are we the embodiment of our civic religious symbols such as the Constitution or the office of the President? Or are we our multi-cultural 'other' as defined by such ethnic hyphens as Chinese-American, Jewish-American, African-American, or Mexican-American?

As Anderson has pointed out in his seminal work *Imagined Communities*, a nation is 'an imagined political community – and imagined as both inherently limited and sovereign' (1991: 6). For the purposes of his definition, a nation is limited by the fact of its boundaries, is made sovereign by its having cast itself in its bid for freedom, and as an *imagined community* in its 'deep, horizontal comradeship,' that makes blood sacrifice possible in defense of it (1991: 7). One is left to ask, however, who gets

---

[7] On 28 July a federal judge in Arizona blocked this requirement. Ms. Brewer expressed her determination to file an expedited appeal at the United States Court of Appeals. http://www.bbc.co.uk/news/world-us-canada-10607927. Criticising the law in his keynote speech and urging for immigration reforms, President Obama pointed out that 'It would tear at the very fabric of this nation because immigrants who are here illegally are already intricately woven into that fabric.' In addition recalling history, president Obama, reminded American people that 'migrant workers, who are mostly in the US illegally had been the labour force for farmers and agricultural producers 'for generations'. http://www.bbc.co.uk/news/10478829 . One may also recall strong historic and cultural ties between the land of Arizona and Mexico. Arizona was one of the Mexican territories prior to the Mexican American War and the Treaty of Guadalupe Hidalgo in 1848.

to chose? Why is one depiction more valid than another? And what happens over time?

We suggest that a closer look at personal experiences can shed light on the complexity of these questions. Given the setting of the online Spanish language courses and being inspired by Michael Apple's rhetorical question, 'How do we enable the histories and cultures of different groups, who are in every communities of population to be taught in responsible and responsive ways?' (39), we have chosen to focus on Spanish-speaking immigrants.[8] The activity, 'Understanding Personal Experience' was created with four purposes in mind: (1) to expand students' knowledge about culture(s) of the Spanish-speaking world and the life of Latinos in the US; (2) to enhance students' critical thinking by engaging them in implicit debates on most controversial topics, including 'natives'/'foreigners' dichotomy and immigration in its relationship to both American politics and globalisation; (3) to develop respect for diverse members of world population, indispensable for the democratic citizenship in the era of globalisation; (4) to foster appreciation of lifelong learning as a life-style, which empowers people of different ages to become independent thinkers and responsible 'doers,' to form their own opinions, and plan their actions in a responsible way. This project has four parts.

Recognising the importance of interpersonal communication in informal settings as a source of learning, in the first part, we asked students to interview a native of a Spanish-speaking country, an immigrant who lives in the US. Biographical stories can be an efficient and personalised way to challenge people to confront complex human issues. With this assumption in mind, we required students to read personal stories from the website 'Undocumented American Dream,' and express their own reflections on immigrants' experiences. The first two parts prepared learners to complete the third part of the assignment, where they offered their opinion about Arizona's new immigration law and explored its relation to globalisation. In the final part, students were asked to reflect on the impact of this learning activity on their views on immigration and their own identity development. In designing this activity, we worked under the

---

[8] Per US Census (2010), 46.9 million of people of Hispanic origin are currently living in the US:
http://search.census.gov/search?entqr=0&ud=1&output=xml_no_dtd&oe=UTF-8&ie=UTF-8&client=2010prod&proxystylesheet=2010prod&site=2010&q=Hispanic .

assumption that democratic transformative education can have an impact on learners' views and beliefs. We see it as instrumental in the development of cosmopolitan outlooks and sensibilities, which we view as a highly desirable goal in advancing learners' growth as democratic citizens who are eager to explore and appreciate the diversity, which surrounds them.

When we designed this project, we knew that according to the Rasmussen Poll 70 per cent of Arizonians and 60 per cent of Americans were in favour of the new Arizona Law. In our view, this data exemplifies the growing sense of insecurity and the renewed emphasis on territorial principle, in response to globalisation. We also suggest that this reaction was influenced by ignorance and apathy, which are results of the acceptance of both the supremacy of the marketplace and the nation-state's need to protect and to regenerate itself. In our opinion, such views impede cross-cultural and cross national understanding and acceptance. Our hypothesis has been that learning experiences which foster critical thinking, empower students to form their own educated opinions, and enhance the development of a cosmopolitan identity position may have an impact on students' perception of the new law. This proved to indeed be the case.

Our findings are based on the review of 42 students' projects. All participants were born in the US, and they are made up of mixed race and gender. The average age of the students was 33. Most students indicated that this activity changed their views on immigration, immigrants and the Arizona Law (39), and several stated that it has been an '*eye-opening learning experience*' (12). As Mezirow points out, transformation implies a deep shift in frame of reference. From the review of students' responses, it became clear that one of the shifts, which took place in many cases (31) is the change in the negative perception of immigrants. As one student, for instance, notices, this activity allowed her to distance herself from the commonly accepted attitude in the area, where she lives,

> *In the area where I live, there is much debate, stigma and even hatred surrounding Hispanics and the issues of illegal immigration . . . Although I never had a very strong opinion on immigration one way or the other, but I experienced many of the same feelings . . . However after interviewing X and getting to know more about his life and culture, and in reading through many of the profiles for the purpose of this project, my attitude towards illegal immigration has began to significantly change . . . I now am more empathetic*

towards those who choose to come here illegally, and better understand the challenges that they faced, both in their countries of origin and in to trying to live a 'hidden existence' here in America.

Another student refers to overgeneralisation and the lack of information as major reasons for his negative approach to immigrants that has been changed,

Had it not been for this essay, I honestly can say that I had a rather negative viewpoint of illegal immigrants in general. That generality generated some negative stereotypes that regrettably I carried over to prejudice. I had a preconception of immigrants that was unfair and based on personal ignorance. I cannot blame someone for wanting a better life for them and their families.

Developing empathy with people different from themselves is one of the important steps for building cross-cultural connections and it is necessary for the formation of cosmopolitan views and sensibilities. Several students indicated that this activity allowed them to view parallels between themselves and immigrants. They discovered that people across the globe have '*common dreams: the better lives for themselves and their families;*' that '*people in North America and South America are not that different,*' and '*[t]hat people are people no matter where they were born and how much money do they have.*' As one student states, '*I have gained a new understanding of immigrants, the activity helped to put me in the shoes of immigrants and their families.*' Thus, an interaction with immigrants as well as the reading of biographical and autobiographical stories allowed students to recognise the universal nature of humanity. Further, discussions of immigrant experiences lead to in-depth thinking about ethical ways of relating to 'the other,' which is a part of the human family as 'myself.' As a student points out, '*This activity inspired me not to think just about immigration and the race, but about humanity and the fair treatment of people. Solidarity helped me to put myself in their shoes [immigrants].*'

The ability to interconnect with people of different backgrounds exemplifies cross-cultural understanding and is an important condition for fostering solidarity, which according to David Held goes further than empathy, '[solidarity is] not just empathetic recognition of another's plight, but the willingness to stand side-by-side with others in the creation of solutions to pressing collective problems' (2007: 241). Students' growing understanding of the necessity to act in order to resolve burning immigration issues, exemplifies solidarity. As several of them noticed (28), the newly gained understanding of the complexity of the issues related to immigration, made learners active advocates for change in immigration policies in the US and critics of the current system.

Almost unanimous criticism, for example, was expressed about the treatment of the children of illegal immigrants. The vast majority of students (40) found the current approach to be a socially unjust violation of human rights, and think that children who were brought to the country illegally should not be accountable under the new immigration law. As one student puts it,

> *I admit that, before now, I had never given much thought to the plight of the millions of children, born in the United States, but who have been denied citizenship due to the status of their illegal immigrant parents . . . I had no idea that these children are denied citizenship and, as a result, are forced to live life as a lie and under the persistent fear of deportation.*

Another student observes that:

> *Deporting someone who has grown up here and only knows the life in the States would be damaging to their life. And there isn't any real way to separate these cases from the ones that the law is trying to target.*

Displaying civil engagement and solidarity as well as distancing themselves from the previous position and opinions, students (22) stress the need to '*fight for the right laws,*' for the new reform. As one student observes, '*My attitude towards immigrants was not changed as much as my attitude towards how US deals with and is prepared to deal with immigration.*' Many students (31) connected the necessity for action, critique and revision of US immigration policy with the fight for social justice. Some students (2) offered creative solutions on incorporating illegal immigrants to the American society, by transforming them into '*tax –revenue sources.*' In this way, learning about 'the other' deepened students' understanding of themselves and their country. The exploration of the topic of immigration became a point of departure for the formation of cosmopolitan thinking through the exploration of such notions as identity, democracy, and social justice.

Furthermore, the discussion of immigrants' experiences unravelled the complexity of the concept of citizenship as a form of a group identity, previously taken for granted. This made several students (21) to face what Mezirow (1995: 50) would call a 'disorienting dilemma,' which emerges when current understandings and frames of reference became problematic. This dilemma became evident when students began asking themselves who real Americans are, what it means to be a citizen and who does deserve this right? As one student questions,

> *Does being born and raised in a place give one more right to belong or does taking an enormous risk and fighting for entry into one's desired place of residence deem one more worthy of being a citizen? I have to say neither carries more weight that the other.*

Another student notices that immigrants' motivation to contribute to the country of their choice should be taken in consideration when a right to citizenship is in question and that overgeneralisation may lead to erroneous decisions. As this student suggests, it is important to differentiate between people who *'take responsibility for their actions versus individuals who seek US citizenship solely because of what they can obtain through the various entitlement programs.'* For another student, the concept of citizenship is intertwined with the appreciation of the American multicultural openness: *'This activity reinforced the concept that the US has a rich heritage of ethnic inclusion and cultural variety.'* Thus, meeting with another culture enhanced identity-renewal through the process of learning, including self-learning, which causes one to rethink things which were previously taken for granted, including one's own culture and system of beliefs.

This learning has also been a key for the transformation of students' perception (31) of the Arizona Law. As one student states,

> *After learning the details of Arizona law and considering the potential pros and cons, I too disagree with it and feel that it is a form of discrimination . . . I also agree that this law would lead to many people being unjustly profiled and harassed, perhaps simply because like this is allowed to take effect, knowing that this is largely based on public opinion, it might lead the way to other unfair laws to be enacted.*

Students answers in favour of the law (6), revealed fear and desire for security to be a major motivation for support. As one student states,

> *I try to be a neutral person I am a type of person that gets nervous for hurting peoples' feelings, although I do think, and I only think this way due to the facts of terror on the USA, that having stricter laws on immigration is only right.*

Several students indicated that the activity allowed them to test their views and to confirm them. Most students agree that the law has some relations with globalisation, and 32 point out that '*it takes us back.*' As one student notices, '*In order to accomplish globalisation there needs to be more a mixture of races and cultures intertwined in different areas and this law is promoting the exact opposite.*'

There is also evidence that students developed an appreciation for life-long learning, instrumental for the development of critical thinking through research and interpersonal interaction, both of which in the case of this activity enhanced independent thinking, engaged citizenship, and facilitated the formation of cosmopolitan views and perceptions. Students developed an understanding of the need not to take any opinion and information for granted and to form their own opinion in a responsible way. As one of the students notices,

> *What struck me as I researched for this essay was the diametric viewpoints on immigration people have. I too must admit that I am guilty of carrying certain prejudices and preconceptions of what, and more importantly who, illegal immigrants are. It was not until reading the viewpoints of both sides of the argument and approaching the topic with an open mind that I was able to formulate an opinion of immigration.*

Due to the impact of the learning experience, another student has chosen to keep informed of current immigration issues, which did not interest her before, '*Because of this assignment I have learned about the Arizona Immigration Law, it will no longer be a headline in the paper that I skim by.*'

This activity, with its infusion of 'heated' topics and dialogue with dominant discourses, real people, and oneself into the online courses, exemplifies foreign language education as an engaging and productive way to enhance identity renewal, the formation of cosmopolitan views and sensibilities, and to foster a democracy-engaged citizenship in a globalised world.

Lifelong-learners as agents of globalisation

Globalisation brings unique challenges to faculty members as they facilitate learning of students with increasingly diverse linguistic, cultural and ethnic backgrounds. To be successful in this task, we suggest that educators need to develop a cosmopolitan identity position, to open themselves to opportunities for identity renewal, and to adopt life-long learning as a life-style. One of the efficient ways to achieve this goal is through experiential learning, which can occur through the immersion in the culture of 'the other,' which is different from one's own. For the faculty members in this study, all of whom are also our colleagues at State University of New York, Empire State College, this immersion took place while teaching with the college's Center for International Programs (IP). Our participants included nine professors, four females, five males, eight whites and one Asian, whose expertise lay in such diverse areas as American History, psychology, business and writing. We asked them to discuss their motivations behind teaching for IP and how this teaching affected them personally and professionally along with their views on international cultures, globalisation, and social justice. In the course of our conversations, it became clear to us that teaching international students in their home countries of Middle East, Latin America, and Eastern Europe had a long lasting impact on the identity development of these educators, whose views and actions proved them to be life-learners and agents of globalisation.

As Jay Lemke and Caspar van Helden perceptively observe, at the age of globalisation, 'Life biographies and learning biographies become increasingly indistinguishable' (2009: 151). Faculty members' responses, which illustrate that the learning experiences gained during their work for IP influenced their identity renewal and the formation of cosmopolitan views, exemplify this statement *par excellence*. This allows us to suggest that in the era of globalisation, when countries become increasingly interconnected and interdependent, the active exposure to other cultures through direct participation is a highly desirable experience. Arguably, we assert that these experiences become indispensable for the personal and professional growth of any faculty member, as they enhance the promotion of cross-cultural understanding and acceptance in any setting.

The desire for experiential learning through the *'experience of other cultures'* has been named as a major motivation for all professors (9), who accepted the teaching position at IP. One of the faculty members discusses the advantages of the work abroad vis-à-vis visiting as a tourist. She points out the benefits of 'participation,' which allows direct communication with international colleagues and students, as opposed to a limited perspective gained through the observation, typical for a tourist: *'Being in the country and the culture as a temporary local is a much richer, often life changing experience. I couldn't ask for more.'*

Becoming aware of the intrinsic embeddedness of the local in the global, another colleague indicated that he wanted to understand better the fellow immigrants in the US, who came from the country, where he was invited to teach. He discusses his motivation as being, *'pure adventure and a desire to learn more about culture of different immigrants. In the US and Canada we are often unaware of our neighbors. US faculty can learn a lot from other countries.'*

All faculty members acknowledged that their work for IP changed them in some way. Most colleagues (7) pointed out that this change had started with the challenge of their frame of reference. For example, one of the faculty members discovered parallels between cultures, about which she was not aware before: *'The culture (of the Dominican Republic) was much more familiar to me than I thought it would be.'* The deeper understanding of North American Culture had been reached through the unique experiences of life and learning in another country. This allowed some professors (4) to develop a critical approach to American mass culture and dominant discourses,

> *It wasn't until I worked with those students that I realized how much my extremely uninformed view of the Middle East had been shaped by the concept of 'terrorism' and many American movies. (This recognition also served as a personal wake-up call about my own ignorance and unexamined assumptions.)*

Another faculty member states that due to her experience teaching with IP, she *'listen[s] to the news with the different ear.'* When one engages in a relationship with members of another culture, there resides the possibility of seeing and understanding the world and therefore oneself differently. As one colleague points out, *'I am more sensitive to how Americans are sometimes too insular in their sensitivity to the world around them.'*

This experience also led to the critical examination and questioning (6) of previous assumptions and beliefs, both personal and professional. As one colleague notices,

> Working with students in IP raised questions I had not previously considered. Questions about language and the requirement that students understand in English, which for some was their second or third language; questions about the nature of American schooling.

The connection between personal renewal and professional development is also evident in another colleague's remark,

> I owe quite a bit of my personal development to my work with international students. They showed me how privileged my life is. I am very careful with any assumptions I make about any student. I don't assume, for example, that what I say is what the person has heard. I think I have become a better listener and, I hope, a better learner . . . I am more aware of cultural differences and how something written can be interpreted differently, when I develop curriculum.

Teaching as a learning process enriched another colleague's perception of the material she teaches, and thus had an impact on her personal intellectual development, as she states,

> it helped me see the material I teach in a new light. I teach American history and culture so it really expanded my ability to concretely compare other cultures and the US with experiential knowledge. I found that extremely valuable for my intellectual development.

Further, the majority of professors (8) developed a vision of themselves as professionals and individuals who enhance cross-cultural understanding and trust. Seven colleagues refer to learning as a key element, which allowed them to achieve this goal. In one case, for example, knowing that common language can work as a bridge between different cultures, which reduces resentment and fear of 'the other,' one professor decided to learn elementary Arabic. This allowed him to create a comfortable atmosphere, conducive to students' learning,

> I did that because I had a student who had never met an American before and was totally intimidated by my presence. We were doing registration and I got one of my prior students to calm the woman down. I'm not an intimidating guy so I said to myself if I just knew a little Arabic it would help so I now have 6 general education credits in Arabic.

Through their personal example as life-long learners who developed a deep appreciation and respect for cultural differences, faculty members felt empowered to challenge the misconceptions many of their students had regarding their perception of North America. This perception was often influenced by accepted negative views and/or dominant discourses. Several professors considered this to be an important step in promoting cross-cultural understanding and acceptance. As one colleague states,

> *what I do helps promote international understanding. When my students sit in a coffee shop in Beirut and the people at the next table start badmouthing Americans I am hoping they are saying, 'Well, you don't know my professor X he's not like that.' . . . To me that is a big thing. Even if it makes one student over there look at us differently, it matters, it matters at least to me.*

This sentiment is shared by another colleague, who notes,

> *I hope as faculty we are ambassadors for a positive view of the American people: not our government, but the everyday American. Personally, I try to be respectful of the cultures where I find myself, learn what I can about them, and try to fit in.*

A conservative perception of the role of women in societies where education for centuries has been a privilege reserved for men is another cultural dogma that one professor wanted to challenge through her work and personal example. As she states,

> *One of the reasons I teach with IP is that we have a presence in areas of the world where education is often reserved for males; where sometimes far less than half of the women in the country are given an education. My presence alone serves as a role model of someone smart, funny, approachable, and educated who has a good life. I don't mean this as a boast: if I can do this, it is possible for the students and I want them to see that. Maybe that's my feminist belief: if we educate women, not only are they able to have a more rewarding life and improve their lot – they are also able to pass this value onto the next generation. Studies have shown that when resources are given to women, they are more equitably distributed among the community – so everyone benefits.*

The striving for the equality of opportunities in education for men and women advances the struggle for social justice. One of the faculty members discusses the impact of IP on this cause,

> *Regarding social justice, I don't know if I personally have an impact but our program has. When I first started in 1999 we had probably 100 plus students. In my first class I had one woman. Now, I would guess it's almost 50/50.*

Promoting equal educational opportunities to people worldwide also serves to the social justice goal, according to another colleague, who is proud of '*[b]ringing opportunities of American education to places, where they otherwise would not have them.*'

These comments also can be viewed as expressions of an act of solidarity with developing countries, which results from the care for students. As one of the faculty members notices, this goes both ways: '*Certainly our worldwide social relations were intensified – we came to care very much about our students . . . we are much more aware of each other.*' One of the faculty members was in the Dominican Republic at the moment when the Haitian earthquake hit. This experience had a profound effect on him and shaped his feeling of enhanced solidarity with the global community, '*Being on the same island had a profound impact on me because I was able to experience even in a tiny way the repercussions from literally the aftershocks of a real global catastrophe.*'

The majority of faculty members (6) indicated that their work for IP influenced their views on globalisation, and made them feel like active participants in this process. One colleague, for instance notices, '*Globalisation has a more real feel for me.*' Another faculty member states that his work allowed him to develop a critical approach toward globalisation, '*My experience in IP has sharpened my awareness of globalisation and encouraged me to develop a critique of it.*' For another colleague, this experience unravelled complexities of globalisation, as a force, which leads to further stratification of society: '*we teach to a small elite group in the countries we visit. That tends to exacerbate the gap between the richest people in the society and the poorest because already, by being bilingual they already have certain kinds of advantages.*'

Thus, teaching international students in their home countries turned out to be an enriching and transformative life and learning experience for faculty members, which enhanced their professional and personal growth. Working as 'agents of globalisation', in addition to sharing their knowledge in specific fields of study, our colleagues opened themselves to integration and co-operation in an aspiration to reduce inequality of opportunities, and enhance intercultural dialogue. This work also deepened their understanding of challenges and rewards of globalisation. There is no doubt that the identity renewal which resulted from this experience will be an asset to their life and work in any setting, and will make them more engaged citizens in a global world.

Conclusion

Globalisation plays an important role in shaping the philosophy and practice of adult education in the USA today. Drawing on two case studies in this chapter, we demonstrated that in a globalised world, both adult educators and students are challenged to test their perceptions of democracy, social justice, and citizenship. This challenge may have a transformative effect on the identities of life-long learners, as it has been the case with two complementary groups of participants in our study from the State University of New York, Empire State College.

Both experiences, in different ways, deepened participants' knowledge about themselves and the larger social world. Whereas in the first group a 'transformation' happened for students while engaging in the formal learning process; with the second group, change was facilitated for a group of faculty while teaching abroad. In both cases, participants confronted and, on several occasions, overcame limitations of their earlier developed views and practices. A close look at these experiences allowed us to illustrate the developing learners' ability to question and critique existent conceptions, foster learners' critical thinking on social justice, and enhance students' understandings of social justice's relationship to diversity, democracy and globalisation. We assert that these values are relevant for adult students and educators alike.

An analysis of the results of this study permit us to suggest that at this time of pressure by the neoliberal discourses for market-oriented pedagogy/education, the tasks of both bringing the equality of opportunities and promoting intercultural dialogue remain to be priorities for adult education, whose major objective and obligation is an expansion of the freedoms of human beings. In the era of globalisation, its fulfilment more than ever depends on fostering cosmopolitan citizenship and enhancing solidarity, developing an ability to interconnect with people of different backgrounds, and making it possible for them to participate in intercultural dialogue on equal terms. These goals deserve a place at the forefront of the agendas of education policy-makers as well as in the work by researchers and practitioners of adult education in the 21st century.

References

Anderson, B. (1991) *Imagined communities*. London: Verso.
Apple, M. (2000) *Official knowledge. Democratic education in a conservative age*. New York: Routledge.
Augé, M. (1995) *Non-places: Introduction to an anthropology of super-modernity*. (J. Howe, Trans.). London: Verso.
Bakhtin, M. (1993) *Toward the philosophy of the act*. Austin, TX: University of Texas Press.
Bauman, Z. (2008) *Does ethics have a chance in a world of consumers?* Cambridge: Harvard University Press.
Bauman, Z. (1998) *Globalisation: the human consequences*. New York: Columbia University Press.
de Certeau, M. (1998) *The Practice of Everyday Life*. (S. F. Rendall, Trans.). Berkeley, CA: University of California Press.
Dubar, C. (1991) *La socialization: Construction des identities*. Paris: Colin.
Held, D. (2007) 'Rethinking global governance: apocalypse soon or reform!' in D. Held and A. McGrew (eds), *Globalisation theory*, 240–61. Cambridge, MA: Polity Press.
Hollinger, D. A. (1995) *Postethnic America: Beyond multiculturalism*. New York: Basic Books.
Houk, K. J. (2005) *New Dictionary of the History of Ideas*, M.C. Horowitz (ed.), 487–9. New York: Charles Scribner's Sons.
Jackson, S. (2010) 'Learning through social spaces: Migrant women and lifelong learning in post-colonial London', *International Journal of Lifelong Learning*, 29: 2, 237–53.
Lemke, J. (2004) 'Language development and identity: Multiple timescales in the social ecology of learning', in C. Kramsch (ed.), *Language acquisition and language socialization*, 68–87. London: Continuum.
Lemke, J. and van Helden, C. (2009) 'New learning cultures: identities, media and networks', in R. Goodfellow and M.N. Lamy (eds) *Learning cultures in online education*, 151–70. London and New York: Continuum,
Marcus, G. (1992) 'Narcissism, roots and postmodernity', in *Modernity and*

identity S. Lash and J. Friedman (eds). Oxford: Oxford University Press.

Mezirow, J. and Associates. (eds) (2000) *Learning as Transformation.* San Francisco: Jossey-Bass.

Mezirow, J. 'Transformation theory of adult learning.' In *Defense of the Lifeworld.* Ed. M.K. Welton (ed.) New York: SUNY Press, 1995.

Mignolo, W. D. (2006) 'Citizenship, knowledge, and the limits of humanity.' *American Literary History*, 18: 2, 312–33.

Mirchandani, R. (July 28, 2010) 'Judge blocks Arizona's controversial immigration law', Retrieved from http://www.bbc.co.uk/news/world-us-canada-10607927.

Norton, B. (2000) *Identity and language learning: Gender, ethnicity and educational change.* Harlow: Longman.

Tomlinson, J. (2007) 'Globalisation and cultural analysis' in D. Held and A. McGrew (eds) *Globalisation theory*, 148–70. Cambridge, MA: Polity Press.

US Census 2010. Retrieved from http://search.census.gov/search?entqr=0&ud=1&output=xml_no_dtd&oe=UTF-8&ie=UTF-8&client=2010prod&proxystylesheet=2010prod&site=2010&q=Hispanic.

CHAPTER NINE

Dialogical processes in adult learning: Teacher identity and professional development in New Zealand's low socioeconomic communities

Vicki M Carpenter

Introduction

> *The question really is not to be free to speak about dialogue, but to fight for the right to participate in a living dialogue* (Freire et al., 1997: 137).

This chapter's focus is on dialogical processes in adult education.[1] I discuss two professional learning situations which involved teachers who were working in New Zealand's urban, low socioeconomic schools. Such schools face social justice challenges related to student underachievement. The argument I advance is that the teachers' involvement in dialogical processes, as part of professional development, helped them become better equipped to work positively towards ameliorating social justice issues. Central to, and underpinning, this chapter is the belief that, where schoolteachers engage in dialogical processes in adult education, their personal, multiple and combined identities are enriched and extended. Concurrently, epistemological understandings are enhanced.

In adult education, every moment of teaching is pressured and precious. There is, however, very little published work on effective and

---

[1] There is much which concerns dialogical practices in adult education which has had to be omitted from this chapter, and the references provide a starting place for further reading.

stimulating ways in which lecturers can help the adults they teach to make a difference in their communities of practice. This chapter contributes to a small, but growing, body of material focused on dialogical practices and identity formation in adult education, and their links to social justice (Carpenter, 2010b; Freire, 1972; Freire, Fraser, Macedo, McKinnon, and Stokes, 1997; Gordon and Whitchurch, 2010; Kincheloe and Steinberg, 1997; Macedo, 1995; Shor and Pari, 1999). Social justice concerns are inevitably surrounded by politics, and the following section contextualises this work in New Zealand's political and economic landscape.

The context and the challenge

In 1984, New Zealand moved politically towards neoliberalism. The Keynesian welfare state's economy was faltering at that time, and increasing globalisation brought additional pressures. From that time onwards, welfare-based state policies were gradually withdrawn or dismantled. The contemporary emphasis, no matter which political party is in power, is on a market economy. Synonymous with the changes has been a strong political thrust for a minimal state, reduced taxation, user pays, and increasing competitiveness in all spheres of life (Barry, 1996).

While it can be argued that the neoliberal agenda was not, and is not, the right one for New Zealand (Kelsey, 1995), its impact, unquestionably, is all pervading. In particular, the gap between the rich and poor has widened considerably, and thousands of children now live in relative poverty (Blaiklock et al., 2002; St John and Wynd, 2008). In a myriad of respects, New Zealand (NZ) can now be described as an unequal society (Wilkinson and Pickett, 2009).

Education, like other NZ state-funded services, has been affected by neoliberalism. In the compulsory primary and secondary school sectors, 'Tomorrow's Schools' (Department of Education, 1988) policies legislated for competition between schools, greater private sector involvement, a national curriculum, external monitoring processes, and school site governance. In the tertiary sector, student tuition fees and loans were introduced; at the same time, state institutional funding was reduced. As in the compulsory education sectors, a competitive model became the norm for universities and polytechnics. In all sectors, compulsory and tertiary, educators were pressured to trim budgets and meet externally imposed outcome requirements. The situation has not eased in recent times; teachers and tertiary educators are now under far more pressure than they were prior to 1984 and their stress is mounting with the seemingly entrenched political climate (Codd, 2008; Sullivan, 1994).

Despite the rhetoric and optimism of neoliberalism, lower socioeconomic compulsory sector students still do not achieve to their potential, while intending tertiary students from this sector tend to be either denied entry due to poor grades, or they are marginalised once in the system. State moves towards neoliberalism have exacerbated already existing problems for the poor and marginalised (Carpenter, 2008). The gap in achievement levels between compulsory sector students from NZ's richer and poorer geographical areas is one of the widest in the western world (Ministry of Education, 2006).

Research findings in NZ, similar to most other western democracies, indicate a strong correlation between poverty and poor educational achievement (Ministry of Education, 2005). In NZ, the children of the poor, and the poor, are failed by the education system. Few low socioeconomic status children graduate to adult education. Those who enter tertiary education often face financial pressures (economic capital related), problems surrounding habitus mismatch (cultural capital), and marginalisation due to their lack of the 'right' connections (social capital). NZ's situation mirrors those of many other western capitalist countries, for instance the UK and the USA. One of the few global exceptions is provided by Finland which largely has retained a strong equity-based education system (OECD, 2007; Sahlberg, 2007).

As identity is a key concept within the poverty and educational achievement discourse, my own perspective follows.

'I am in the text'

My identity and politics influence all that I do, including research and writings. As Jones (1992) states, 'I am in the text'. I have a personal and schooling background in a low socioeconomic community, and I identify as a lesbian feminist with working-class roots. I have a long history of teaching in the compulsory sector in low socioeconomic schools, and a more recent history of working in adult education in the field of social justice. My current teaching is in a Faculty of Education at a NZ university.

A critical reading of Freire (1972; 2005) and other related works (for example: Anyon *et al.*, 2009; Hammersley, 2000; Weiler, 1988; Young, 1998), combined with a lived awareness of the impact of neoliberal policies on those in poverty, helped me decide to revisit my personal pedagogy. My classroom, whether it comprises children or adults, is a very privileged place for me to be. This is the ambit where I can close the door, and together we, the students and I, can be learners and change the world. The belief shared by many (for instance, Chitty, 2002; Hawk and Hill, 2000; Kumashiro, 2009) that education can contribute significantly to a positive social justice difference impacts on how I frame and undertake my professional work.

Schoolteachers generally undertake Professional Development (PD) as their form of adult education. PD often includes research projects and further education for qualifications. A PD-related research project and a postgraduate class are presented below as case study contexts for the examination of dialogical processes in adult education. In both cases, our ultimate and shared goal was social justice related: raising the educational achievement of children from low socioeconomic backgrounds. My identity plus the identities of the case study teachers I worked with all intersected in a variety of ways, and dialogical processes brought our commonalities to the fore.

Freire and dialogue

Most descriptors of dialogue stem from the work of the late Brazilian educator Paulo Freire. His words and practices are cited by educators and activists throughout western and third world countries (Becker, 1995; Esposito and Evans-Winters, 2007; Galguera, 2005; Gandin and Fischman, 2006; hooks, 1994; Roberts, 2008). Politics, history, identity, place, education, oppression, silence, knowing, and conversations are all addressed by Freire. Carefully crafted and published Freirean words resonate, in particular, with those who care about social justice. His ideas speak of empowerment: Freire posits that people should learn from each other, be proud of their identity (class, in particular); should know and speak of injustice, and actively work to make the world a better, more socially just place. Identity is central to Freire's thinking, without a sense of identity, there can be no real struggle (Freire, 1972).

Pedagogy of the Oppressed (Freire, 1972), Freire's most widely known work, clarifies his interpretation of dialogue:

> ... *dialogue is the encounter in which the united reflection and action of the dialoguers are addressed to the world which is to be transformed and humanized, this dialogue cannot be reduced to the act of one person's*

> *'depositing' ideas in another, nor can it become a simple exchange of ideas to be 'consumed' by the participants in the discussion . . . [Dialogue] is an act of creation; it must not serve as a crafty instrument for the domination of one man [sic] by another. The domination implicit in dialogue is that of the world by those who enter into dialogue, it is the conquest of the world for the liberation of men* (Freire, 1972: 61–2).

Arguably, many adult education encounters involve banking and deposits; the teacher lectures while students take notes, with the latter prepared to regurgitate their banked knowledge in examination or essay form. In contrast, in a dialogical classroom situation, words and worlds intermingle as epistemologies and personal understandings are shared and critiqued (Freire, 1972; Freire *et al.*, 1997; Macedo, 1995; Shor and Freire, 1987; Shor and Pari, 1999).

Donaldo Macedo interviewed Freire and published 'A dialogue: Culture, language and race' (Macedo, 1995). That publication, plus Freire's final chapter in *Mentoring the mentor* (Freire *et al.*, 1997), Shor and Freire's *A pedagogy for liberation* (1987) and Shor's *Empowering education* (1992) provide the foundation for my interpretation of dialogue. Shor contextualises dialogic pedagogy in adult education:

> *Mutual discussion is the heart of the method. Dialogue is simultaneously structured and creative. It is initiated and directed by a critical teacher but is democratically open to student intervention. Co-developed by the teacher and the students, dialogue is neither a freewheeling conversation nor a teacher-dominated exchange. Balancing the teacher's authority and the students' input is the key to making the process both critical and democratic. Dialogic teachers offer students an open structure in which to develop. This openness includes their right to question the content and the process of dialogue, and even to reject them* (Shor, 1992: 85–86).

The more widespread banking model, indicated above, can alienate and disenfranchise those who have historically been marginalised; generally this includes those who identify as women (see Jackson, 2004), working-class, non-white, or intersections of all of these. The tension between the banking model and dialogic pedagogy signals a potential rift. Teaching differently – for instance using dialogical practices – may well be empowering, but it can also engender various forms of institutional and student resistance. Dialogue may be too different, too unusual, too hard and therefore too challenging. There are risks, tensions and exciting opportunities involved in changing accustomed practices, as my students and I discovered.

The students and the methods

The two groups involved were working on either the Te Whakapakari (the Strengthening) research project (coded as 'Res') (six teachers) which a colleague and I initiated; or studying in a postgraduate class ('PgC') (21 students, many of whom were teachers) I taught. My work with the two groups was between 2007 and 2009, and my involvement in both was part of my university work.

The research group worked with a colleague, Colleen, and me on the Te Whakapakari project (Carpenter and McMurchy-Pilkington, 2007) (Res). The funded project aimed to raise the achievement levels of Maori (indigenous) children in the compulsory schooling sector. Six women were involved as teacher action researchers: two identified as Maori; two were school administrators (a Principal and a Deputy Principal); and all taught in what are described internationally as urban schools. The women taught economically poor children of mixed ethnicities, including a large percentage of Maori children. Facing the effects of childhood poverty (hunger, poor health, inadequate clothing, and crowded housing) and dealing with tensions in the playground were normal daily activities for the teachers. Our meetings and activities covered one calendar year. Time together included group meetings; one-to-one time between a lead researcher (Colleen or me) and a teacher researcher; communal times spent eating meals or experiencing an overnight stay in a *marae* (Maori meeting house); and presentations of our work. Colleen and I researched the Te Whakapakari project and selected findings are included here as research data.

The postgraduate class (PgC) worked with me as the lecturer. The 21 students opted to study in the six-month course, 'Low decile education', with three-hour classes held on 12 occasions. The course's purpose is to critically examine research, theory and good practice related to NZ's urban schools, with an emphasis on Freirean ideas and processes. All students either taught in urban schools or were closely associated with such contexts. Students identified in particular with their ethnic origins (Maori [indigenous New Zealanders], Pakeha [white, usually of European ancestry], Pacific Islands or Pasifika [Samoan, Nuiean, Cook Islanders, Tongan], and Canadian) and genders (17 were women). Many speak English as a second language, but all are fluent speakers of English which is the accepted and usual language of instruction in NZ's state schools. Maori and sign language also have legal status. As I have indicated, economically poor and marginalised students gain entry to NZ universities, albeit with considerable obstacles prior to, and during, their studies. Many such postgraduate students teach in low socioeconomic schools and can thus be attracted to the 'Low decile education' course. I kept a reflective research diary during the course timeframe, and some diary content is included in this chapter as data.

Freire's ideas perhaps have stronger relevance to the observably oppressed than they do to those like Res and PgC members who have succeeded in becoming university students or qualified teachers. He first implemented his adult education theories in informal contexts, often amongst those who could not read and write. Unlike Freire, and more like his colleague Ira Shor, my context is the university, a privileged form of adult education. While some Res and PgC members may be marginalised in their daily lives due to their ethnic, sexual or gendered identities, all have potential power in their professional lives due to their teacher identities. The solidarity implicit in teaching, but particularly in urban, low socioeconomic school teaching, suggests a particular and empowering identity is possible for those wishing to pursue issues of social justice. Addressing and enabling such a possibility was central to our classroom processes.

Dialogical processes

Incorporating Freirean dialogical practices can constitute a worthwhile and empowering challenge for most learners and educators. As indicated above, Freire's work and ideas can resonate both with those who have power and those who do not. The former are able to replicate and perhaps take his methods into other, possibly oppressed, contexts. Res and PgC members undoubtedly had some power, and potential agency, in their urban school domains.

Selected aspects of dialogical processes from both cases are examined in the following sections. Theory is interspersed for illumination and reflection. The examples are presented according to five significant themes: 1) our communities and relationships; 2) politics and theory; 3) action research; 4) my role and pedagogy; and 5) the 'game' of university education.

Our communities and relationships

Despite very careful planning and preparation I rarely sleep well the night before first teaching any class; I am invariably anxious. Just like other classes, the most important sessions for both Res and PgC were the initial ones. They were the sessions where the groundwork was laid and the patterns set. In both cases, Res and PgC, not only was I teaching new classes for the first time, I was also challenging myself and the students to a new way of working, and I was not sure that it would succeed. A body of research testifies to the importance of relationships for effective teaching of marginalised groups (Carpenter, McMurchy-Pilkington, and Sutherland, 2004; Coleman, 1997; Hawk, Cowley, Hill, and Sutherland, 2002), and the first sessions were integral to our relationship forming.

Students arrived at both contexts with expectations of some form of lecture. In the case of PgC, paper or electronic notebooks were at the ready and pens or fingers poised. Students expected to be provided, at the very least, with a list of readings and the assessment requirements. Res arrived differently. They were more in a problem-solving mode. They were aware that they were going to be involved in action research and, as busy and task-focused women, they were ready to 'get on with it'. Res expected information on action research methodology and methods. In brief, both groups arrived expecting to experience a banking model of education.

Freire notes that 'there is no education that is non-directive' and 'the radical educator has to be an active presence in educational practice' (Macedo, 1995: 378–379). Building communities and relationships, establishing safe places for dialogue, and modelling how we could proceed without using a banking model were my intentions in those first two gatherings. While I undoubtedly had authority, I believed that my teaching could be done in a different way from the university norm and expectations.

The seemingly informal atmospheres of those two first sessions were in fact, carefully planned. I aimed to construct environments where there were conceptual spaces for affirmation of identities and respect for the same. I also hoped to develop critical consciousness and extend intellectuality. The planned activities were in no way 'laissez faire'. The latter types of methods, according to Freire, reproduce the values of the power structure (Macedo, 1995).

The groups and I spent sufficient time at the beginning mixing, mingling and getting to know each other. Res participated in a formal *powhiri* (welcome by indigenous Maori) as it was their first time on the university campus. Back in class the students met, shook hands/hongied (rubbed noses, Maori greeting) and talked with every other person in the room, me included.

In the case of PgC, meeting and greeting took a long time, almost an hour, but it was time well spent. We learned each other's names, workplaces, ethnicities, passions and expectations. We shared a little of our identities and worlds, and connections – sometimes historical – were made. A level of comfort was already evident as chairs and tables were then moved into a circular setting. Our sharing processes then continued, although in a somewhat more formal manner. Simple ground rules were co-established, such as not interrupting speakers and the non-necessity of routing all comments and questions though me, the lecturer. Conversations were vital for our epistemological journeys, our object was knowledge and everyone's worlds and words (not just mine) were critical. We all had expertise and experiences, and we could all learn from each other. While I probably had a stronger theoretical and research knowledge than the students there was much that I could learn about practice. The first sessions were also the appropriate places to introduce students to Freirean pedagogy; to not do this would be disingenuous and could risk alienating some students.

Res' feedback on the positive aspects of their first day included:

thinking, learning, reflection time away from work;
knowing what it is and not being 'afraid' of it now!!
great group of people, good discussions, relaxed and humorous interaction;
working with people who are passionate about the same thing, meeting people, working with others from other schools;
interactive group work, enjoying the company of the group, listening to the experiences shared by the group;
taking part in a powhiri *(formal Maori welcome ceremony);*
the all-women environment.

What is especially pleasing about the feedback from the first day of Res is that Colleen's and my names were not mentioned. We were there, we took part, we were involved in the dialogical processes, but we did not bank knowledge and we were not the centre of attention.

PgC also provided feedback on aspects helpful to their learning in the early sessions:

Clarity of information shared;
Interactive classroom environment;
Felt free to ask questions;
Passion.

Relationship-forming on the first days and throughout the following sessions was partially aimed at increasing social capital. Social capital is about the connections, usually positive, that we have and make as we live our lives (Baron, Field, and Schuller, 2000; Coleman, 1997; Putnam, 2000). Just like economic capital, social capital compounds – the more people we know, the more connections we have, the more connections we are likely to accumulate. Research has demonstrated that an increase in social capital results in an improved ability to be successful and live a long and healthy life (Putnam, 2000). Teachers from both groups had huge potential for social capital gains: '. . . [as] teachers actively and routinely collaborate to innovate and share knowledge – social capital becomes a lubricant of knowledge transfer and development, and it pays considerable educational dividends' (Halpern, 2005: 159).

A key component in social capital building for Res was the *marae* overnight experience. The main purpose of the overnight stay was to introduce students to the lived realities of many Maori students who have strong connections to *marae* in rural areas; forming relationships and building social capital were extra dividends. Preparing and eating food together, then sleeping on mattresses on the floor in a communal space provided opportunities for us to understand and know each other better.

Mention must be made of food. There are no cultures in the world that I am aware of who do not place some significance on food. In both cases, food and the sharing of it played an integral part in cementing our relationships. For the Res group, the occasional trip to a restaurant (funded by the research budget) complemented the women's busy lives and indicated to them that we valued them and respected their energy. Their positive feedback noted such things as the *kai* (food) and *lovely morning tea and lunch*. For PgC, food was always waiting on the table for students when they arrived at 4:30pm after their busy days in schools. The food said to them, 'you must be tired and this will help sustain you through the next few hours'.

These pedagogical situations, which facilitated the building of social capital, juxtapose with the ghetto-like situations which have evolved in recent years regarding PD for urban schoolteachers. The tight monetary constraints of neoliberal policies have meant poorer schools cannot afford what they would like to offer professionals and this has resulted in limited PD opportunities. While teachers sensed that their work was becoming more technocratic, and their levels of autonomy were declining, most did not have the words or political understanding to describe their situations.

Politics and theory

Ameliorating education-related social justice issues was the underpinning purpose of our time together. To fight oppression (in our case, underachievement by children in poverty) one must first critically understand any underpinning causes and effects. This calls for the development of what Freire describes as 'epistemological curiosity – a curiosity that is often missing in dialogue as conversation' (Macedo, 1995: 382). Such curiosity needs feeding, and the necessary nurturing comes from practice (or worlds), and from historical, theoretical and political understandings (or words).

> *It's good to be able to talk with other teachers, instead of just being in your own world or your own class. I mean talking to the other teachers on the project. We talk a lot about what we're doing. If they (the other teachers in the school) had been on some sort of project they might talk too – it widens your horizons; you see the school from a different angle, we're talking about learning* (notes from the reflective journal teacher researcher A, Res group)

PgC students' feedback on what was most helpful for their learning:

> *Discussion on readings;*
> *The readings, the discussions;*
> *Student to student discourse, then summarising and questioning from lecturer;*
> *The interactive 'Freirean' approach;*
> *A mix of theory and practice. I particularly enjoyed the theory aspects.*

Our engagement with theory gives rise to our intellectuality and a good teacher is an intellectual; someone who engages critically with all she or he reads, observes and hears. Is it possible to learn of history, urban-school-related theory, and politics if someone with more knowledge than us does not suggest to us what we need to know, or indicate what we could read?

While such practices do not gel easily with the notion of dialogical teaching, theory in some form is indispensible. Kanu and Glor (2006) argue that teachers, using a range of tools including the theoretical, need to transform themselves into amateur intellectuals. Such intellectuals are sceptical of political and social trends, and they raise any moral issues at the heart of technical and professional activities. According to Kanu and Glor, teachers must learn to 'teach in ways they were not taught, commit to continuous learning and reflection, and work and learn both alone and in professional teams where they can raise moral questions about practice and access knowledge from the collective intelligence of the team' (Kanu and Glor, 2006: 103).

Teaching is highly complex work and the additional requirements of the neoliberal based knowledge economy mean that teachers often have to function in fragmented ways (Kanu and Glor, 2006). We had to find a range of ways of accessing and sharing knowledge. Both Res and PgC students had minimal understanding of how the global and NZ's political systems worked. Many of the younger students in particular were not aware of how political moves to the left or the right impact on teachers' professional lives, urban schools and children in poverty. Teachers' work was at the micro level and the issues there were so great that little time was left in normal working days for teachers to reflect on macro political or economic issues.

Our own practice and theory-related knowledge, shared through dialogue, was preceded or followed by readings of works by critical theorists in education such as Jean Anyon (1997, 2005), Michael Apple (2004), John Codd (2008) and Roger Dale (1989, 2008). The important point, the point which precludes a banking methodology, is the use in the previous sentence of the word *critical*. In other words, all readings shared with students were positioned as problematic and open to critique (Shor, 1992: 35).

> *... what is important, what is indispensible, is to be critical. Criticism creates the necessary intellectual discipline, asking questions to the reading, to the writing, to the book, to the text. We should not submit to the text or be submissive in front of the text. The thing is to fight with the text, even though loving it, no? To engage in conflict with the text . . . it is a very, very, very demanding operation. The question then is not just to impose on the students quantities of chapters from books, but to demand that students confront seriously the texts* (Freire in Shor and Freire, 1987: 11).

Textual and theoretical confrontation:

How to achieve this? One method I used to facilitate serious textual confrontation was the co-operative jigsaw learning technique (Van der Kley, 1991). In PgC I sometimes chose four articles or book chapters centred on a topic, for instance gender or race issues in education. The class was divided into four groups and each group read, outside of class and without any prior input from me, one of the four writings.

At the following class the students first spent time – at least an hour but however much was necessary – with peers in their group who had read the same work. Groups were encouraged to engage critically with their readings, and to see the works as problematic.

> *In the readings you gave us, the one I had to interpret (for a sharing session with the group) I thought 'I do this! I do this!'* (notes from the reflective journal of teacher researcher C, Res group)

PgC students' feedback on what was most helpful for their learning:

> *Class discussions and sharing of our understandings of readings;*
> *Access to lots of high quality readings;*
> *The readings added significantly to my knowledge;*
> *The political issues in education shared by various researchers.*

Questions such as the following guided discussions: Do we understand this reading? Why or why not? Can we translate it into language which reaches us all? Who wrote it? How does the writer's bias show? Whose interests are served by the writings? What is the argument which holds this writing together? How well is the argument expressed? Is the evidence for the argument enough? How does this work relate to our existing understandings and knowledge? How does this work have relevance to our contexts? What can I/we learn from this reading? How does this writing encourage us to read/learn more? How does this work link into other reading we have done? So what? Has this article moved my understandings?

Freire describes the possibilities offered by theory:

> *I cannot conceive of the possibility that a written dialogue – just because it is fixed in time – ceases being alive or loses its dynamism. The task and challenge*

> ... *is to rewrite the text by dialoguing with its author via the written text ... and with the potential incompleteness of the ideas ... though its initial force may be fixed in time, it is a historical document, emerging from a specific historical context, and that at the same time it is a document that provides the possibility of unveiling in new ways in a different historical time.* (Freire et al., 1997: 319).

The second stage of the co-operative learning technique involves mixing the groups. Each new group has one or some representatives from the original four groups; in other words one or more people are present in the new groups who have read and discussed each one of the original four works. This stage can take upwards of two hours or more, as the original readers share their understandings, translate and critically reflect on the work they have read and discussed. Experience has shown me that, despite the scaffolding of the first stage, some students are reticent about speaking and sharing their epistemological perspectives – they prefer and have every right to remain silent. Pairing or larger clustering takes tensions away for some, and it keeps the focus on the true purpose of the exercise.

The final stage often, but not always, is a class discussion. The mood of the class, and the feeling I have as I circulate amongst the groups in both of the previous stages, helps my decision making at the time. Whether or not we conclude with a class discussion the co-operative learning exercise usually means a deeper critical understanding of the texts by students, an understanding that sometimes takes them from a dichotomous position regarding theory and practice to some sense of unity and possibility.

The place of the lecture in a dialogic approach:

Despite some misgivings I occasionally present a lecture. I acknowledge there is a place for such pedagogy, particularly in PgC and especially if the lecture engages, enlightens and challenges thinking. What I find crucial is the tenor of any lecture, and its critical engagement with students' minds. Nobody likes to be told things they already know, and that is always a risk with a lecture model.

For some sessions I prepared a lecture in the normal manner. This can take many, many hours. However, before presenting the lecture, I engage the students in dialogue surrounding the lecture topic. An example was a lecture on the relevance of capital (cultural, human, social and economic), which I researched and prepared for PgC. Rather than simply presenting the lecture, the class and I first talked. We established what the class knew (a great deal, on a personal and school/community level), and I then adapted and extended my lecture to fill in the spaces, make links, build bridges from student knowledge bases, and pose appropriate problems. Students could interrupt my lecture at will, and many did – for clarification or to provide greater depth by contributing their knowledge and understandings.

Such a lecturing strategy, while meeting student epistemological needs, reduced the possibility of communicating materials and facts the students already knew. Lecturing in this way is a very delicate and intricate dance as the lecturer never knows and cannot predict the direction that learning will take. Humbleness is necessary, plus a willingness to be open regarding one's own knowledge limitations. In many ways such lecturing was a personal pedagogical challenge and a highlight for me. If a lecture was successful, both the students and I emerged from it intellectually exhausted.

Action research

Teachers in the Res programme each completed an action research project. As indicated, the projects were aimed at raising the achievement levels of Maori students, promoting a social justice related agenda. Being involved in research was a major undertaking for group members, most of whom had not been involved in any postgraduate study since gaining their initial teaching qualifications. Many writers assert the importance of teachers being also researchers (for examples see Butler, 1992; Kincheloe, 2003; Robinson, 2003). In his work, Joe Kincheloe acknowledges the importance of the teacher researcher, but also shares his fears surrounding teachers being positioned, in this neoliberal age, as technocrats; workers who spend their days with students attempting to meet externally imposed standards:

> *Promoting teachers as researchers is a fundamental way of cleaning up the damage of technical standards. Deskilling of teachers and dumbing-down of the curriculum take place when teachers are seen as receivers not producers of knowledge. A vibrant professional culture depends on a group of practitioners who have the freedom to continuously reinvent themselves via their research and knowledge production. Teachers engaged in complex, critical practice find it difficult to allow positivistic standards and their poisonous*

> *effects to go unchallenged. Such teachers cannot abide the deskilling and reduction in professional status that accompany these top-down reforms* (Kincheloe, 2003: 19).

A dialogical and power-sharing/empowering process best describes our way of working with action research. While the women's multiple identities often centred on that of *teacher*, we wished to include *researcher* in those repertoires. Colleen and I shared Kincheloe's belief (2003) that best possible results emerge, for teachers and students, when teachers research their own practice (rather than external researchers entering classrooms to conduct research).

Theory-based readings and discussions ensured we all had a good understanding of NZ's urban school context. This knowledge was complemented by the examination of a range of theory plus researched explanations and solutions for the problems we saw in the system. Only then did the women begin to talk through and share their prospective classroom, or school-based, research questions. Our deliberating and dialogical processes were very important, and they needed to take as long as was necessary. We all helped ensure that each teacher researcher's focus came from her experience and knowledge base, that it was focused enough, and that her question or problem was researchable. Colleen and I wanted the best possible prior conditions to be in place to enable positive outcomes for the action researchers and their participants. All of us played 'devil's advocate' for each other's ideas and eventually six problems were identified and ready for the university ethics committee's approval.

Gaining ethics approval was a stressful and very much a top-down procedure. Awareness grew exponentially about university politics and requirements. One teacher researcher, at the end of the research process, rightfully criticised the committee's requirements. The committee obliged the teacher researcher to send a formal participant information letter to parents of the children in her class. After receiving the letter, one parent contacted the teacher, very pleased. As the letter was written on university letterhead, the parent thought her child had early acceptance to university. Distressing and embarrassing as this issue was for the researcher and participants, its sharing meant that Res members learned how language and symbols, despite people's best intentions, can be confusing, alienating and possibly oppressive. Res members reflected on the distance between what they described as the 'ivory towers' of the university and their own workplaces/schools and communities; and a sense of solidarity was seeded. Recognition of the need for attention to openness and social justice is evident in the following:

> *Communication needs to be in a language or manner that parents understand. Communicating appropriately will diffuse any misconceptions, and provide the community with the knowledge they need in order to understand and participate in future research programmes* (notes from the reflective journal of teacher researcher C, Res group).

Dialogical processes ensued throughout the various research activities — as indicated, often these were over meals, and sometimes they occurred during smaller meetings. Much of the talk involved the sharing of both fears and findings, and the meaning of the latter related to strategies to deal with them. The final stage of the research involved presentations and this meant teacher researchers had the opportunity to present their research and findings to a range of audiences. All agreed to present together at a public university forum and, although daunting, it was a very successful and bonding event. The teacher researchers invited their peers, colleagues and families, and there was the usual eclectic mix of university and Ministry of Education people present. The public university presentations sealed and enhanced participants' identities as teacher researchers as well as teachers.

> *Another teacher has come up to me and asked how we're doing it, the action research. She has some problems and wants me to help her, but I told her I may not have the answers* (notes from the reflective journal teacher researcher A, Res group)

After the public presentations some took a further step and chose to publish their work for an even wider audience. This aspect is an ongoing process and Colleen and I are sometimes involved as co-authors. An excerpt from a co-publication is included below. Chris is a school principal who set up a programme to work with a disruptive group of boys in her school:

> *The critical consciousness provided through the professional development and the research community processes of Te Whakapakari was central to the success of the project. The nature of the critical action research meant that Chris was able to share her concerns, joys, directions and fears in a safe way with a*

professional and critically reflective group . . . The critical action research process meant that Chris acknowledged to the research community that the boys' interests were not being served by the status quo; in turn the community's dialogical processes gave her support to take the courageous action necessary for positive results. (Carpenter and Cooper, 2009: 611).

My role and pedagogy

I was not in class to be the friend of the students or to enter and take from their worlds. I was the lecturer and as such had an important role to perform. This role includes, as Shor (1992) suggests, problematising students' realities and engaging students in problem-posing and problem-solving.

To do this I needed to help students take a critical perspective on the seemingly common-sense and taken for granted, on issues which had social justice related dimensions. My reflection below is reasonably typical; it demonstrates that my journey was not easy, and nor should it have been.

> *. . . a discussion-lecture on critical theory. Again, I felt I talked too much. However right near the end Fatu (Samoan) and Sonja (Paheka) (pseudonyms) engaged in a debate re ethnicity – the atmosphere was tense, and time was running out, unfortunately (or fortunately?). We will need to work on this more next time – the importance of debate and how we can discuss ideas and not get too personal. There was a little tension as people left, some discomfort; I need to remind the class of the importance of disequilibrium for personal growth* (my notes, PgC class).

In a sense I wanted Res and PgC members to move beyond possibly fixed internal positions, their ethnic and gender identities for instance, to the production of new ways of seeing themselves in relation to the world; to identify also as proud professionals – working alongside colleagues, parents, communities and students in low socioeconomic schools – who were able to make a positive difference to their students' lives.

My role in all of this was not that of a facilitator:

> *Teachers maintain a certain level of authority through the depth and breadth of knowledge of the subject matter that they teach. The teacher who claims to be a facilitator and not a teacher is renouncing, for reasons unbeknownst to us,*

the task of teaching and, hence, the task of dialogue (Freire's words, in Macedo, 1995: 378).

I have already signalled the importance of co-operative learning activities. I learned most of what I know about such activities from reading (Van der Kley, 1991), experiments and experiences. All co-operative learning 'recipes' need adaption in some way to fit students' and teachers' learning needs. Sometimes we do not need theory or prior experience to guide us; our instincts simply tell us how to be co-operative and inclusive, or the students show the way. Particularly noticeable in my classes were Maori and Pasifika ways of knowing how to work in supportive ways. On many occasions Polynesian students taught us all. In a sense the tables were turned in Res and PgC. The people who shared their wisdom and insights, and guided us all, tended to be those whose voices are not often heard in NZ's mainstream banking classes; those who identified as Maori, Pasifika, and women. Our dialogical processes worked particularly well with those whose identities are usually marginalised.

> *A Maori woman spoke passionately about how she and her village succeeded in school – she gave credit to their teachers in a low socioeconomic innovative school who had high expectations. Our classroom discussions took us to the realization that there is no one answer (to underachievement) for all people at all times, and that politics is always involved* (my notes, PgC class).

> *Lots of laughing and banter tonight, particularly from Maori and Pasifika students – Pakeha are quiet by comparison. I wonder why? I suspect the theory and concepts are disconcerting for some, and challenging* (my notes, PgC class).

Learning to be silent, learning to wait, and engineering respectful spaces where all can share their worlds and thoughts were amongst my biggest challenges. As an experienced teacher, and used to being the 'font of all knowledge', it is difficult for me to be silent. I usually know the answer, therefore is it not better to use the classroom time wisely and impart my knowledge? Also, the students expected me to know; why else would I be paid to teach them?

One PgC student suggested in her/his feedback that there needed to be *'more structure in classes rather than just discussion'*. This student was alone with this suggestion, and the inclusion of the words here is illustrative of the possible tensions which can emerge. In contrast to this, another student found *'the Freire approaches used by Vicki'*, and *'open discussions'* to be helpful for learning. Despite appearances, teaching in a dialogical manner is far from easy. Student thinking and reflection take time, and all work differently. For some students, English is not their first language, some ideas that people shared were very complex, and others just needed the time to gather their thoughts together. While circle seating was used in most teaching situations there was still a tendency to route conversation through me as a kind of conduit.

My personal head space was what I had to deal with in my reaction to classroom silence, and my concerns regarding student deferrals to my position. Self talk, combined with a studious gaze out the window at times meant that silence became important spaces in our sounds, and deferrals to me were minimised.

> *I really have to control myself as I can feel tense, wanting to get on with my banking model. But – their sharing can be so profound. Last night we learned of transient people sleeping in fields while other family members picked vegetables. I had never heard of this happening in our country, and I suspect it was news to most of the class* (my notes, PgC class).

> *The wisdom of the older women in the class is evident – they know and have lived the history* (my notes, PgC class).

The 'game' of university education

Delpit (1995, 2006, 1997) writes of students who are failed by education systems. Influenced by Freire, she maintains that alternative world views (to those of the majority or those who have power) need to be included in classrooms. At the same time as accepting and valuing students' own languages and styles we need to ensure that they know that there is a political power game being played. If we teach well, then students will learn other games as well as their own. Marginalised and less powerful students should ideally be taught the codes of those with power; this will enable the marginalised or oppressed to participate more fully in mainstream life. Codes are arbitrary and they represent power relations. High expectations of all students are essential, and good liberal intentions on the part of educators are not enough.

The reason so much of Delpit is included in this section is that her messages, in particular, resonated and spoke to both the Res and PgC students, and with me. Sometimes students will have what is often described as an 'Aha!' moment, and the deconstruction of Delpit's ideas achieved that, particularly for white, middle-class students. Students who identified as brown, working-class and women oft-times already instinctively understood Delpit's messages.

As a teacher of adults, Delpit's messages prompt me to think very deeply about the students I work with and our learning context. What is the political 'game' of the university? Are my practices or the university's alienating some students? Which ones? How? Concerns surrounding the university's ethics procedures have already been discussed. I reflect quite often on the assessment tasks I use: Could they be more 'user friendly'? Do I want to test English essay writing skills, or do I really want to know how well students have critically come to grips with material the course is centred on. Do assessment tasks have to be individual and seemingly competitive? Are group and oral presentations possible? Should I be the only person who assesses student work? Do I always need to be involved in the assessment processes? How could peer assessment work? Why do marginalised students and women in particular, often comment negatively about their work as they hand in their submissions? How can I be more inclusive of students who struggle with English as a second language? I further explore the answers to these questions in other publications (Carpenter, 2010a, 2010b), but in the two classes described above, in some way or another, we confronted them all.

Conclusion

The underlying argument in this chapter is that the dialogical processes in Res and PgC were instrumental in producing new and additional forms of solidarity and identity. Those new identities included teacher researcher, advocate for low socioeconomic schools and communities, teacher intellectual, academic, and fighter for the oppressed. Kincheloe and Steinberg (1997: 27) write of the production of identity, and describe it as the way we see ourselves in relation to the world. They suggest that, for solidarity, we need sometimes to move beyond fixed identity positions, and they warn of the dangers inherent when only those who belong to privileged groups are able to analyse and speak. New identity formation enabled solidarity within the PgC and Res groups. Ultimately student and teacher feedback indicated that PgC and Res members felt better equipped to 'pursue an egalitarian, democratic vision' (Kincheloe and Steinberg, 1997) for low socioeconomic schools and communities.

PgC student course evaluation comments:

> *This course has given me access to literature important to the educational context I work in. It's given me a much deeper understanding of the impact of society, economics and politics play in education. I feel like it's refreshed me in a sense, I'm really motivated to get back into the classroom next year and do what I do best.*

> *During the open discussions I came to realise how my colleagues felt about their students and other teachers.*

> *The course grounds us/reminds us as teachers of the reason why we choose to be teachers in the first place – to humanise, make people whole and ourselves whole in the process.*

A critical reader may reflect on the potential portability of NZ-based classroom approaches. Will the ideas and specific strategies work with different students, in perhaps work-based or non-university-based programmes, on the other side of the world? I believe all of the strategies can be adapted, and every one is transportable in some way. While most European tertiary institutions are unlikely to have students who identify as Maori or Pasifika, their cohorts will probably include those whose identities are perhaps non-white, women, or marginalised. Generic pedagogical practices, such as dialogical methods, can be adapted and will work in adult education in most countries and contexts.

Will such practices help adult education students work towards ameliorating social justice issues? Feedback indicates that the participants' tangles of perceptions and understandings were both sorted and clarified, partly due to our dialogical methods. At the same time, our ways of working provided models which can be emulated in all schools. Teachers returned to their workplaces equipped with optimism, a critical theory based stance, and experience with dialogical strategies. Underachievement by children in poverty was unacceptable to them; PgC and Res members' identities were extended and enriched with their new sense of solidarity, and they were more aware of positive ways they could work towards social justice.

Working in a dialogical manner is not something that can be read about and learned overnight. My experience tells me it is a journey which is best undertaken with small and measured steps, with a focus on the learners, their identities, their worlds, and social justice. During the past three years my work in adult education has changed to such an extent that I am now uncomfortable teaching in any way other than the dialogical. Even in undergraduate lectures, to perhaps 400 students, I seek ways to be inclusive, to merge, in a critical manner, my words and worlds with those of the audience. I continue to learn and grow – currently my thoughts centre on how technology and web-based teaching can be more dialogical, and on the range of possibilities offered by interactive web sites. Information is now available everywhere, the world's bank of knowledge is available at the push of a button through the internet on home computers. A banking model of education is therefore passé. It is time for teachers of adults to internalise that their evolving and central role, more and more, is to encourage critical thinking.

I have varying levels of success with my teaching and I have much to learn. In many ways the market model, which justifies large classes on the basis of economics, has the potential to preclude the intimacy and relationships which are essential and desirable in identity enhancement and formation, and the pedagogical exchange. We must know where we stand and fight for the right to engage, debate, and work for social justice.

References

Anyon, J. (1997) *Ghetto schooling. A political economy of urban educational reform.* New York: Teachers College Press.

Anyon, J. (2005) *Radical possibilities. Public policy, urban education and a new social movement.* New York: Routledge.

Anyon, J., Dumas, M. J., Linville, D., Nolan, K., Perez, M., Tuck, E. et al. (2009) *Theory and educational research. Toward critical social explanation.* New York: Routledge.

Apple, M. W. (2004) *Ideology and Curriculum* (Third Edition). New York: RoutledgeFalmer.

Baron, S., Field, J. and Schuller, T. (eds) (2000) *Social capital. Critical perspectives.* Oxford: Oxford University Press.

Barry, A. (1996) *Someone else's country* [DVD]. Wellington: Community Media Trust.

Becker, J. R. (1995) 'Women's ways of knowing in mathematics', in Rogers, P. and Kaiser G. (eds), (1995) *Equity in mathematics education*, 163–74. London: Falmer.

Blaiklock, A. J., Kiro, C. A., Belgrave, M., Low, W., Davenport, E., and Hassall, I. B. (2002) *When the invisible hand rocks the cradle: New Zealand children in a time of change* (No. 93 Innocenti Working Papers). Florence: UNICEF Innocenti Research Centre.

Butler, J. (1992) 'Teacher professional development: an Australian case study', *Journal of Education for Teaching*, 18: 3, 221–38.

Carpenter, V. M. (2008) 'Teaching New Zealand's 'children of the poor'', in Carpenter *et al.*, 109–21.

Carpenter, V. M., Jesson J., Roberts P. and M. Stephenson (eds) (2008) *Ngā Kaupapa Here; connections and contradictions in education*. South Melbourne: Cengage Learning.

Carpenter, V. M. (2010a) 'Opening eyes to different worlds', *Waikato Journal of Education*, 15: 1, 121–33.

Carpenter, V. M. (2010b) 'Worlds and words: education for social justice', in Jesson J., V. M. Carpenter, M. McLean, M. Stephenson and Airini (eds) *University teaching reconsidered. Justice, practice, inquiry*. Palmerston North, NZ: Dunmore Press.

Carpenter, V. M. and Cooper, C. (2009) 'Critical action research: the achievement group', *Educational Action Research*, 17: 4, 601–13.

Carpenter, V. M., and McMurchy–Pilkington, C. (2007) *Te Whakapakari: Pouako me nga akonga. The strengthening: learners and teachers. Project report for the Manurewa Enhancement Initiative (MEI)*. Auckland: Manurewa Enhancement Initiative.

Carpenter, V. M., McMurchy–Pilkington, C. and Sutherland, S. (2004) *Kaiako Toa* (ACEpapers monograph series No. 6). Auckland: Faculty of Education, University of Auckland.

Chitty, C. (2002) 'Education and social class', *Political Quarterly*, 73: 2, 208–10.

Codd, J. (2008) 'Neoliberalism, globalisation and the deprofessionalisation of teachers', in Carpenter *et al.*, 14–24.

Coleman, J. S. (1997) 'Social capital in the creation of human capital', in Halsey *et al.*, 80–95. Oxford: Oxford University Press.

Dale, R. (1989) *The state and education policy*. Milton Keynes: Open University Press.

Dale, R. (2008) 'Globalisation and education in Aotearoa/New Zealand', in Carpenter *et al.*, 25–35.

Delpit, L. (1995) *Other people's children. Cultural conflict in the classroom.* New York: The New Press.

Delpit, L. (2006) 'Lessons from teachers', *Journal of Teacher Education*, 57: 3, 220–31.

Delpit, L. D. (1997) 'The silenced dialogue: power and pedagogy in educating other people's children', in Halsey *et al.*, 582–94.

Department of Education. (1988) *Tomorrow's Schools. The reform of education administration in New Zealand.* Wellington: Department of Education.

Esposito, J. and Evans-Winters, V. (2007) 'Contextualising critical action research: lessons from urban educators'. *Educational Action Research*, 15: 2, 221–37.

Freire, P. (1972) *The pedagogy of the oppressed.* London: Penguin Books.

Freire, P. (2005) *Teachers as cultural workers. Letters to those who dare teach.* Boulder: Westview Press.

Freire, P., Fraser, J. W., Macedo, D., McKinnon, T., and Stokes, W. T. (eds) (1997) *Mentoring the mentor: a critical dialogue with Paulo Freire.* New York: Peter Lang.

Galguera, T. (2005) 'Learning to see the invisible', in Kroll, L. R., Cossey, R., Donahue, D. M., Galguera, T., LaBoskey, V. K., Richert, A. E. and Tucher, P. (eds) *Teaching as principled practice. Managing complexity for social justice*, 121–41. Thousand Oaks, California: Sage.

Gandin, L. A. and Fischman, G. E. (2006) 'Participatory democratic education: Is the utopia possible? Porto Alegre's citizen school project', in Kincheloe, J. L., Hayes, K., Rose, K. and Anderson, P. M. (eds) *The Praeger handbook of urban education*, Volume 1, 135–141. Westport, CT: Greenwood Press.

Gordon, G. and Whitchurch, C. (eds). (2010) *Academic and professional identities in higher education. The challenges of a diversifying workforce.* New York: Routledge.

Halpern, D. (2005) *Social capital.* Cambridge: Polity Press.

Halsey, A. H., Lauder, H., Brown, P. and Wells, A. S. (eds) (1997) *Education. Culture, economy and society.* Oxford: Oxford University Press.

Hammersley, M. (2000) 'Critical or uncritical, is that the question? On researchers as public intellectuals engaged in social criticism', paper presented at the BERA conference, Cardiff University.

Hawk, K., Cowley, E. T., Hill, J. and Sutherland, S. (2002) The importance of the teacher/student relationship for Maori and Pasifika students. *Set: Research Information for Teachers*, 3: 44–9.

Hawk, K. and Hill, J. (2000) *Making a Difference in the Classrooms* (AIMHI report). Wellington: Ministry of Education.

hooks, b. (1994) *Teaching to transgress. Education as the practice of freedom.* New York: Routledge.

Jackson, S. (2004) *Differently academic: developing lifelong learning for women in higher education.* Dordrecht, the Netherlands: Kluwer.

Jones, A. (1992) 'Writing feminist educational research: Am "I" in the text?' in Middleton, S. and Jones, A. (eds) *Women and Education in Aotearoa*, Vol. 2, 18–32. Wellington: Bridget Williams Books.

Kanu, Y. and Glor, M. (2006) '"Currere" to the rescue? Teachers as "amateur intellectuals" in a knowledge society', *Journal of the Canadian Association for Curriculum Studies*, 4: 2, 101–22.

Kelsey, J. (1995) *The New Zealand experiment. A world model for structural adjustment?* Auckland: Auckland University Press and Bridget Williams Books.

Kincheloe, J. L. and Steinberg, S. R. (1997) *Changing multiculturalism.* Buckingham UK: Open University Press.

Kincheloe, J. (2003) *Teachers as researchers. Qualitative inquiry as a path to empowerment* (second edn). London: RoutledgeFalmer.

Kumashiro, K. K. (2009) *Against common sense. Teaching and learning toward social justice* (revised edn). New York: Routledge.

Macedo, D. P. (1995) 'A dialogue: culture, language and race', *Harvard Educational Review*, 65: 3, 377–93.

Ministry of Education (2005) *Briefing for the incoming Minister of Education.* Wellington: Ministry of Education.

Ministry of Education (2006) *The big picture: student outcome overview 2001–2005.* Wellington: Ministry of Education.

OECD (2007) *Top–performer Finland improves further in PISA survey as gap between countries widens.* www://www.oecd.org/document/28/0,2340,en_2649_201185_34010524_1_1_1_1,00.html.

Putnam, R. D. (2000) *Bowling alone.* New York: Simon and Schuster.

Roberts, P. (2008) 'Teaching as an ethical and political process: a Freirean perspective', in Carpenter *et al.*, 99–108.

Robinson, V. (2003) Teachers as researchers: a professional necessity? *Set: Research Information for Teachers*, 1, 27–29.

Sahlberg, P. (2007) 'Education policies for raising student learning: the Finnish approach', *Journal of Education Policy*, 22: 2, 147–71.

Shor, I. (1992) *Empowering education. Critical teaching for social change.* Chicago: University of Chicago Press.

Shor, I. (1996) *When students have power. Negotiating authority in a critical pedagogy*. Chicago: The University of Chicago Press.

Shor, I. and Freire, P. (1987) *A pedagogy for liberation. Dialogues on transforming education*. Westport, CT: Bergin and Garvey.

Shor, I. and Pari, C. (eds) (1999) *Critical literacy in action. Writing words, changing worlds*. Portsmouth, NH: Boynton and Cook.

St John, S. and Wynd, D. (eds) (2008) *Left behind: How social and income inequalities damage New Zealand children*. Auckland: Child Poverty Action Group.

Sullivan, K. (1994) 'The impact of educational reform on teachers' professional ideologies', *New Zealand Journal of Educational Studies*, 29: 1, 3–20.

Van der Kley, M. (1991) *Co–operative learning, and how to make it happen in your classroom*. Christchurch, NZ: M. Van der Kley.

Weiler, K. (1988) *Women teaching for change*. Massachusetts: Bergin and Garvey.

Wilkinson, R. and Pickett, K. (2009). *The spirit level. Why more equal societies almost always do better*. London: Penguin.

Young, M. F. D. (1998) *The curriculum of the future. From the 'new sociology of education' to a critical theory of learning*. London: Falmer.

CHAPTER TEN

Challenging constructed learner identities: Women's informal learning

HELEN ABERTON

Introduction

> *I had a guy ring up last night and he was doing a Gallup Poll. And it was –* *'What standard of education did you go to? Did you go to Tertiary Education?' And I said – 'No'. But it's like – well if you don't, you have got nothing. You're not recognised at all in what you have achieved* (Sarah: Int 1, 2007).

According to the dominant epistemology of learning, the learning which resides in individual minds is the traditional benchmark for judging the worth of learning (Hager, 2005). Lifelong learning rhetoric has extended to lifelong and lifewide learning, and now pays more attention to 'informal' learning. However, while the discourse continues to privilege assumptions and practices of educational institutions, the unplanned, *ad hoc* nature of everyday learning is seen as weak, trivial and lacking authenticity as legitimate learning. For example, adult education discourse focuses on the construct of identity, or more specifically 'learner identity' which assumes the dominance of cognitive learning and formal learning discourse. Furthermore, policies and practices of lifelong learning hide multiple layers of injustices that operate around processes of identity formation (Burke and Jackson, 2007). Constructs of learner identity do not encompass all adult learning, and therefore are not all inclusive. Additionally, constructed labels such as reluctant learners, resistant learners, non-traditional learners, and 'non-learners' create a deficit model of learners who need education. Binaries are rampant. People in the 'knowledge society' are either constructed as educable subjects (Fejes, 2006) or 'other'. Individual identities are either learners or non-learners.

Alternatively, learning can be considered as an outcome of activities or sets of practices which are practically and discursively performed and performative. These practices connect and overlap in hybrid spaces where realities not governed by traditional discourse are enacted and emerge into view. It involves the recognition and understanding of local places as nodal points in networks of social relations, discourses, material resources and representations (Nespor, 2002). From an actor-network viewpoint of learning, the psychological conception of the 'learner' as an 'individual', discrete entity is not accepted. Instead, actors are seen as 'distributed' with shifting boundaries and compositions that spread across space and as well as time (Nespor, 1994). In this chapter I argue that actor-network theory affords an alternative framing for the study of learning and identity formation and opens up the possibility to challenge educational constructs and associated limiting dualisms.

This chapter is divided into four sections. After an initial discussion of identity and learning in everyday life, the next section provides a brief outline of changes in learning theory and how an actor-network approach opens up new possibilities for researching learning. This is followed by a description of my doctoral study (in-process) and an analysis of empirical data. I conclude with a discussion of different ways learning is viewed and the implications for social justice.

Identity and learning

Assuming a poststructuralist understanding of identity as unfixed, unstable, contradictory, complex and contingent on external factors, I argue that mainstream educational research constructs, subject to the way in which we frame an understanding of lifelong learning and context, are limited and limiting. But the crucial question is: what really counts as learning?

> *What counts as learning is highly contested and is tied in with competing constructions of who is a learner, what learning means and where learning can take place. These conceptions are always classed, gendered and racialised. In the current hegemonic discourses of lifelong learning, what counts as learning*

is bound up with particular middle-classed values and perspectives around the decontextualized individual learner; notions of citizenship that are tied in with lifelong learning; neoliberal constructions of the flexible learner/worker; and learning that happens in the public rather than the private sphere of social life (Burke and Jackson, 2007: 13).

The lifelong learning policy of Australia's adult and community education (ACE) sector is based on the Delors (1996) pillars of learning. The government:

supports a collaborative approach to ACE, particularly in relation to its role in the provision of vocationally focused education and training and fostering the development of skills required for individuals to participate fully in their communities and the economy (Ministerial declaration on adult community education, 2008).

ACE programmes tend to privilege vocational learning and 'second chance' learners for training, and 'supporting productivity in Australia' (Julia Gillard, Deputy Prime Minister, Media release, 2009) at the expense of educating for well-being and full participation in communities. Australia's apparent emphasis on gaining vocational skills and qualifications also reflects the current government policy in the United Kingdom (Burke and Jackson, 2007: 11).

At the same time, learning takes place outside education as people participate in everyday living – pursuing new adventures, interests or social experiences in practices such as: working allotments and caravanning (Crouch, 2003); dancing and frequenting local markets (de Carteret, 2008); participating in men's sheds (Golding, 2009); home-making (Eichler, 2005b); participating in local institutions, churches or related projects (Conradson, 2003; Willis, 2000); and in community organisations (Mündel and Schugurensky, 2005). In contexts in which women predominate as unpaid workers, such as in the homeplace, learning is devalued or ignored (Gouthro, 2005), even though it is real work in terms of the time and energy it requires, in terms of the goods and services it produces, and in terms of its economic impact. It is not regarded as such (Eichler, 2005a). These comprise some of the practices with which many lifelong learners identify: practices through which they develop and maintain a sense of self and place. The argument is made that as learning in these practices is not restricted to the traditional knowledge-making discourses and the development of an identifiable, decontextualised learner identity, there is a need to look at learning, and identity formation in different ways. Furthermore, an alternative way of looking at learning and identity formation creates the possibility to challenge learner identity constructs and the dominance of a classification system which excludes different forms of learning and knowledges.

By implication, a more inclusive view of learning, both inside and outside formal education, leads to recognising the legitimacy of studying 'informal learning' as authentic learning. Definitions vary, but for the purposes of this chapter it is sufficient to define informal learning as that which may be unplanned, incidental, embodied and affective and takes place, but not exclusively, in the wider society rather than within formal learning institutions which focus on curriculum planning, pedagogy, assessment and qualifications. For further discussion of 'informal learning', and its relationship to formal and non-formal learning, see Colley, Hodkinson and Malcolm (2002).

In education circles, the study of informal learning and identity formation is limited by the certainty of conventional framings and the traditional evidence-based research methods of the dominant epistemological paradigm. The over-riding assumption is that there is one best mode of learning which is best studied scientifically in the context of educational institutions. In some 'informal learning' research the difficulty in identifying and quantifying informal learning through surveys was acknowledged, because of the way in which learning was defined, verbalised and construed by the researchers and the research participants. For example, some people can verbalise learning only in terms of their school experiences (Livingstone, 2006). Boud and Solomon (2003) found that identifying as learners at work is also problematic and is resisted at times when politics and identity tensions are involved. Others (McGivney, 2006; Sawchuk, 2008) have experienced difficulties with research methods which are inadequate for studying the ephemeral, the indefinite and the irregular (Law, 2004: 4). Accordingly, only 'the tip of the iceberg' (Livingstone, 2002) has been exposed. Furthermore, Livingstone (2006) acknowledged that failure to carry out empirical research in the context or 'activity structure' of respondents' daily lives was a limitation.

Having established that 'informal learning' counts as learning, it can be argued that it is not distinct from established learning theory. In order to identify practices of learning and to articulate informal everyday learning and identity formation it is necessary to include and draw on established and evolving learning theories. The next section gives a brief overview of developments in adult learning theory showing how the dominant paradigm of learning has been contested by evolving learning theories: situated learning in sociocultural practices, and actor-network theory (ANT), with alternative paradigms for conceptualising learning.

Developments in adult learning theory

According to the dominant epistemology, the best way to study learning is through science. Following the Cartesian mind/body, inner/outer dualisms, scientific learning is a purely rational process of knowing separable from (irrational) human emotions and embodiment. This learning can be conceptualised as acquisition of a product (Sfard, 1998) which is transparent to the learner and can be measured and standardised. Founded in behaviourist and cognitive psychology, learning is seen to be essentially an individual cognitive act of acquiring replicable knowledge, true facts or skills which are codifiable, objective, stable, universal and replicable, and occurring in formal educational institutions. Furthermore, 'othered' learning not transparent to the learner, such as tacit knowledge, is considered inferior. At the same time identity is seen to be a stable construct.

A growing dissatisfaction with the standard paradigm based on the notion of self as essentially individualistic and learning as mentalistic, while ignoring how human beings lived and worked in a socially structured world, led to a paradigm shift. Lave and Wenger (1991) challenged traditional learning theory by suggesting an alternative situative perspective on learning as participation in a community of practice. Active social participation became a primary condition for learning processes, while decentring common notions of mastery and pedagogy.

Situated learning – Legitimate peripheral participation, (Lave and Wenger, 1991) was originally based on Jean Lave's anthropological study of apprentices in the workplace, but this theory has also been applied widely in education communities. This theory triggered a conceptual shift from the traditional view of 'the individual as learner to learning as participation in the social world, and from the concept of cognitive process to the more-encompassing view of social practice' (Lave and Wenger, 1991: 43), but participants are still to be taken to be unitary or self-standing subjects.

Space does not permit an extended critique of community of practice theory (see Hughes, Jewson, and Unwin, 2007), but a significant criticism is that it fails to explain the circulation of power, learning and change within and across communities of practice (Fox, 2000). This is addressed by ANT, which, like the communities of practice approach, focuses on concrete practices, but it locates learning across networks rather than in bounded communities, and considers that learning and identity are the co-production of people, processes and objects. Agency is accorded to humans, as well as to non-humans, including objects. For a simple example of how this works, take Magritte's (1928–9) *Ceci n'est pas une pipe*: a painting of a pipe which he provocatively calls 'This is not a pipe'. The painting plus title *forces* the viewer to engage, or not, in a puzzle. How do our brains treat the image of an object as if it were that object, and how does it happen automatically without our being aware of it?

An ANT perspective suggests that 'knowing is not a static embedded capability or stable disposition of actors, but rather an ongoing social accomplishment constituted and reconstituted as actors engage the world in practice' (Orlikowski, 2002: 249). The material semiotic framing of ANT has the potential to address learning as a phenomenon by giving attention to its sociality (e.g. social interaction, dialogue) *as well as* its materiality (e.g. artifacts, bodily encounters). Sociomaterial practices encompass more than sociocultural practices in that materiality, objects, are given equal weight, whereas in sociocultural practices the humanist interpretation of meanings through language and discourse are privileged while discounting non-human objects. Therefore ANT dissolves the assumed mandatory boundaries between humans and non-humans, which can, and do, form through practice. Accordingly, by focusing on the entanglement of human activity with artifacts in everyday practices, and the agentive role that artifacts can play in this activity, learning and identity formation can be viewed differently, as demonstrated in Larissa's story which follows. ANT breaks down an ontological and epistemological binary (Orlikowski, 2002), allowing learning (knowing) and identity formation (being) to emerge co-constructed and situated in everyday sociomaterial practices.

Central to actor-network theory is the notion of *performativity*. This term is used to accent *practice* – to indicate that reality is brought into being: is enacted, fashioned or done. Learning does not exist outside its 'doing' in various and different practices. It is the object or effect of networks or arrangements or assemblages of many and diverse practices (e.g. textual, technical, social, spatial, temporal, corporeal, institutional . . .) which enact or allow learning and identities to emerge. The concept of identity, understood from a poststructural approach, accepts that identities are multiple, constructed across different discourses, material practices and positions. While a form of poststructuralism, a material semiotic way of thinking gives particular attention to the material constitution of identity. This thinking 'challenges modernist notions of the unitary knowing subject, [and] most particularly that this knowing is done in exclusively mindful ways' (Mulcahy, forthcoming).

I have argued that informal learning, and particularly that of women, has largely been neglected in lifelong learning literature. Research methodologies influenced by dominant learning theories have been inadequate for studying learning and identity formation. However, a sensitivity to ANT promises to be a useful tool for making sense (Law, 1994) of the social and for investigating how things, people and ideas become connected and assembled, (see Latour, 2005). This chapter is based on my research which focuses on women's informal learning in voluntary community organisations in an Australian rural town. I used a practice-based (Gherardi, 2006) and sociomaterial (actor-network theory) approach as an alternative methodology. This approach has provided a window on emergent learning in practices often too mundane or unworthy of being noticed in terms of the hierarchy of the dominant epistemology in educational discourse.

The research

> *My interest in the learning of rural women was aroused by reflection on my mother's life as a farmer's wife and mother of six children. She was unable to continue formal education beyond the age of 14 years, but led a very active life in practices such as: being a farmer's wife, being a mother, being a gardener, being a good cook, being a carer and participating in many community organisations which led her as far afield as a World Conference of the Associated Country Women of the World. My mother, and father, made it possible for my siblings and me to have the educational opportunities which through family circumstances were unavailable to my mother. She was proud of our educational achievements. However, I found it rather poignant that when she compared herself (and her life-time achievements) with those of her children, she said 'but I'm not clever'. From a perspective that privileges the practices of educational institutions, she did not have a 'learner identity' and consequently undervalued herself. This left me with the questions: what about informal/ incidental/practical learning in everyday life? How does it count? Sarah,*

(quoted above) a participant in my study expressed a similar view. Without tertiary education it is as though 'you have got nothing'. Sarah (55–65) has a history of very active involvement in her church, and in local and district community organisations. She has been recognised in the Lakeview Shire as 'Citizen of the Year'.

My doctoral study, in process

Informal learning, the object of this study, is 'not easy to pin down' (Law, 2007: 599). Accordingly, following Mol, (2002) I adopted the stance of a 'praxiographer/ethnographer ... [who] stubbornly takes notice of the techniques that make things visible, audible, tangible [and] knowable' (*ibid*: 33) by using a variety of methods to trace the interactions of human and non-human actors in actor-networks.

The ethnographic, qualitative research study focuses on the activities of 17 'older women', aged 55–97, in the district of the Victorian rural town called Lakeview, for research purposes, with a population of five thousand people. Considering it advantageous for an ethnographic study, I chose the district where my mother was known for her community involvement, and where I went to school. My focus was on 'older women' because in lifelong learning and widening participation literature, not only women who are not in the labour force are excluded, but also those not sufficiently valued to be eligible for 'second chance' education and training. My focus on activities provides a way to study the informal learning of women as they voluntarily participate in community organisations and carry out their everyday practices. The data were obtained through documents (newspaper accounts, archives) and semi-structured interviews (narrative) with 17 women, my mother's diary and memories of practices in which my mother was involved. As the units of analysis of the study are the practices, the interviews were conducted by focusing on the participants' everyday activities at home and in the community, without foregrounding learning (Boud and Solomon, 2003), or knowledge accumulated through their lives (St Pierre, 1997). Enactments of embodied learning were accessed by following one (or groups) of those 17 participants to different community sites, that is to the places where knowledge was constructed, while the women were involved in community activities. Following Gherardi's (2006) lead, research started from practices – as sets of seeing, doing and saying – not from the individual or the collective actor, and materiality was considered to be 'tangible knowledge'.

These practices were observed, photographed or recorded on video or audio tapes. In most instances the interviews were conducted in the participants' homes which also added a related dimension to their sociomaterial practices. I was able to hear, see (and photograph) things in their homes with which they identified. The interview narratives complemented data collection by providing more information about practices which I had observed (or participated in) – such as a Country Women's Association (CWA) meeting. CWA is similar to Women's Institutes in the UK (Jackson, 2006). In addition, the narratives made more practices 'viewable', which otherwise were temporally and physically inaccessible to me during my limited time as a participant observer in the field.

In being able to focus on the participants' recollection of and meaning making around 'concrete' activities, '[t]he concrete activity of producing and using knowledge becomes visible and observable, as well as describable [and one does not have] to assume the intentionality of people or [have] to delve into what goes on inside their heads' (Gherardi, 2006). By observing concrete activities, it was possible to view participants interacting with the world, i.e. learning (Mol, 2008). Activities and actions are 'materially mediated [and] situated within a field of practices' (Gherardi, 2006: xiv). As Gherardi and Nicolini (2000) explain:

> *Since media are always socially constituted and sustained, it follows that action is always social action, even when it is performed individually . . . [and] everyday action is also based on the use of discursive and material artifacts which embody not only practical knowledge and experience but also the history and social relations implicit in the mediating artifact (331).*

Through the readings of narratives in conjunction with other material data, patterns of sociomaterial practices emerged, were identified and organised in categories. By drawing on established learning theory, instances of learning could be identified in practices, and as practices, along with identity formation.

Additionally, in line with actor-network theory's concern with the 'productivity of practice' (Law, 2009: 144), an in-depth examination of the practices of six particular participants was made. The material performances of learning and identities were traced in sociomaterial practices and relationships. Whilst not being constrained by concepts drawn from practices within educational institutions, I have by necessity called on learning theory and its language to describe instances of learning.

The following empirical data focuses on one of the 17 study participants. I consider that the story of one unique person is representative of the way in which learning and identity formation emerged. Following the normal structure of discursive writing, the 'storying' is assembled in a linear way, according to identity-related themes defined by the activity. The selected illustrations are my attempt to convey the immediacy and materiality of learning and identity formation, which is a continuous process of enacting. There can be no claim to absolute 'truth' or certainty. Accordingly, I have taken 'poetic licence' with the English language by expressing continuing activities of being, doing and saying, through the use of the present participle '-ing'.

Larissa's story – being a country woman

Larissa (in the 55–65 age bracket) was born and attended secondary school in Melbourne, Victoria's capital city with a population of more than three million. She was employed as a seamstress. At approximately 30 years of age, when they married, she and her husband moved from Melbourne to live on a newly purchased rural property near Lakeview. This was a deviation from the traditional practice of patrilineal inheritance prevailing in agriculture, that ensured women's continuing subordinated position in farm management (Alston, 1995), thus Larissa was not setting out on a usual rural farm woman's 'becoming' and identification as a 'farmer's wife'. Country living, animal husbandry and farming were new ventures. Furthermore, Larissa's husband was predominantly occupied in his retail business in the nearest rural city. Larissa said that in her quest to 'be country' and to belong, she had 'the thought that you conjure up in your mind of what it is like when it is beyond you and you have never been there'.

There are various linked networks in which Larissa enacted 'being country', at home, and in community organisations.

Doing domestic things

> When I moved up here, I thought 'RIGHT'. You have to make bread, you have to make soup, you have to do this, you have to do that. So I really got into things which I thought were typically 'country'. I had such an awakening one day when I mentioned to someone (a regular country woman) that I make my own bread, and she said – 'I have never made bread in my life'. That kind of slowed me up for the moment . . .

Challenging constructed learner identities

It is apparent that Larissa's goal or quest is to shape her identity as a country woman by participating in sociomaterial practices, yet she discovered that what she idealised/constructed was not necessarily lived out by everybody who lived in the country.

Doing CWA – 'CWA-ing'

Larissa joined the CWA – 'another country thing that you do'. A neighbour invited her and it looked 'like a bit of fun' ('learning something new . . . something you have probably thought about for a while, or you saw when you were younger and all of a sudden you think – 'Ooh, I can do that'). Larissa explained that:

> *all the people there were older than me, but I didn't mind that. I never find a divider between age. There is so much we can learn and enjoy from all ages. Some people just say – 'They're a bit old for you' and I say – 'No they're not. I'm learning heaps all the time'.*

Larissa resisted the behavioural expectation implicit in what 'some people' said about CWA members being 'a bit old'. By identifying with CWA, Larissa recognised learning possibilities through participation in activities which exposed her to 'the ways in which rural women reinforce and contest dominant constructions of rural femininity as they negotiate their identity' (Hughes, 1997: 119). Although she makes soup and bakes bread (imagined typically 'country' practices), unlike other women in the study who connect competency in cooking with their identity as women, Larissa does not 'do gender' as a good cook: 'I am not a cook. I only cook to eat for survival. I don't survive to cook'.

CWA provides learning spaces during meetings and over shared afternoon teas. During meetings, the set agenda items are interspersed with comments:

> *[Sometimes you think] who wants to do what I am doing, or who wants to know what I know? They [might] think it's unimportant but – you can always get something out of someone – whether you thought at the time 'that was a load of – rubbish' . . . (laughter) . . . And something will pop up. It might even come up later on in a conversation and you think 'ooh, someone said that – yes, that* really *does apply – it's not as bad as I thought it was'.*

Alternatively, 'if someone requests something, someone will know the answer or know where to get it from' and general discussion, or chat in the meeting provides 'spaces of participation' (Jupp, 2008: 334) or 'conversational learning spaces' (Baker, Jensen, and Kolb, 2002). Chat in those 'in-between spaces' (Boud, Rooney, and Solomon, 2009: 325) 'indicates particular kinds of social connections and interpersonal relationships that allow for talk to be spontaneous, free-flowing and seemingly without surveillance' and plays a critical role in identity formation and everyday learning.

Furthermore, Larissa explained that during chat, 'you have got to learn to listen as well. That's important. Everyone has a talk, chat about something, then listen' and even though she might not think the information was correct at the time. 'But down the track you go "aha!" when you come to a situation where if fits and you can use it'.

Exhibiting home produce

Additionally, as a CWA member, Larissa in supporting established practices (exhibitions of home produce), participates by putting:

> *cakes and plants [flowers and vegetables] in the Show, mainly to keep up the numbers. But also it gives me a bit of a buzz when you think . . . 'I went to the bother and took the time to do that'.*

As Larissa said, when there is a limited number of entries, 'it would be awful if there was only one entry'. Furthermore, anyone seeing her entries would consider it good that she participates and puts time into doing 'country things' well. Her learning trajectory is propelled by 'a buzz' when she can 'measure up' with the practices of other (country) women around her and therefore legitimise (Parker, 2007) her country identity and reinforce a sense of 'being country'. Like learning, becoming or identity transformation is a social (and one must add, material) practice. Larissa cannot be a 'real country person' unless she is appropriately recognised by 'real country people' in the practices of doing being-and-becoming this person in particular situations and spaces.

Volunteering

Besides joining women's groups Larissa has found that voluntary work offers a way into the rural community – 'a way of becoming accepted ... especially important for those moving in with no existing ties' (Little, 1997: 146). For in not having children, Larissa has not had the automatic progression of involvement in rural voluntary work through school committees and support of children's activities. As she said:

> *when you do volunteer at things people are so happy to have you in as a volunteer. When people don't know you, they say – 'Ooh, I haven't seen you before. Where are you from? Who are you?' and – 'Thanks very much for coming to volunteer.' That could well be the thing that makes you feel [you belong]. And then of course when you have done that, when you have been there long enough, you greet other people that come in. So I guess you are a* second *generation of volunteers, or a second intake of volunteers. So you feel – 'Oh. It's what they did for me, I'll do for them. I could be in.'*

Larissa's experience is consistent with participation in a community of practice (Lave and Wenger, 1991). She moved from peripheral participation to the centre, and acceptance – to be 'in' (identifying as a volunteer) and then she was able to see the process being repeated for novices. This is also how she experienced other women's groups.

Belonging to sewing, spinning and patchwork quilting groups

Before marriage, Larissa was a seamstress by trade who started at the bottom and progressed to become a cutter. When she first moved to the country she volunteered to run dressmaking classes at the Lakeview Learning Centre because: 'a lot of people don't sew these days and it is very sad. It is beyond a craft and is a *necessary* field that women need to know'. She also joined a Spinners' and Weavers' group in order to learn to spin and weave her own fabrics.

Larissa has 'never forgotten' the welcome she received when she joined the spinners' group. As she first walked in:

> *one lady jumped up, and said – 'Ooh, we've got a new face here. Come in, welcome, we love to see you.' ... And so when something like that has been done for you, you do it back to someone else don't you? I guess that's belonging or being involved in an area ... And I am* still *there (about 30 years later) and that's a wonderful feeling.*

And history repeated itself recently when 30 year old Naomi, who reminded Larissa of her 'younger self', joined the group. 'We have got her as Secretary already!' In going through the 'rites of passage' (Munro, 1997), or in ANT terms, 'obligatory point of passage' (Callon, 1986: 205), Naomi is being drawn into and accepted in the group in the same way as Larissa was. Now, when Larissa identifies as an experienced participant who belongs, she has new understandings:

> *I can understand how the women of my age or older just enjoyed having a young person* there, *that was interested in the* craft *that is not all that popular . . . I guess, in a way, that's another belonging and local feeling.*

In identifying with the groups of women, Larissa was 'pushed on' to make quilts and has 'been shamed into' knitting some of her home-spun [wool] 'which she has accumulated. 'I haven't done enough for long enough'.

> *Particular enactments are learnt so that necessary competence is acquired, and the suitability of the performance is also likely to be subject to the disciplinary gaze of co-participants and onlookers* (Edensor, 2006: 486).

As already stated, Larissa was new to farm life but adapted with a passion.

Doing farm things – Caring for stud Poll Dorset Horn sheep – 'animal husbandrying'

'Working with animals is corporeal work containing aspects of care work and emotional work' (Brandth, 2006: 20). Larissa explains:

> *And so I learned how to pare their feet and crutch.*[1] *I had a go at shearing too. A friend came along and taught me. I had to sit down for the next three days because the muscles that I used with bending were upsetting me so much that I decided that I can't do that and would leave shearing to someone else.*

Crutching is the removal of wool from the crutch of a sheep to keep the area dry and less attractive to blowfly strike. With a little practice, the owner could do this with a pair of sheep shears or large scissors. http://www2.dpi.qld.gov.au/sheep/4909.html retrieved 26 August 2009.

Larissa did not refer to herself as a 'farmer'. For the 'true' farmer, 'control over land and stock' (Liepins, 2000: 612) is important in rural discourses and practices of masculinity. But as a farmer, or carer, Larissa's fulfilment of that role was not restricted by her embodied difficulties in shearing sheep. Unencumbered by the dominant discourse that a (good) farmer 'is tough and strong, able to endure long hours, arduous labour and extreme weather' (Little, 2002: 666), Larissa forged her own 'farmer' identity within the constraints imposed by her body and prevailing sociomaterial farm-related practices.

Larissa bought sheep at the municipal sale yards. There were rules prohibiting the sale of sheep with the dreaded disease foot rot, which causes the sheep to suffer due to lameness, severe economic loss to sheep owners and disruption to normal farm operations. But, as Larissa explained, the sheep – perhaps 200 purchased at a time – 'always had bad feet', and she 'used to always do their feet'. It 'was a good experience' because she 'had never done anything like that before' (nor was that a job commonly performed by local farm women at that time, but '(g)ender and rurality are not fixed, [they are] rather constructed through social and cultural practices which have given them meaning in everyday life' (Hughes, 1997: 119). Larissa felt 'quite happy' when she had 'straightened up the feet and the sheep could walk better and straighter'. It seems that without complaint, Larissa resisted the 'unruly contingencies' (Suchman, 2003: 189) of footrot, disabled sheep and farmers who ignored the rules. It was normal for farmers to infringe the by-laws, and Larissa would not have publicly contested the 'normal' practices of (male) farmers. In other words she was enrolled in or translated by the network of footrot-infected sheep; she learned through becoming an active agent in shaping the health and well-being of these sheep.

When the sheep threatened to eat the trees she grew from seed, Larissa watched a friend build a fence, and went on to construct fences to protect the trees. For Larissa, farming practices were: 'a lot of fun' because she had to work out a lot of things herself . . . [particularly] if things were going wrong'. Larissa's second husband is a 'real farmer' who has always been farming. Larissa no longer has the sheep, and has adopted a more 'traditional' farmer's wife role (Alston, 1995; Brandth, 2006). Bob ploughs the paddocks, sows the pastures; he constructed the 'chook sheds' and she works alongside him, in a supportive role, in activities such as the recent planting of hundreds of trees on their property. But Larissa still fixes things herself, and when she shares her practical knowledge, and explains how to make something work, people respond: 'Well how do *you* know?' and she, in turn, replies: 'Well I was really stuck one day, and I *had to work it out*. And I *did* it!' Larissa enjoys the challenge of learning as she enacts her identity as a practical, self-sufficient 'country person', with the ability to surprise and impress other 'country people'. As (Brown and Duguid, 2001) suggest: '[l]earning... involves acquiring identities that reflect both how a learner sees the world and how the world sees the learner' (ibid.: 200). Accordingly, it is the recognition and acceptance by others who count (i.e. the country people with whom she identifies) that matter to Larissa.

> *Recognition from others helps the self to make meaning of its own actions, feelings and intentions. However, this recognition can only come from another individual whom we recognize as a person in his or her own right'* (Benjamin, 1988, cited by Baker, Jensen, and Kolb, 2002: 21).

Meeting with chooks (poultry)

Larissa described the 'Black Orpington' as the 'matron of chooks' and hers 'are very big plump ladies with a big chest... and quite beautiful.' She is proud of their healthy appearance. Furthermore, 'when people come to have a look at my chooks, they say – 'I have *never seen* such big chooks!"' Larissa's validity is reinforced by others' recognition of her practices.

On joining the 'Victorian Chooks Society' (the Victorian Poultry Society), Larissa learned 'what you need to do if you want to 'show' your chooks' – which 'sounded like a bit of fun'. In preparation for showing they had to be washed:

Figure 1: The 'matron of chooks'.

Challenging constructed learner identities

Figure 2: Chooks scratching in the paddock.

And of course chooks, like all beings, have personalities. There were some roosters with such personalities! You washed them! But you can't do everything at once. I would say, 'Just stay there, I'll be back with the towel', and they would ... stand dripping on the perch, obviously just happy to stand still. Or whether they were petrified [because] they were so cold, I don't know. But I dried them off with towels, then got out the hair drier and used it as you would with your own hair and fluffed the feathers up. Once they are fully dry and fluffed up, they strut around, and of course they do look beautiful! This particular rooster would just stand on the bench and I could just lean over him to pull out [extend] each wing, dry under each wing, pull out and get the drier through his tail feathers, which are very thick and fluffy, without having to hold his legs or anything. I washed him a few times because I took him to a few shows.

Larissa's story re-enacts the practice – the embodied entanglement with heterogenous actors (human, other 'beings with personalities,' and drips, towels, feathers, hair dryer, bench) and affect ('happy to stand still', 'look beautiful' and 'they strut around'). Similarly Larissa found that the rams (male sheep) used 'to love attention' as well, and when she 'tickled them under the chin, they would just stand there', compared with 'the girls' (ewes) which, like the hens, 'could be a bit flighty'. It is through socio-material practices – being in the chook society, chook showing, washing roosters, relating to the rams with a 'tickle under the chin', keeping the 'chooks happy and healthy' with their daily mix of hot pollard in winter, before being released to scratch in the paddock (field) all day, that Larissa meets the 'gaze' (Haraway, 2008: 21) of other species. In other words, according to Haraway (2008), animals are not objects of vision, but are 'beings who look back and whose look ... intersects [with humans], with consequences for all that follows' (ibid.: 21). Furthermore, the meetings of humans and animals 'make us who and what we are in the avid contact zones [entanglements] that are the world' (ibid.: 287). Accordingly Larissa's curiosity and 'responsive relationship[s]' (ibid.: 25) with non-human animals shape her identity. She cares and learns a way of coexisting well in the world in which 'diverse bodies and meanings co-shape one another' (ibid.: 4).

Productive learning in everyday spaces

The pervasiveness and continuous enactments of Larissa's learning and identity formation demonstrate that the everyday is a productive space for learning. Although Larissa did not identify as a learner, the learning becomes visible. Some of the study participants unselfconsciously used terms like 'grow', and 'see outside the square', but the observation of practices liberated the study from constraining constructs such as 'reluctant learner' which implies a deficit model of learning. Accordingly, thinking materially can help surface multiple forms of learning in everyday practices and provide understandings of learning outside such constructs or categories which are 'historically situated artefacts and, like all artefacts, are learned as part of membership in communities of practice' (Bowker and Star, 1999: 287). By paying attention to sociomaterial practices, a less categorical view of learning is afforded, although entwined and entangled, categories do some useful work in describing learning theories or contested definitions of formal/informal and non-formal learning (Colley, Hodkinson and Malcolm, 2002). However, one needs to consider that 'the 'invisibility' that pervades classifications [categories] make it difficult to see how they work' (Waterton, 2003: 113) and how they hide social injustices.

Having taken heed of Billett's (2002) suggestion that it is probably not helpful to describe or discuss learning outside educational institutions through concepts drawn uncritically from practice within educational institutions, I use 'educational' language to conceptualise and challenge understandings of learning and learning identities with caution. Sometimes in adult education literature 'informal learners' are 'othered'; they are invited to be 'second chance' learners or are categorised as 'non-learners', unless they have engaged in formal learning (Hodkinson, 2006); or they remain excluded from 'Statcan' (2008) *Education Matters* webpage, although 'informal learning' was mentioned in a description of adult learning. Examples such as these show how the 'invisible' power of the dominant paradigm hovers in educational research and excludes Larissa's informal learning. Accordingly, Larissa would have been a 'non-learner' or does not count at all.

Nonetheless, as postmodern critique rejects locating human actions, including learning, within any foundational certainty, I consider the empirical data, by bringing informal learning into view, provide an avenue for challenging existing framings. Larissa's story emphasises the gap between informal learning embedded in the community, and education. They can exist separately, but by bringing the differences to view it increases awareness of how injustices and exclusions work in practice. In adult learning literature, different gaps emerge 'between policy priorities, and those of providers, as well as between what policy makers and institutions value and promote and what learners value and want to achieve' (McGivney, 2002: 2). Furthermore, a power imbalance exists in educational policy discourses by virtue of 'devaluing and excluding informal learning' (Golding et al., 2009: 49).

In analysing Larissa's identity formation, the standard theoretical story of narrative identity as enacted, performed and reinvented is of some use. However, from a poststructuralist view, identity is shifting, relational, multiple, contingent on circumstances and understood through difference. In the circumstances of everyday life, empirical data show that identity is performative and worked in different ways. For example, Larissa's identity formation was true to her passion for practical material experiences which 'look like fun'. The generativity and creativity of identity formation emerged through the dynamics of sociomaterial practices. By necessity I have assembled Larissa's multiple and shifting identities in a linear fashion in stories. The assembled stories demonstrate how Larissa's life has been subjected to several intersecting axes of differentiation and power (Moser, 2006) – gender identity, age, rural and class dynamics. Norms, values and sociomaterial practices shape, change and sustain activities and interactions. It is in these interactions with the world that identity and learning are completely entwined without the 'interference', exclusions or separation imposed by a 'learner identity' construct, which in adult learning theory attempts to signify foundational certainty (Kang, 2007).

The data demonstrate the liveliness, immediacy, corporeality and fluidity of learning which is a broad and all-encompassing effect of everyday life. Larissa's trajectory shows that learning is not reserved for particular learning moments (Billett and Somerville, 2004), or settings (Billett, 2006), as in school, or the workplace. Larissa's learning is mobilised, moving 'hand-in-hand' (ibid.: 16) and from place to place in 'nomadic movements' (Fenwick, 2006: 23), as she participates in activities and sociomaterial practices. She appears to flow into and out of networks of practices (CWA, keeping farm animals happy and healthy, 'Chook' Society Shows), while learning and identity is distributed through the interconnecting range of networks (Edwards and Nicoll, 2006) which require effort to maintain. Both the complexity of emergent learning, and the entanglement of learning and identity formation, challenge the notion of a constructed learner identity in isolation (Tanggaard, 2000), and the associated limitations and exclusions.

The learning which emerged can be considered 'informal' because it is not necessarily mediated, or planned by adult educators to have a proscribed outcome. Nor is it necessarily a thing (or construct) for which all people strive. In this regard these data challenge lifelong learning discourse which creates the educable adult (Fejes, 2006), who is forced to identify as a learner, and, in failing to do so, becomes 'othered', targeted or invisible like Larissa because her learning falls outside the boundaries of adult education.

Conclusion

Ouane, (2009) the Director of the Institute of Lifelong Learning within UNESCO, suggested the need:

> *to recognise that we are not simply producers and consumers, but citizens with families and personal lives. We are also participants in diverse communities of practice. We need to learn in these communities: across the lifespan: about health and wellbeing; to re-create lives beyond work; to age, to enhance social, civic and family roles and responsibilities; to strengthen and develop personal identities, family, community, national and international relationships* (cited by Golding and Campbell, 2009: 422).

Larissa, (like the other 16 participants in my study) is 'not simply a producer and consumer', but is an active citizen, engaging in volunteering, enjoying relationships with family and social networks and enjoying physical and mental well-being. In other words she shares, but without necessarily identifying as a learner, the attributes of the 'lifelong learners' to whom Schuller (2004) refers. By airing her story, I hope that it contributes to finding a way towards the recognition of how her learning and being can contribute to social equity for those who are excluded by government education policy.

Currently, in Australian public policy and the wider community, there is lack of recognition of the importance of lifelong and lifewide learning for maintenance of people's identities and well-being (Golding and Campbell, 2009). The availability of adult and community education (ACE) programmes is limited. A three tiered programme comprised of vocational education and training (VET), community participation and community learning is offered. But:

> *the categories of access and equity in Australian adult education and training policies assume that the stable centre or dominant discourse in Australian adult education and training is Anglo-Saxon, male, physically and mentally able, situated in urban communities and employed on a full-time and fulfilling basis* (Townsend, 2006: 166).

It is 'a system that values highly structured, systematised, outcome-driven approaches to young people's learning' (Golding *et al.*, 2009: 53) and consequently learning facilities are not necessarily appropriate to the interests of 'othered' individuals. For example, as older people usually do not require 'retraining' for employment they prefer less formal activities in which learning is a by-product. Jackson (2006) describes how, in the UK, the Women's Institute members, many of whom are 'older' women, have the opportunity to participate in fulfilling and interesting non-formal programmes at the organisation's own Denman College. Limited adult education funding is available for accredited courses. The dilemma lies in the reality that many older learners join in for reasons other than 'retraining' and/or successful completion of courses. Once again, the conceptualisation of 'successful learning' becomes problematic (McGivney, 2002). Policy requirements exclude people who do not 'fit' into learner identity constructs or the participation discourse of lifelong learning. Participation counts more than the effects of particular learning programmes (Schuller, 2004), or the needs of individuals when courses are translated into statistics which are analysed, quantified and justified as the good. Community education ACE centres in Australia face a similar dilemma (Rooney, 2007) along with the Men's Sheds movement (Golding *et al.*, 2009). The needs of Larissa, like many other older rural women and men, remain ignored by government policy, unless the institutions and courses become 'accredited'.

Larissa's informal learning in the context of everyday community life, in being considered less economically profitable than formal learning, is located outside policy priorities. Situated in this way, informal learners are further disempowered and devalued because as Golding *et al.*, (2009) argue, informal learning:

> *is currently dis/identified through hegemonic discourses and policy contexts that constrain, devalue and reduce opportunities for different learning preferences, opportunities and possibilities to be presented to different learners* (ibid.: 50).

It is necessary to raise awareness of social injustice, through research and publications, as well as to provide opportunities, or support in the way of acknowledgement, affirmation, confirmation or validation, and to help in the pursuit of interests and practices 'nested' (Wojecki, 2007) in the world of those for whom current adult education facilities are not available or appropriate. As suggested above, the provision of support is problematic. (Vickers, 2007) suggests the establishment of educational partnerships, but in a rural area there are limited possibilities and interest. During my study it emerged that there is a procedure in the Lakeview Shire for not-for-profit community organisations to apply for grants to help support activities. This in effect is a way of valuing selected local groups (and embedded informal learning). However, other organisations, for example one of the CWA branches, comprised of ageing members with limited financial means, recently disbanded because of costs involved in maintaining affiliation with the parent group. Other groups are similarly threatened. One of Larissa's craft organisations faces rising costs which could deter and/or exclude old as well as new members. In such instances a subsidy could enable the continuation of such organisations.

Social injustice continues while government funding for adult learning centres is dictated by current lifelong learning discourse. Therein lies the challenge for research – to raise awareness of how 'regimes of truth' about learning operate (Edwards and Nicoll, 2006: 182), and how injustices occur as a result of educational discourse and policy. If research is framed from within traditional educational research paradigms there is the danger of codifying informal learning to meet academic requirements and in so doing reinforce the notion that only the latter counts (Fraser, 1995 cited by McGivney, 2006: 21). As a 'valued knowledge domain' (Harman, 2007:

72), everyday learning could be supported and promoted, by fostering its conditions, spaces and relationships through structured learning initiatives (Boud et al.: 2009: 333) and not colonised or reshaped to fit with current lifelong learning policy. My presentation of Larissa, who does not have a constructed 'learner identity', has shown that it is possible to bring the skills and knowledges of ordinary people to view and recognise that their stake in the world is just as great as the stake of those who are paid to comment upon it (Thrift, 1997: 126 cited by Nash, 2000: 655). Larissa's story contributes to the recognition of everyday learners and their needs. Hopefully more stories like hers will encourage educators to reexamine some of the assumptions that have been taken for granted about the role of educators, and 'the dominance of an exclusively educational perspective' (Boud, 2006: 83) on learning and learner identities.

Acknowledgements

I am grateful to my PhD supervisor Dianne Mulcahy, for her guidance in the use of actor-network theory as a research tool, Larissa for so freely sharing her experiences, and Sue Jackson for her editorial advice.

References

Alston, M. (1995) 'Women and their work on Australian farms', *Rural Sociology*, 60: 3, 521–32.

Baker, A., Jensen, P., and Kolb, D. (2002) *Conversational learning: An experiential approach to knowledge creation*. Westport, CT: Quorum Books.

Benjamin, J. (1988) *The bonds of love, psychoanalysis, feminism, and the problems of domination*. New York: Pantheon Books.

Billett, S. (2002) 'Critiquing workplace learning discourses: Participation and continuity at work', *Studies in the Education of Adults*, 34: 1, 56–67.

Billett, S. (2006) 'Work, subjectivity and learning', in S. Billett, T. Fenwick and M. Somerville (eds), *Work, subjectivity and learning: Understanding learning through working life*, 1–20. Dordrecht: Springer.

Billett, S. and Somerville, M. (2004) 'Transformations at work: Identity and learning', *Studies in Continuing Education*, 26: 2, 309–26.

Boud, D. (2006) 'Combining work and learning. The disturbing challenge of practice', in R. Edwards, J. Gallagher and S. Whittaker (eds),

Learning outside the academy: International research perspectives on lifelong learning, 77–89. Milton Park: Routledge.

Boud, D., Rooney, D. and Solomon, N. (2009) 'Talking up learning at work: Cautionary tales in co-opting everyday learning', *International Journal of Lifelong Education*, 28: 3, 323–34.

Boud, D., and Solomon, N. (2003) '"I don't think I am a learner": Acts of naming learners at work', *Journal of Workplace Learning*, 15: 7/8, 326–31.

Bowker, G. and Star, S. (1999) *Sorting things out: Classification and its consequences*. Cambridge, MA: MIT Press.

Brandth, B. (2006) 'Agricultural body-building: Incorporations of gender, body and work', *Journal of Rural Studies*, 22: 1, 17–27.

Brown, J. and Duguid, P. (2001) 'Knowledge and organisation: A social-practice perspective', *Organisation Science*, 12: 2, 198–213.

Burke, P. and Jackson, S. (2007) *Reconceptualising lifelong learning: Feminist interventions*. London: Routledge.

Callon, M. (1986) 'Some elements of a sociology of translation: Domestication of the scallops and the fishermen of St Brieuc Bay', in J. Law (ed.), *Power, action and belief: A new sociology of knowledge*, 196–233. London: Routledge and Kegan Paul.

Colley, H., Hodkinson, P. and Malcolm, J. (2002) *Non-formal learning: Mapping the conceptual terrain. A consultation report*. Leeds: University of Leeds.

Conradson, D. (2003) 'Doing organisational space: Practices of voluntary welfare in the city', *Environment and Planning A*, 35: 11, 1975–92.

Crouch, D. (2003) 'Spacing, performing, and becoming: Tangles in the mundane', *Environment and Planning A*, 35: 11, 1945–1960.

de Carteret, P. (2008) 'Diverse pleasures: Informal learning in community', *Australian Journal of Adult Learning*, 48: 3, 502–21.

Delors, J. (1996) *Learning: the treasure within – Highlights: A report to UNESCO of the International Commission on Education for the Twenty-first Century*. Hamburg: UNESCO.

Edensor, T. (2006) 'Performing rurality', in P. Cloke, T. Marsden and P. Mooney (eds), *Handbook of rural studies*, 484–95. London: Sage.

Edwards, R. and Nicoll, K. (2006) 'Action at a distance: governmentality, subjectivity and workplace learning', in S. Billett, T. Fenwick and M. Somerville (eds), *Work, subjectivity and learning: Understanding learning through working life*, 179–193. Dordrecht: Springer.

Eichler, M. (2005a) 'The other half (or more) of the story: Unpaid household and care work and lifelong learning', in N. Bascia, A. Cumming, A. Datnow, K. Leithwood and D. Livingstone (eds), *International handbook of educational policy: Part Two*, 1023–41. Dordrecht: Springer.

Eichler, M. (2005b) 'Unpaid housework and lifelong learning', paper presented at 'The Future of Lifelong Learning and Work OISE/UT Conference', Toronto.

Fejes, A. (2006) 'The planetspeak discourse of lifelong learning in Sweden: What is an educable adult?' *Journal of Education Policy*, 21: 6, 697–716.

Fenwick, T. (2006) 'Escaping/becoming subjects: Learning to work the boundaries in boundaryless work', in S. Billett, T. Fenwick and M. Somerville (eds), *Work, subjectivity and learning: Understanding learning through working life*, 21–36. Dordrecht: Springer.

Fox, S. (2000) 'Communities of practice, Foucault and actor–network theory', *Journal of Management Studies*, 37: 6, 853–67.

Fraser, W. (1995) *Learning from experience: Empowerment or incorporation*. Leicester: NIACE.

Gherardi, S. (2006) *Organisational knowledge: The texture of workplace learning*. Malden, MA: Blackwell Publishing.

Gherardi, S., and Nicolini, D. (2000) 'To transfer is to transform: The circulation of safety knowledge', *Organisation*, 7: 2, 329–48.

Golding, B. (2009) 'Older men's lifelong learning: Common threads/sheds', in J. Field, J. Gallagher and R. Ingram (eds), *Researching transitions in lifelong learning*, 65–75. Abingdon: Routledge.

Golding, B., Brown, M., and Foley, A. (2009) 'Informal learning: A discussion around defining and researching its breadth and importance, *Australian Journal of Adult Learning*, 49: 1, 34–56.

Golding, B., and Campbell, C. (2009) 'Editorial', *Australian Journal of Adult Learning*, 49: 3, 417–22.

Gouthro, P. (2005) 'A critical feminist analysis of the homeplace as learning site: Expanding the discourse of lifelong learning to consider adult women learners', *International Journal of Lifelong Education*, 24: 1, 5–19.

Hager, P. (2005) 'Philosophical accounts of learning', *Educational Philosophy and Theory*, 37: 5, 649–66.

Harman, K. (2007) 'Re-thinking workplace learning: Worker subjectivity/ies as sites of alignment and resistance', unpublished PhD Thesis, University of Technology, Sydney.

Haraway, D. (2008) *When species meet*. Minneapolis: University of Minnesota Press.

Hodkinson, H. (2006) 'Older people as learners: Identity, life change and well being', Paper presented at the International Conference of the Association of Education and Ageing 'Later Life Learning – fit for purpose', Brighton.

Hughes, A. (1997) 'Rurality and "cultures of womanhood": Domestic identities and moral order in village life', in P. Cloke and J. Little (eds), *Contested countryside cultures: Otherness, marginalisation and rurality*, 118–32. London: Routledge.

Hughes, J., Jewson, N. and Unwin, L. (eds) (2007) *Communities of practice: Critical perspectives*. London: Routledge.

Jackson, S. (2006) 'Jam, Jerusalem and calendar girls: Lifelong learning and the Women's Institutes (WI)', *Studies in the Education of Adults*, 38: 1, 74–90.

Jupp, E. (2008) 'The feeling of participation: Everyday spaces and urban change', *Geoforum*, 39, 331–43.

Kang, D. (2007) 'Rhizoactivity: Toward a postmodern theory of lifelong learning', *Adult Education Quarterly*, 57: 3, 205–20.

Latour, B. (2005) *Reassembling the social: An introduction to actor–network-theory*. Oxford: Oxford University Press.

Lave, J. and Wenger, E. (1991) *Situated learning – Legitimate peripheral participation*. Cambridge: Cambridge University Press.

Law, J. (1994) *Organising modernity*. Oxford: Blackwell.

Law, J.(2004) *After method: Mess in social science research*. London: Routledge.

Law, J. (2007) 'Making a mess with method', in W. Outhwaite and S. Turner (eds), *The SAGE handbook of social science methodology*, 595–606. Los Angeles: Sage.

Law, J. (2009) 'Actor network theory and material semiotics', in B. Turner (ed.), *The new Blackwell companion to social theory*, 131–58. Chichester, U.K.: Wiley-Blackwell.

Liepins, R. (2000) 'Making man: The construction and representation of agriculture-based masculinities in Australia and New Zealand'. *Rural Sociology*, 65: 4, 605–20.

Little, J. (1997) 'Employment marginality and women's self-identity', in P. Cloke and J. Little (eds), *Contested countryside cultures: Otherness, marginalisation and rurality*, 133–51. London: Routledge.

Little, J. (2002) 'Rural geography: Rural gender identity and the performance of masculinity and femininity in the countryside', *Progress in Human Geography*, 26: 5, 665–70.

Livingstone, D. (2002) *Mapping the iceberg*. http://www.oise.utoronto.ca/depts/sese/csew/nall/res/54DavidLivingstone.pdf

Livingstone, D. (2006) 'Informal learning: conceptual distinctions and preliminary findings', in Z. Bekerman, N. Burbules and D. Silberman-Keller (eds), *Learning in places: The informal education reader*, 203–27) New York: Peter Lang.

Magritte, R. (1928–9) *Ceci n'est pas une pipe*. http://en.wikipedia.org/wiki/The_Treachery_of_Images

McGivney, V. (2002) *A question of value: Achievement and progression in adult learning. A discussion paper*. Leicester: NIACE.

McGivney, V. (2006) 'Informal learning: The challenge for research', in R. Edwards, J. Gallacher and S. Whittaker (eds), *Learning outside the academy: International research perspectives on lifelong learning*, 11–23) Milton Park: Routledge.

Ministerial declaration on adult community education. (2008) Canberra: Department of Education, Employment and Workplace Relations.

Mol, A. (2002) *The body multiple: Ontology in medical practice*. Durham NC: Duke University Press.

Mol, A. (2008) Response to provocation questions for 'A turn to ontology in STS' workshop at Said Business School, Oxford. Retrieved 14 July, 2009, from http://www.sbs.ox.ac.uk/NR/rdonlyres/9B397CCA-D926-463B-8372-08AF1D0F658D/5181/AnnemarieMol2.doc

Moser, I. (2006) 'Sociotechnical practices and difference: On the interferences between disability, gender, and class'. *Science, Technology, and Human Values*, 31: 5, 537–64.

Mulcahy, D. (forthcoming) 'Teacher professional becoming: A practice-based, actor–network theory perspective', in L. Scanlon (ed.), *Becoming a professional: An interdisciplinary analysis of professional learning*. Dordrecht: Springer.

Mündel, K., and Schugurensky, D. (2005) 'The "accidental learning" of volunteers: The case of community-based organisations in Ontario', in K. Künzel (ed.), *International Yearbook of Adult Education*, 183–205. Cologne: Böhlau-Verlag.

Munro, R. (1997) 'Ideas of difference: Stability, social spaces and the labour of division', in K. Hetherington and R. Munro (eds), *Ideas of difference: Social spaces and the labour of division*, 3–26. Oxford: Blackwell Publishers/The Sociological Review.

Nash, C. (2000) 'Performativity in practice: Some recent work in cultural geography' *Progress in Human Geography*, 24: 4, 653–64.

Nespor, J. (1994) *Knowledge in motion: Space, time and curriculum in undergraduate physics and management.* London: Falmer Press.

Nespor, J. (2002) 'Studying the spacialities of schooling', *Pedagogy, Culture and Society*, 10: 3, 483–91.

Orlikowski, W. (2002) 'Knowing in practice: Enacting a collective capability in distributed organising', *Organisation Science*, 13: 3, 249–73.

Ouane, A. (2009) *Only through adult education can we address the real problems of society.* http://www.unesco.org/fileadmin/MULTIMEDIA/INSTITUTES/UIL/confintea/pdf/press/confinteavi_interview_ouane_en.pdf

Parker, M. (2007) 'Identification: Organisations and structuralism', in A. Pullen, N. Beech and D. Sims (eds), *Exploring identity: Concepts and methods*, 61–82. Basingstoke: Palgrave Macmillan.

Rooney, D. (2007) 'Bridges: Linking the work of NSW neighbourhood centres to education', Paper presented at the 37th Annual SCUTREA Conference, Belfast.

Sawchuk, P. (2008) 'Theories and methods for research on informal learning and work: Towards cross-fertilization', *Studies in Continuing Education*, 30: 1, 1–16.

Schuller, T. (2004) 'Studying benefits', in T. Schuller, J. Preston, C. Hammond, A. Brassett-Grundy and J. Bynner (eds), *The benefits of learning: The impact of education on health, family life and social capital*, 3–11. London: RoutledgeFalmer.

Sfard, A. (1998) 'On two metaphors for learning and the dangers of choosing just one', *Educational Researcher*, 27: 2, 4–13.

St Pierre, E. (1997) 'Circling the text: Nomadic writing practices (exploratory writing as a research technique)', *Qualitative Inquiry*, 3: 4, 403–18.

Statcan. (2008) *Adult learning in Canada: Characteristics of learners.* http://www.statcan.gc.ca/pub/81-004-x/2008001/article/10560-eng.htm#b

Suchman, L. (2003) 'Organising alignment: The case of bridge-building', in D. Nicolini, S. Gherardi and D. Yanow (eds), *Knowing in organisations: A practice-based approach*, 187–203. New York: M.E. Sharpe.

Tanggaard, L. (2000) 'Resisting an isolated learning discourse', *International Journal of Lifelong Education*, 28: 6, 693–703.

Thrift, N. (1997) 'The still point: Resistance, expressive embodiment and dance', in S. Pile and M. Keith (eds), *Geographies of resistance*, 124–51. London: Routledge.

Townsend, R. (2006) 'Adult, community and public education as primary sites for the development of social capital', *Australian Journal of Adult Learning*, 46: 2, 153–74.

Vickers, A. (2007) 'Partnerships with local community groups – a new direction for adult education?' Paper presented at the 37th Annual SCUTREA Conference, Belfast.

Waterton, C. (2003) 'Performing the classification of nature', in S. Bronislaw, W. Heim and C. Waterton (eds), *Nature performed; Environment, culture and performance*, 111–29. Oxford: Blackwell Publishing.

Willis, P. (2000) 'Expressive and arts-based research: Presenting lived experience in qualitative research', in P. Willis, R. Smith and E. Collins (eds), *Being, seeking, telling: Expressive approaches to qualitative adult education research*, 35–65. Flaxton, Queensland: Post Pressed.

Wojecki, A. (2007) '"What's identity got to do with it, anyway?" Constructing adult learner identities in the workplace'. *Studies in the Education of Adults*, 39: 2, 168–82.

CHAPTER ELEVEN

Love in a cold climate: Mental illness and learning to write 'I love you'

OLIVIA SAGAN

Introduction: The geography: mental illness, narrative, learning

Much has been written, particularly in the past two decades, about mental illness and the urge to narrate, with the narrative in question usually, but not always, being expressed through writing. In compiling the formidable *Bibliography of First-Person Narratives of Madness In English*, now in its 4th edition, Gail Hornstein (2002) provides testament to the inexorable tide of efforts to accomplish what one of the people in this study described as 'getting it down on paper'. This 'it', being accompanied by a vague hand gesture in the direction of the head, a gesture I have seen replicated dozens of times in my research when I ask mentally ill adults why they want to write, or in this case, learn to write. The 'it' it would seem, is the subject that won't go away: my mental state, my illness, my madness. The story is one of how a condition became one's life and how that life either buckled under the strain of it or found astonishing resources to survive it and to narrate that survival.

This need to write 'it' out has been described as a desire for 'a re-negotiating of the spaces of the self in which suffering is, or was, experienced' (Stone, 2004: 50). It can also be seen as a need for the narrative to form part of one's quest or restitution narrative (Frank, 1997), through which one invests in a reconstructed narrative as part of the envisaging of a point beyond illness in its current form. Stories also give voice; as Frank notes (1997: xii), through illness, people 'need to become storytellers in order to recover the voices that illness and its treatment often take away.' From the psychosocial perspective adhered to in this study, the need to write it out can, for one example, meet a desire and urge for reparation (Sagan, 2008) through which the damaged objects of one's internal world begin to be met and repaired. In each of these possible explanations the sequencing and structure inherent in writing plays a powerful role in counteracting the disintegrating, fragmentary state of mind often experienced when mental illness takes hold. As this hold is tightened, the mind's fabric begins to splinter, sometimes opening up a kaleidoscopic vista of newly imagined forms, other times, enmeshing you 'in the blackest caves of the mind' (Jamison, 1995) with the experience of *dis*integration being overwhelmingly reported. The sentence, as Derrida commented (1978: 54–5), by its very essence, carries 'normality within it' and is therefore, almost certainly, the desired tool, if not always the most able, for the job of describing that which lies outside the mainstream.

Largely missing, however, from the literature which explores the narrative writing of the mentally ill is consideration of first person written narratives of people who have very low levels of literacy, and sometimes, low levels of verbal articulation. This study was often troubled by this lack of access to words and the gateway to subjective expression they offered; troubled by what Laplanche and Pontalis (1973: 168) called 'symbolic abolition' – the being left with experience that you have no way of symbolising. This trouble was felt and in some cases tentatively described, in hard wrought sentences, by people in this study.

The production of both spoken and written narrative is commonly agreed to be fulfilling a creative or human urge, as Barthes observes, *'there does not exist, and never has existed, a people without narratives'* (Barthes, cited in Polkinghorne, 1988: 14). And in producing narratives, people with mental illness do indeed often find catharsis, relief or simply pleasure in an otherwise 'storm of murk' (Styron, 2004: 46). So how then is it that narrative practices are so routinely denied to certain adults? These are individuals who have low levels of literacy either due to lifecourse factors, such as disrupted childhoods; structural factors, such as inadequate educational provision; health impacts, such as mental illness attacking previously adequate levels of literacy, or 'simply' the isolation of a social exclusion which renders them not only excluded, but unheard and *unlistened* to. While in England strategies such as Skills for life (2001) have triggered funding for provision, and the 2001 Special Educational Needs and Disabilities Act (SENDA) has ensured awareness raising and training, there are people for whom such provision is unbefitting. Further Education settings and their pedagogic approach are found alienating and threatening, and the Adult Literacy Curriculum with its regulative discourse and basis in political and economic rationales (Taylor, 2008) is largely inappropriate. What if you are long term mentally ill, have a physical illness which impedes your mobility, have lower than average literacy skills, yet want to learn to write 'I love you' to a special person? A person who, in your vision, has done more than anyone else or anything else to help you survive, and through whom you have co-constructed a vital counter-narrative? This paper is about one such couple. It is also about the way the UK welfare state increasingly depends on such love, and yet puts little love into those on whom we depend to love one another. The role, use and function of love as an adjunct to welfare support in international contexts and cultures varies; but it is safe to comment that as economic tightening is enforced, the demands on those who love, to love 'better', increase.

This research began at the height of policy concern with providing adult basic skills provision; a concern generated through the 'shock' findings of the Moser report (1999) which claimed to have found evidence of 7 million 'functionally illiterate' adults in England. It also found itself at the confluence of concerns regarding links between mental illness, low educational attainment and social exclusion. Some of the research claims of this time (early 2000s) have been found to be lacking in evidence or robustness (see, inter alia Payne, 2006) while much New Labour educational rhetoric has also been critiqued as generating a discourse of derision, and a culture of blame which targets individuals such as those in this study, and obscures the shortcomings of welfare and education (Ball, 2006). Moral panics over the apparent weaknesses of Care in the Community had, in addition, reignited a culture of fear and loathing regarding the mentally ill, through which they again became recipients of society's projected fears regarding our own decay, instability, and anger (Harper, 2005).

What was happening meanwhile, in the lives of thousands of people living in the 'psychiatric gulag' (Hartill, 1998) was their voices, and their own representations of self continued to be largely unheard (and unwritten), while discourse positioned them as multiple Other (Shakespeare, 2000) – other to the sane, to the included, and now, to the skilled. This suturing (Lacan, 1977) of the mentally ill subject denies expression of counter-narrative, and eventually, such denial ensures that even counter-*thought* becomes restrained (Sagan, 2009). Amongst the narratives from this study in which people referred, in sometimes mystified terms, to the apparent colonisation of their minds by mental illness, there emerged another form of colonisation: of people's internal pictures of themselves. They now often 'saw' themselves as being 'unskilled' and 'socially excluded' – words and images which were incongruent with more authentically generated versions of their identity. As Hoggett (2000: 169) points out:

> *there is something seriously wrong with a society in which the bestowal of full citizenship is contingent upon fitness to join a labour market which increasingly has the feel of a jungle.*

This strident skills and fitness agenda with its stultifying discourse and prescriptive vision of learning also worked against a more humane and hopeful focus developing within mental health, one of recovery (Ralph, 2000; DoH, 2001).

The research: who, how

The study drawn on in this chapter explored the experiences of a group of 14 mentally ill adults, aged between 24 and 65, as they undertook a basic literacy/creative writing course at their local mental health drop-in centre. All individuals in the study were in receipt of disability allowance and held diagnoses from a range of mental illness including schizophrenia, psychosis, chronic depression, BPD and anxiety. Such diagnoses are notoriously contested and shifting, the 'wholesale comings and goings of disease classifications' (Porter, 2002) of the Diagnostic and Statistical Manual of Mental Disorders (DSM IV) in themselves testament to the rapidity of changes and uncertainty of diagnostic knowledge. Common to all individuals, however, was a long term battle with depression and they had each been hospitalised several times for treatment.

Most of the group, including the couple in this paper, were from a white British background. Consent was gained for each set of data (interviews, observations, written work) and participants were regularly reminded of my role, the scope of the research and their right to withdraw from all or parts of the research. While most gave full consent, in some cases participants were happy for me to observe sessions and read their work, but they did not feel able to take part in the interviews. Tili and Dexter (not their real names) were part of the 'core group' who gave full consent to each part of the research for a full five years.

The research applied a psychosocial (Hoggett, 2004) analysis to the data. This assumes a psychosocial subject, through which 'the real events of the external, social world are desirously and defensively, as well as discursively, appropriated.' (Hollway, 2004: 7). This meant being mindful throughout of factors such as meaning-making, behaviours and perceptions which could be seen to be products of a particular class and its discourse, of growing up in a particular time and culture (Sagan, 2007), but also of factors which seemed to suggest unconscious behaviours and responses. As researchers in the psychosocial paradigm attest, this is not a straightforward process. This study revealed time and again, for example, that the difficult relationship with formal education shared by the people in this group was forged through a long and troublesome combination of socioeconomic background *and* early behaviours and emotional responses. Such particular responses might be the result, of, for example, a lifelong problematic relationship with authority, or even with food and the taking in of nourishment (Eigen, 1999). In the case of the two people in this paper, the question of what role love was performing in enabling learning and a shift to a new narrative, was important. Throughout my work with them, however, the need for a strong tolerance for 'unresolvedness' and for 'negative capability' (Bion, 1970, after Keats, 1817) in research processes was evident, in order to stay with, and be thoughtful of, the apparent contradictions, silences, gaps, repetitions and reluctances of this couple's learning and narrative involvement. Such unresolvedness in narrative structure reminds us that for many, a life story is best told through what is *unsaid*, *non-textual* and *withheld*; requiring particular skills and spaces in the listener, the reader and the research methodology.

The analysis included a tracking of the 'identity work' apparently being carried out across the three data domains of narrative interview, observations of learning sessions and the writing produced therein. This enabled a picture to emerge of how identities were being performed through varying engagements with opportunity for narrative. The weighting was deliberately uneven, however, with interview data being seen as the primary source, to be either contradicted by or concurred with through the other data. Although a well-worn research tool in investigating the lives of the vulnerable and the excluded (Chamberlayne, Rustin et al., 2002) biographic interviewing did not come easily to the people with whom I spoke, unaccustomed as they were to the 'talking cure' paradigm and its corollaries, be it autobiographic writing, oral history or counselling. The expression that such activities were *'not for the likes of me'* was common. This was, I found, a salutary reminder that such reflexivity, or rather, opportunities for it, are class-based; and their survival ever more tenuous in the present cold climate.

We met in the psychiatric ward: Romantic narratives

> ... *the romance growing up in the interstices of a mass of hard, prosaic reality*
> (Thomas Hardy, Far from the Madding Crowd).

Tili and Dexter met during one of their many stays in a local hospital. Both were recovering from breakdowns and had long histories of mental illness. Tili had a history of psychoticism and Dexter suffered from chronic depression and anxiety. Their 'love at first sight at the psychiatric hospital' narrative was well-rehearsed and known to all at the day centre where I met them. It was always retold and relistened to with companionable enjoyment, and had importantly become part of the fabric of circulating stories from the users. These, in themselves, made up the hopeful (and often recovery focussed) narrative of the day centre itself. These appeared early on to directly counter the narratives *of* rather than *from* the 'mentally ill adult learner' I was to hear from some professionals, particularly, regrettably, in education. Tili and Dexter's romantic narrative had become a way of offering to others an idiom through which to source a seam of good outcome in otherwise bleak stories. Both in their late forties, Tili and Dexter had been married a couple of years, and for Tili the marriage had meant a move away, at last, from her oppressive parents' home. This home ran a harsh religious regime with little tolerance for amongst many things, emotional fragility.

Dexter was known as a bit of a wordsmith, being able to conjure up short, pithy rhymes. He was personable and always put on a brave face, despite his many ailments both mental and physical, some of which were life-threatening and sadly increased as the study progressed. He was well-liked and sociable. He appeared relatively secure in Tili's brief absences, but talk of himself, his illness or his writing would be brief before returning to generous mention of Tili, their life together, or his concern for her and what he regarded as a loss of her talent – for writing, for learning, for life. Dexter invariably had a plan for Tili: *'I'm trying to make sure she gets out . . . she should be doing some voluntary work, other things, too, I need to get her to go . . .'*

Tili herself was darker, both in appearance and character. Swarthy and heavy set, she looked out timidly from troubled, dark eyes and spoke in a thick, slow and reticent speech, often slurred by heavy medication. Her narrative was deferential to Dexter(s). Praise of him and his talents was lavish, and expressions of her concern for his well-being abundant. Both Dexter and Tili spoke *lovingly* – but the stakes appeared higher for Tili who made no secret of her being *'completely dependent on him, for everything'*. She made no secret of the fact that he saved her from continued belittlement and isolation at the hands of her parents.

Over the five years of this study it became increasingly difficult to interview Tili and Dexter separately. In fact, after the second year I stopped trying, following a particularly difficult interview with Tili during which her levels of anxiety at being separated from Dexter and not *'there if he needs me'* became palpable. She was physically uncomfortable, unable to settle in her chair, her eye contact became erratic and her facial features tense. She was distracted; unable to maintain a narrative thread, frequently losing track of what she had said and limiting her responses to sentence fragments. I was reminded of the flapping desperation of a fish out of water, and indeed, when I 'released' her back into the water of being with Dexter, she relaxed immediately, and swam away gratefully. From then on, my interviews were taken with them both. This, however, rendered even more porous the boundaries between Tili's narrative and that of her husband. Questions regarding 'whose' narrative was being performed, and thus co-creating the narrator, came to the fore. Narrative researchers interviewing couples will be familiar with the frequently self-referential content of the narrative. Here, remembered stories are co-constructed in a delicate play-off and collaboration between facial gesture and other non-verbal signal, voice tone and straightforward dismissal or negation:

Tili: It happened when we were at Bournemouth, we were . . .
Dexter: (looks at Tili and raises eyebrows) . . . er, no love, it wasn't that year . . .
Tili: (Pauses, looks at Dexter) . . . it was, 'cos we bought that tea cosy . . .
Dexter: (shifts in his seat) no, no, it definitely wasn't Bournemouth, not that year neither . . .
Tili: (laughs, shrugs, looks at me apologetically) . . . my memory . . .

it's bad Olivia, getting really bad . . . I forget things! It wasn't Bournemouth . . . not that year . . . (pause)

A pursuit of 'truth' (i.e. what happened at Bournemouth, if it was Bournemouth, if not where/ when) was not at stake in the research, but there was an attempt being made to map *individual* stories of motivation for learning and writing, within the quagmire of mental illness. It was clear that such an 'individual' mapping was untenable, given the dominance of a *joint* story and the simple acknowledgement that all narrative is built on the borders of another life, other lives – or indeed their absence. It also appeared that Tili's narrative was elusive and diminishing – what scraps emerged were being subsumed by the couple's narrative, and that, largely driven by Dexter. The narrative reproduced in the sessions by both the couple and, gradually, by narrative osmosis, the other members of the group was that:

Dexter was a good writer and writing helped his health through helping him relax and express himself.
Tili wrote because she wanted to write for Dexter (find new ways of praising him/saying I love you).
She attended sessions to be near him and help him if/when he needed her. They did everything together.
Tili was nobody and nothing before she met Dexter.
She owed him her life.

There were, however, a number of contradictions in this narrative. Tili was, at least on paper, the better educated, and had spent more actual time in formal primary and secondary education. She was younger and not unattractive. Although ill in terms of *mental* illness, Dexter was far more immobile and incapacitated by heart problems, asthma and the effects of at least one minor stroke. While Dexter wrote rhyming verse with wide popular appeal, Tili's work, confined in the main to activities suggestive of an unyielding obsession with a single person, characteristic of the state of *limerance* (Tennov, 1999), consisted of poems about Dexter, his characteristics and their love affair. Such written work, while repetitive and often monotonous in its unchanging content and thrust, was no less fluent or competent than Dexter's. And yet the *package* of Tili and Dexter presented to the centre, the users and indeed to the research, was one which fore grounded Dexter's narrative; his life; writing and talents, while over-shadowing a figure of Tili as the more needy, less capable, weaker and more ill. This may well have constituted an apparent 'bad faith narrative' (Craib, 2000) in which there is an attempt to *'deny agency and the possibility of change'* (p. 67) and one more case of women's narrative identity being colonised by the male, sequestered into a default position of lack and dependency. The suppressed within a story, however, nevertheless *'continues to affect the character of the whole'* (Chessick, 1999: 65) and, in cases of co-dependency, it is the nature of the *co* which is less easily addressed. Dependency itself is often more overt than the ways in, and through which it is enacted. How the whole of the Tili and Dexter narrative was operating on each respective life became an increasingly important question, as indeed did the question of how and if this co-dependency was helping or hindering the survival and learning of each.

It appeared that in this limited, constricting realm of activity the depleting pressure of subtle male influence joined forces with the cultural view of emotionality and mental illness as more debilitating than physical infirmity. While one could speculate endlessly about who or what Tili would be without Dexter, working *within* the highly dependent dynamic it is still vital to identify which, if any, were the survival strategies being deployed by Tili and where, if anywhere, lay the spaces for agency. Learning, tied so traditionally to notions of empowerment, even while it routinely sabotages this by reproducing power structures intact, was one potential way in which a breathing space might be allowed for the emergence of an alternative narrative of Tili.

The price of love

> *Who am I to tell my private nightmares to if I can't tell them to you?*
> (Estragon, Act 1, Waiting for Godot by Samuel Beckett)

Tili and Dexter were enrolled on a once weekly course which ran three times a year for approximately 10 weeks. Funding was secured for the course at the time by demonstrating that it would help increase literacy levels of marginalised, mentally ill adults in the borough. It was thus in line with the vision of the Skills for Life Strategy which was saturating practice with its provisos and prescriptive pedagogy. While working within the restrictions attached to the funding, however, the centre and its teacher became adept at inbuilding adequate fluidity and sensitivity of content to give at least a veneer of learner-centredness and provide what seemed, after the term of the study, to be a sustained, good-enough experience of learning. Individual aspirations (learning to write 'I love you') were to some extent catered for, even while none of these aspirations included passing the level 2 Adult literacy test and thus contributing to the government's targets and its clamorous campaign for skills (Leitch, 2006). Neither Tili nor Dexter showed any interest in attending the local college, expressing instead a marked disinclination for learning in what they considered to be a stigmatising, threatening environment in which *'They'd make us do stuff we're not interested in . . . What I don't want to do . . .'*

It was striking how the narrower the remit of education became (the language of learning, rehabilitation and leisure being replaced by the language of upskilling, employability and competence) the wider was the gap between the 'self as learner' envisaged by Tili and Dexter and the image of learner being promoted both locally and nationally. This polarity became, it seemed, one more mechanism through which the mentally ill individual, as mentioned earlier, was positioned as other and effectively barred access to participation in education. As I (Sagan, 2009) and others before have observed (Rustin, 2001), such bi-polar, frequently minutely obsessive characteristics of sclerotic educational policy and provision are particularly unhelpful and yet ironic in their bizarre reflection of symptoms of mental illness itself.

Paradoxically, while these two learners were involved in adult learning, the factors which appeared to keep them involved were more to do with love and its corollaries than skills. Dexter 'loved writing' and Tili loved Dexter. They were both, in their ways, involved in a prolonged campaign to improve or at least maintain their health *'to make the most of the years we've got, now that we've found each other'*. Coming to the centre and participating in its activities with their peers in the struggle for mental health was very much a labour of love – one which they spoke of in strong 'we' terms of survival, with regular question-tags of affinity and collaboration:

We've got to get out of the house . . . haven't we?
If we miss a week, it's bad . . .
We go right down, don't we, Dex, if we don't go?
We make sure we get there, don't we Tili?

Both Tili and Dexter described *loving* 'learning' and 'words' and, for Tili in particular, being able to expand her repertoire of loving words to

Dexter was crucial to her involvement – as was loving *'seeing 'im busy in the lessons . . .'* While the writing and the sessions, including the group dynamic, appeared to simply offer *'more ways to say I love you'* (and it would be easy to denigrate or pathologise this), the trajectory of Tili's depression and mental illness was such that it was extremely unlikely that she would have left the house at all, let alone engage in the learning and writing, without Dexter, and without this one reason to persevere. Although through the five years of the study there was no noticeable shift in Tili's narrative, she did, from time to time, allude to *what had been* 'her story' – one of illness, subjugation to a harsh religious dogma in her parent's house, and stigma. Out of this – she and Dexter had constructed a very different story, one of love, support, care, possible recovery and latterly, learning; aspects missing, from her narrative prior to falling *into* love, a narrative which, in her words was a: *'no story . . . I didn't have a story, it was . . . just nothing . . .'* In this story the transformative power of learning can claim no great victory; yet the incremental nature of recovery and learning against such odds as Tili's suggest that learning to say I love you, just may, given time, given safety and stability of provision and life factors, lead to a riskier exploration of the 'I' in I love you.

The price of love, it seemed, was not as high as the price of being alone with a deteriorating mental illness and a bleaker and bleaker 'no-story'. Given *this* configuration, the relationship and its maintenance, in all its apparent subservience, can be construed as a valuable survival strategy, a resource deployed from within a small and shrinking range of possibilities.

Elements of love and its language were not confined to Tili and Dexter. Over the five years of the study, a forceful anchor in the group and stimulant of the motivation of its members was the social capital it engendered. Whilst much has been written about this aspect of community learning (Schuller *et al.*, 2004), a belief that marginalised groups are thereby given either recognition or power outside of these settings through such capital is erroneous. Such capital and the networks which webbed it, nevertheless did allow a cohesive learning setting to be sustained. This nurtured shoots of other projects through which the feelings of safety and being held enabled a learning, if not of spelling, of peripheral, yet vital lessons: learning strategies for survival, learning to voice an 'I', learning to say I love you, differently.

The mutuality and recognition amongst a group of adults each of whom had a long history of stigma through mental illness was referred to by each as a vital component of their learning. It was, importantly, one which they felt was unquestionably *not* forthcoming or even potential in the more formal learning settings into which several of them had experimentally strayed at some point in the recent past. The love of the group, in this case, was a further indirect outcome of the way in which this provision was managed – and this management in turn was another product of a labour of love, expressed by the teacher and the centre volunteers throughout the term of the study in words with which community and voluntary practitioners and researchers will be familiar: words of passion; compassion; dedication; sympathy; belief; indignation at injustice and discrimination. In a recently argued plea for a return to an appreciation of the role of love in pedagogy, Halpin (2009: 94) rightly draws our attention to the importance in pedagogy of the responsibilities of love. These include the need 'to be open; to be sensitive; to be sincere; to be concerned; to be connected; to be empathic; to be tolerant; to be respectful'. Despite its continually threatened funding, its shoe-string resources, heavy reliance on over-worked and underpaid personnel and the day to day resilience needed to work with some of the borough's most ill, distressed and sometimes desperate citizens, the centre in this study managed to function in a spirit of good-enough education and welfare. This, as Hoggett (2008) points out, is perhaps because '... for many public service workers care is inseparable from social justice,' he adds that workers on such front lines embody an 'angry compassion' which fuses an ethics of care with a passion for justice.

This care, this 'angry compassion' enabled the centre in this research to provide learning where more well resourced, staffed and recognised educational facilities in the area could not. The price for individual professionals, however, of such emotional labour was *not* explored in this research – although there undoubtedly is one. What is also not in doubt is that the loving and holding function of small pockets of provision for the mentally ill and marginalised adult learner problematically allow other educational organisations and institutions to continue in an abjuration of such responsibilities. It allows too, a continued fetishised adherence to a neoliberal managerialism and technicist pedagogy which effectively foreclose on developing processes, metrics and environments which might contain and hold the delicate hurts of complex lives.

The cost of care

> *The managerialisation of welfare has led to a situation in which the amount of one-to-one contact between clients/service users and professionals has been systematically reduced – on the ward, in the classroom, between offender and probation officer, client and social worker, troubled adolescent and youth worker* (Hoggett, 2008).

Our continued love/hate relationship with love in the philosophical nerve centre of western society has meant that considerations of what love is, how it, in Puccini's words, turns to anguish, but also how it sustains and repairs, have become part of the bedrock inquiry of anthropology, epistemology, sociology and art. And of all our disciplines, psychoanalysis, perhaps, has had the most to say about love. Much of the time, however, we are clearly not talking about the same thing, and there have been pains taken to separate romantic love from altruistic love, for example. Less time has been spent on looking at classed notions of love, and, for example, the disdain regularly expressed about the love of others. Recently, the love of parents who 'allow' their children to become obese has been questioned. The stereotyped 'tough love' of the working class towards their kids as they 'clip em round the ear' has also been regarded as somewhat 'other' to the love of the middle classes who are routinely portrayed as having a more complex and rich emotional life compared with the 'psychological simplicity' of the working class (Steedman, 1986). But most staggering, still, is our view of the almost taboo love of the disabled and the mentally ill. Murphy (1987: 92) analyses how the disabled have to 'protect' society from their social relations:

> *'they must comfort others about their own condition. They cannot show fear, sorrow, depression, sexuality, or anger, for this disturbs the able-bodied'*

Tili and Dexter, poor, marginalised and ill, had, despite this managed to create a counter-narrative with their 'we met in psychiatric hospital' story. This story, fascinatingly, had come to surpass their own individual stories of sad childhoods, trauma, illness, poverty, and enduring battles with systems, services and institutionalised lovelessness.

Melanie Klein's (1998) distinction between *eros* and *caritas* is useful for this paper, not only in offering a more rounded way to think about Tili and Dexter's love but also to think about the welfare of compassion, and its requisite reparative culture (Froggett, 2002). In this perspective, Eros is the greedy, more selfish and 'paranoid-schizoid' of loves, idealising and energised in its fundamentally narcissistic quest. Caritas, on the other hand represents a move to Klein's depressive position, where a more reflective subjectivity is enabled, one which allows for a recognition of the other as separate and unique. Far from denigrating Tili and Dexter's love, co-dependent as it appeared, subjugating of Tili's narrative as it arguably was, classically male defined and led, as it was, it nevertheless appeared to enable survival. And while Estragon and Vladimir's cruel but touching co-dependent relationship sustained them, in all its tricks, abuses and small generosities, throughout their long wait for Godot (Beckett, 1954), Tili and Dexter's love similarly provided a *raison d'être*, literally, a reason to be, when prevailing discourses were telling them all they were *not*.

In a cold climate with little love in welfare and in a postmodern time of liquid, shifting, greedy and conditional love (Bauman, 2003), Tili and Dexter's self-referential love story of Bournemouth holidays, shared medical appointments, and once-weekly writing class where they learned to write I love you better, saved lives. It saved Tili and Dexter from the cold climate that was the best our current education and welfare services could offer; one of isolation, stigma, poverty, and last but not least, loneliness, identified as a source of considerable distress in mental illness (Lynch, 2000).

One of the arguments against increased welfare has traditionally been the question of the creation or encouragement of dependence. As with a reading of Tili and Dexter's own co-dependence, which could simplistically be seen as maintaining Tili in particular in a position of inferiority and weakness, such binary formulations are unhelpful in understanding human needs and the intertwined nature of welfare, agency and health. Perhaps we need to turn our attention to the interface, the inter*play* of binaries:

> *Rather than promoting the dependency/independence dichotomy, we could propose interdependence as the principle which brings into play all those emotional, material, physical networks of unequal reciprocity, and creates the basis for autonomy* (Williams, 1999: 677).

Through the construction and maintenance of their narrative, Tili and Dexter performed, for each other, a crucial task of recognition (Benjamin,

1998). In this, they both saw each other, and themselves, as other to their historic (troubled) selves but crucially, other to the ill. Whilst psychic health may indeed lie, eventually, in the replacement of fantasy with reality, and the erosion of denial at the service of 'truth' – Tili and Dexter's fight for life, particularly Tili's, was much more at a basic survival level. And precisely because of the lack of love in our communities, the scarcity of caritas in our evidence-based welfare (Froggett, 2002) and the subservience of love to notions of 'hard' skills in our pedagogic approaches, this love affair was also acting as community, family, welfare and teacher.

Endings: Love in a cold climate

> *The 'I' in illness is isolation, and the crucial letters in wellness are we.* (Mimi Guarneri)

Towards the end of this research my father was diagnosed with Alzheimers. In some ways, this was a blessing. We, his beleaguered family, had struggled through many years of an undefined, shifting mental illness which had eroded the love, nerves and hope of us all by its subtle stealing of memory and its playing havoc on narrative coherence, empathetic capability and even basic processes of thought. These were also years which enmeshed me in a personal and professional absorption in the strategies, sometimes unconscious, which are deployed as an individual attempts to make sense of the non-sensible, while remaining, or indeed becoming, the 'narratively dispossessed' (Baldwin, 2006).

What was clear, however, from early on in the diagnosis, was that as his mental faculties were weakening, the 'love' of the family was being hailed by a health and welfare service unable to address the largely unanticipated 21st-century phenomenon of huge increases in dementia within a growing aged population. According to one report, by 2025, there will be over one million dementia sufferers in the UK and currently family carers of people with dementia save the UK over £6 billion a year (Knapp and Prince, 2007). Increases in life expectancy in other postindustrial countries are likely to lead to a similar reality having to be faced, with ageing populations of physically able but mentally impaired elderly people needing specialised care. The love of families and friends will be instrumental in contributing to quality of later-life. In the case of my family, this love of ours was to be redefined, stretched, tested and reconfigured as new and often seemingly unfair demands were put on it to deliver, in order to help someone increasingly unable to survive, survive. As Wolff, (2007) argues:

> *The love, compassion, kindness, familiarity and trustworthiness provided by a family member contribute value in ways that are difficult to quantify and value through impersonal market forces. Likewise, the pain and suffering of family members who internalise the suffering of their chronically ill family member are also unrecognised by replacement valuation. In essence, these intangible attributes of caregiving services, which are produced in informal markets, are assumed to be valueless.*

In the case of Tili and Dexter, struggling with deteriorating mental health, as in my father's case, it was clear that our weakening and much commodified welfare and education provision was falling short. Less and less able to hold and to contain, it was calling hard and fast on families and individuals to pick up the slack. In so doing, entire narratives were being constructed by people whose language now became one of care, responsibility and providing, rather than a language of choice. Choice remains a characteristic of privilege; and contrary to Bauman's (2003) description of a nonchalant, individualistic and self-interested subject dropping love like a hot potato when it gets tough, for class and cultural reasons, many people treat, and need love differently. If, as Bauman maintains, we are nomads in the brave new world, swanning through love affairs, commitments and relationships in a virtual whirl, then that nomadic freedom is still limited to some, and largely deprived others. Tili and Dexter, in loving each other in a cold climate, and committing, in Bauman's description, rather old-fashionedly, to looking after each other, paid the price in terms of the precious autobiographic 'I'. Such an 'I', prized achievement that it has become, and much sought-after accomplishment of a postmodern fragmented self, is a privilege; one not yet on the radar of those for whom making it through to tomorrow is achievement enough.

References

Baldwin, C. (2006) 'The narrative dispossession of people living with dementia: thinking about the theory and method of narrative', in *Narrative, memory, knowledge: representations, aesthetics, contexts*. University of Huddersfield, pp. 101–9.

Ball, J. S. (2006) *Education policy and social class: the selected works of Stephen J. Ball*. London: Routledge.

Bauman, Z. (2003) *Liquid love*. Cambridge: Polity.

Chamberlayne, P., Rustin, M. et al. (2002) *Biography and social exclusion in Europe; experiences and life journeys*. Bristol: The Policy Press.

Craib, I. (2000) 'Narratives as bad faith', in S. D. Sclater, C. Squire and A. Treacher (eds), *Lines of narrative: psychosocial perspectives*, 67–74. London, Routledge.

Frank, A. W. (1997) *The wounded storyteller: body, illness and ethic*. Chicago and London: The University of Chicago Press.

Halpin, D. (2009) 'Pedagogy and romantic love', *Pedagogy, Culture and Society* 17: 1, 89–102.

Hartill, G. (1998) 'The web of words: collaborative writing and mental health', in C. Hunt and F. Sampson (eds), *The self on the page: theory and practice of creative writing in personal development*, 47–61. London, Jessica Kingsley Publishers

Hoggett, P. (2000) *Emotional life and the politics of welfare*. Basingstoke: Macmillan.

Hoggett, P. (2004) 'Strange attractors: politics and psychoanalysis', *Psychoanalysis, Culture and Society*, 9, 74–86.

Hoggett, P., Clarke, S. and Thompson, S. (eds) (2008) *Emotion, Politics and Society*. Basingstoke: Palgrave Macmillan.

Hornstein, G. (2002) 'Narratives of madness, as told from within', *The Chronicle of Higher Education*, 25, 7–10.

Knapp, M. and Prince, M. (2007) *Dementia UK*. London: Alzheimer's Society.

Lacan, J. (1977) *Écrits: a selection*. New York: Norton.

Leitch, S. (2006) *The Leitch review of skills: Prosperity for all in the global economy*. Norwich: The Stationery Office.

Murphy, R. F. (1987) *The body silent*. London: J. M. Dent and Sons,

Payne, G. (2006) 'Re-counting "illiteracy": literacy skills in the sociology of social inequality', *The British Journal of Sociology*, 57: 2, 220–40.

Polkinghorne, D. E. (1988) *Narrative knowing and the human sciences*. Albany: SUNY Press.

Porter, R. (2002) *Madness: a brief history*. Oxford: Oxford University Press.

Rustin, M. (2001) *Reason and unreason: psychoanalysis, science and politics*. London: Continuum.

Sagan, O. (2007) 'An interplay of learning, creativity and narrative biography in a mental health setting: Bertie's story', *Journal of Social Work Practice* 21: 3, 311–21.

Sagan, O. (2008) 'The loneliness of the long-anxious learner: mental illness, narrative biography and learning to write', *Psychodynamic Practice*, 14: 1, 43–58.

Sagan, O. (2009) Anxious provision and discourses of certainty: The sutured subject of mentally ill learner', *International Journal of Lifelong Education* 28(5): 615–29.

Stone, B. (2004) 'Towards a writing without power: notes on the narration of madness', *Auto/Biography* 12: 1, 16–33.

Styron, W. (2004) *Darkness visible*. London: Vintage.

Taylor, N. (2008) 'Critical analysis of the adult literacy curriculum: instructive or regulative?' *Research in Post-Compulsory Education*, 13: 3, 307–14.

Tennov, D. (1999) *Love and limerence: the experience of being in love*. Chelsea, MI: Scarborough House Publishing.

Williams, F. (1999) 'Good-enough principles for welfare', *Journal of Social Policy*, 28: 4, 667–87.

Wolff, N. (2007) 'The social construction of the cost of mental illness', *Evidence and Policy*, 3: 1, 67–78.

Identities: Conclusion

SUE JACKSON

In this section the authors have explored both learner identities and teacher identities, whilst recognising that many of us are both learners *and* teachers, teachers *and* learners. In particular, the section's chapters have been interested in transformations: transformations of identities through lifelong learning; and transformations of lifelong learning through those to whom striving for social justice is part of their personal, professional and political identities. They have demonstrated how identity formation takes place within neoliberal global discourses and policies of individualism, marketisation and competition, with widening gaps between rich and poor. Yet despite this, or maybe because of it, the authors in this section have also shown ways in which identity formation takes place through critical engagement with the growing awareness of inequalities that learning can bring, whether in the classroom or outside of it. They have shown how this leads to increasing commitments to strive for social justice, especially when learners share something of their identities and their social and political worlds.

The authors have been interested, too, in power and power relations, and the relationships between constructions of power and identities in localised/globalised societies and their places and spaces of learning. They have shown how power exists within social interactions, with people responding to power, exercising or resisting it, according to social, cultural and political contexts, as well as to identity formations. These are themes with which I will engage in the book's final chapter, its conclusions.

Lifelong learning and social justice: Conclusion

SUE JACKSON

Olssen *et al.* (2004) argue that education – and particularly education policy – is key to sustainability in a globalised world (see also Chapter One of this book). The era of globalisation, they say, brings an urgency for a new world order, and 'education policies are central to such a global mission' (p. 1). A question for the authors of this book has been whether a model for lifelong learning can be developed that does not take neoliberalism as the accepted truth of globalisation. To what extent are models of lifelong learning still possible that continue from some of their more radical routes in their concern with equality and social justice? Several of the chapter authors call for a model of lifelong learning that embraces alternative visions for learning as participation through concerns with equality and social justice (see, e.g., Chapters Two, Three, Eight and Nine). As some of the authors here have shown, learning can be revolutionary, responding and acting to bring about change. Nevertheless, it has also been argued that lifelong learning aims to discipline subjects (Fejes and Nicholl, 2008; see also Chapter Five) through governmentality of activities which guide and shape the permissible conduct of individuals. This book has critically engaged with contradictions such as these, considering power and resistances to power in its exploration of lifelong learning and social justice in a globalised world.

As several of the chapter authors have demonstrated, power is everywhere. It exists within all (local and global) social structures and interactions, and people respond to it, exercise it or resist it according to social, cultural, political and educational contexts, and within constructs of difference. According to Foucault, power 'incites, it induces, it seduces, it makes it easier or more difficult; in the extreme it constrains or forbids absolutely' (Foucault, 1982: 219). Power demands conformity to dominant ideas: this can be resisted but may result in punishment. It can be direct but can also be insidious, creeping and hidden.

According to Foucault, subjects are constituted through power. Unlike Marx, for example, he does not locate power within classes: rather it is located within individuals and their activities and institutions, although some people occupy more significant positions in society to exercise power than others. As this book has shown, it is impossible to separate discussions of lifelong learning and/or social justice from discussions of power. Foucault describes power/knowledge as one: knowledge and truth are produced out of power struggles between different fields of knowledge. There is, he says:

> *no power relation without the correlative constitution of a field of knowledge, nor any knowledge that does not presuppose and constitute at the same time power relations* (Foucault, 1977: 27).

Foucault (1977) has demonstrated how the power of normalising discourse can create an illusion of normality against which we judge claims to truth, which constructs people as both subjects and objects of power and knowledge. It is the constitution of knowledge claims as 'truth' that is linked to systems of power: those who have the power – structurally and institutionally as well as individually – to determine and legitimise 'truth' also have the power to determine dominant discourses (Jackson, 2004). As Jarvis (2007: 15) argues, power is also constituted through control of social and cultural agendas. It is the resources of power and authority that determine decisions which appear as if they are 'normal'.

Foucault notes that the normalising judgement has become one of the central elements of our society (although, as below, he often normalises male ways of being, showing women as 'Other' in his writing). He says:

> *The judges of normality are everywhere . . . it is on them that the universal reign of the normative is based; and each individual, wherever he may find himself, subjects it to his body, his gestures, his behaviour, his aptitudes, his achievements* (Foucault, 1977: 304).

However, there is always the possibility of resistance. As Avtar Brah argues:

> *Conscious agency and unconscious subjective forces are enmeshed in everyday rituals such as those surrounding . . . social activity. These rituals provide the site on which a sense of belonging, a sense of 'identity', may be forged in the process of articulating its difference from other people's way of doing things* (Brah, 2007: 143).

As the authors of these chapters have shown, whilst we do all have agentic possibilities, self-understanding arises not just from how one is prepared to act (Brubaker and Cooper, 2000: 17) but how one is *able* to act. In part, the ability to act depends on the resources available to us, the capital we are able to accumulate through our various and varying positionings.

Capital can be understood as an amount or volume of wealth held by particular agents, and is a social relationship that thus permeates the social world (Beasley-Murray, 2000). The concept of capital is about its accumulation not just to exchange, but also to invest. It is possibly most commonly understood in relation to financial resources, but can also be understood in relation to ways in which we accumulate other types of 'wealth' and resources, for example social capital (see, e.g., Putman, 1995; also Chapters Three, Six and Nine); human capital (see, e.g., Becker, 1964; also Chapters Four and Six); cultural capital (see, e.g., Bourdieu, 1973; and Chapter Nine); identity capital (see, e.g., Côté and Levene, 2002; see also Chapter Eight); emotional capital (Nowotny, 1981; see also Chapter Eleven) and more recently relational capital (Jackson, 2010 – see below).

Social capital, often discussed in relation to lifelong learning (see, e.g., Field, 2006), is central to the promotion of civil society, and involves moral obligations and norms, social values and trust, and social networks. Putman (2007) argues that a central challenge is for modern, diversifying societies to create a new, broader sense of 'we'. However, as several of the chapters in this book have shown, a sense of 'we' may be located in the discursive spaces of dominant groups (see for example Chapters One, Three, Six and Nine). Brubaker and Cooper are interested in exploring what this means with regard to identities, arguing that a strongly bonded sense of community, a 'sense of 'we', may depend on a 'powerfully imagined and strongly felt commonality' (2007: 20). A 'powerfully imagined and strongly felt commonality' is evident in some of the chapters here (see Chapters Two, Three and Ten), where authors describe learning communities and communal spaces of learning. However, this can sometimes lead to a sense of identity developed through being only with 'people like us', to sectionality rather than intersectionality, to accounts of insider/ outsider, or belonging and unbelonging. In turn, this may normalise hegemonic ways of being where marginalised groups little recognise themselves. As these chapters have shown, groups and individuals of unequal power and unequal access to resources can struggle to find meaningful engagement with learning 'opportunities' which can often seem at odds with an agenda of social justice.

Social divisions of difference become negotiated and constructed through constructions of 'we' and although this is empowering for some it is disempowering for others (see Brah, 1996: 184). Additionally, a sense of 'we' may be part of the 'imagined communities' to which people feel affiliated. Imagined communities have been described as the images of affinity between community members that members of a community hold in their mind (Anderson, 2006), whether or not that affinity exists (Jackson, 2008; see also Chapter 8). Yet communities are also imagined in relation to our position within them: imagined as male, for example, or 'white', or imagined as a space where social justice prevails, where meaningful learning is available to all, and where connections with others are made.

In considering such connections, I have recently developed the notion of relational capital: a notion of capital that is about the accumulation of *shared* or collective stocks, rather than individual, that may be developed through communities of practice (Jackson, 2010: 250). Relational capital:

> *enables the accumulation of collective stocks of understandings that arise from the relational understandings of and between . . . different voices, histories and memories . . . Relational capital, then, is political, and relational understandings, per se, are about an investment in the development of shared consciousness* (Jackson, 2010: 250).

It enables clearer understandings of the ways we live our lives in localised/ globalised worlds. As such, a determination to strive for social justice can become central to lifelong learning, enabling the alternative ways of seeing for which several of the chapters have called.

This book has been interested in the ways in which identities and sense of self develop through engagement with lifelong learning, in work and in communities. Its authors have recognised that different identities are prioritised in different ways, and at different times, by different groups and individuals, and for different purposes. They have argued that this should send a note of caution to policymakers, with regard to their use of, or creation of categories that do not correspond to 'practice'. Education policy may be key to sustainability in a globalised world (Olssen et al., 2004), yet there is little evidence that policy makers are concerned with policies that embed critical engagement with social justice and lifelong learning.

This book has argued for the development of lifelong learning that offers the potential for new beginnings, finding different ways of belonging and developing alternative ways of being, through real and imagined communities and places of work. It has explored how new belongings and identities are negotiated and constructed through engagements with a critically focussed lifelong learning, that has a concern for social justice at its core. The book's authors have been interested in the multiple encounters which form and inform lifelong learning and social justice: the encounters between individuals and groups; between the private and public; between the personal, political, social, cultural and economic; between home and community; local and global. They have engaged with encounters between competing theoretical and conceptual perspectives and – perhaps most relevant here – encounters between communities, work and identities in a localised/globalised world. As these chapters have so powerfully argued, it is time to explore lifelong learning and social justice through alternative visions for transformative action. Such visions would open possibilities for the development of new knowledges based in critiques of power and holistic understandings of the relations of difference in a globalised world.

References

Anderson, B (2006) *Imagined communities*. London: Verso.
Beasley-Murray, J. (2000) 'Value and capital in Bourdieu and Marx', in Brown, N., and Szeman, I. (eds) *Pierre Bourdieu: fieldwork in culture*, 100–19. Maryland: Rowman and Littlefield.
Becker, G (1964) *Human capital: a theoretical and empirical analysis with special reference to education*. Chicago: University of Chicago Press.
Bourdieu, P. (1973), 'Cultural reproduction and social reproduction', in Brown, R. (ed). *Knowledge, Education and Cultural Change*, London: Tavistock.
Brah, A. (2007) 'Non-binaried identities of similarity and difference', in

Wetherell, M., Lafleche, M. and Berkley, R. (eds), *Identity, ethnic diversity and community cohesion*. London: Sage.

Brah, A. (1996) *Cartographies of diaspora: contesting identities*. London: Routledge.

Brubaker, R. and Cooper F. (2000) 'Beyond Identity', *Theory and Society*: 29: 1, 1–47.

Commission on Integration and Cohesion (2007) *Our shared future*. Wetherby: CIC.

Côté, J. and Levene C., (2002), *Identity formation, agency and culture*, New Jersey: Lawrence Erlbaum.

Fejes, A. and Nicholl, K. (2008) *Foucault and Lifelong Learning: governing the subject*, Abingdon: Routledge.

Field, J. (2004) *Lifelong learning and the new educational order*. Stoke-on-Trent: Trentham Books.

Foucault, M. (1977) *Discipline and punish*. London: Tavistock.

Foucault, M. (1982) 'The subject and power: an afterword', in Dreyfus, H. and Rabinow, P., *Michel Foucault: beyond structuralism and hermeneutics*. Brighton: Harvester Press.

Jackson, S. (2010) 'Learning through social spaces: migrant women and lifelong learning in post–colonial London', *International Journal of Lifelong Education*, 29: 2, 237–54.

Jackson S (2008) 'Diversity, identity and belonging: women's spaces of sociality', *8th International Conference on Diversity in Organisations, Communities and Nations*, University of Montreal, June 17–20.

Jackson, S. (2004), *Differently academic? Developing lifelong learning for women in higher education*. Dordrecht: Kluwer Academic Press.

Jarvis, P. (2007) *Globalisation, lifelong learning and the learning society: sociological perspectives*. London: Routledge.

Olssen, M., Codd, J. and O'Neill, A. (2004) *Reading education policy in the global era Education policy: globalisation, citizenship and democracy*. London: Sage.

Putman, R. (1995) 'Bowling alone: America's declining social capital', *Journal of Democracy*, January, 65–78.

Putnam, R. (2007) *'E Pluribus Unum*: diversity and community in the twenty–first century The 2006 Johan Skytte Prize Lecture', *Scandinavian Political Studies*, 30: 2, 137–74.

Nowotny, H. (1981) 'Women in public life in Austria', in Epstein, C and Coser, R (eds) *Access to power: cross–national studies of women and elites*, eds Cynthia London: Allen and Unwin.

Index

Page numbers in *Italics* represent tables.
Page numbers in **Bold** represent figures.

Aberton, H. 187–8, 237–59
Acker, J. 106
active labour market 110
actor–network theory (ANT) 241, 245
actor–network viewpoint of learning 238
adult and community education (ACE): programmes 257; sector 239
adult education 156; encounters 214; facilities 258
adult learning 78; and dialogical processes 210–32
adult learning theory 241–3
adult literacy 15, 43, 55; education 52–3; and numeracy 150; social practice account of 56
Adult Literacy Curriculum 268
The Age of the Stupid (Documentary) 35
Agnew, R. 67
Agyeman, J. 30
Alzheimers 280
American mass culture 203
American multicultural openness 200
Anderson, B.: *Imagined Communities* 195
Annette, J. 13
Apffel-Marglin, F.: and Bowers, C. 5
Apple, M. 193
Arabic 204
Archer, L. 2
Arendt, H. 61

Aretxaga, B.: *Shattering Silence* 59
Arizona Law of Immigration 195
Armstrong, F. 35
artistic representation 51
Australia 239
autobiographical stories 198
autonomous and ideological model 44
autonomous motivations 145

Baker, J.: et al 46
Bakhtin, M. 191
Ballymac Women's Group 75
banking model of education 217
Barr, J. 71
Barthes, R. 267
Bauman, Z. 25, 191, 281
Beckett, S.: *Waiting for Godot* 274
Belfrage, S.M.: *The Crack–A Belfast Year* 77
Benhabib, S. 61
Bibliography of First Person Narratives of Madness in English (Hornstein) 266
Billett, S. 254
biographical stories 196
Blewitt, J. 18–38
Boshier, R. 138
Boud, D.: and Solomon, N. 240
Bourdieu, P. 76
Boutros-Ghali, B. 46
Bowers, C. 32; and Apffel-Marglin, F. 5
Bradley Report 89
Brah, A. 287
Brine, J. 105
Brown, P.: and Hesketh, A. 88

Index

Canada 155–75; 'head tax' 158; workplace arrangements 163
Canadian context 171
Canadian culture 169
Canadian immigration policies 172
Canadian labour market 156
Canadian society 155
Canadian Survey on Work and Lifelong Learning (2004) 156
Canadian Work In Lifelong Learning Survey (WALL) 159
capital relevance 223–4
Carbon Accounting Systems 35–6
carbon emissions 36
Care in the Community 268
carework 157
Carpenter, V. 187, 210–32
Categorical Imperative notion 91
Catholic University of Ireland 91
Catholic women 72–3
Center for International Programs (IP) 202
child care 151, 167–72
childhood poverty 215
China 162
Chinese culture 172
Chinese immigrant parents 170
Chinese immigrants 157–9; grocery shopping 165; informal learning *161*; informal learning participation *162*; reasons for immigration 169
Chinese medical beliefs 167
Chinese women 158
choice discourse 2–3
Churchwell Women's Centre 76
Churchwell Women's Group 75
civic education 43
civil engagement 199
civil society 287
climate change 27
Clinton, H. 60
co-operative learning technique 223
Cockburn, C. 66, 70
collective intelligence 221
colleges 149
colonialism 6–7
common-sense 227
communicating materials and facts 224
communities 8, 13–16, 288; of practice 288

community engagement 82, 96
Community Engagement Classification 94
community gardens 14–15, 33
community learning 276
Community Learning and Development 148
community of practice 249
community-based women's centres 64–7
conditionality 118
conformity 286
Connolly, L. 62
Corporate Citizenship Company 95
Corrigan, M. 68
cosmopolitan citizenship 187
Country Women's Association (CWA) 245
The Crack—A Belfast Year (Belfrage) 77
creative methodologies 50, 52
Creole 4
critical theory based stance 231
critical thinking 201, 207
cross-cultural connections 198
cross-cultural understanding 205
cultural agendas 286
'Curriculum of Excellence' 148–9

Delors, P. 239
Delpit, L. 229–30
dematerialisation (the economy) 27
dementia sufferers 280
democracy-engaged citizenship 201
democratic society 194
Denman College 257
Department for Work and Pensions (DWP) 113
Derrida, J. 267
Derry Peace Women 68
developing countries 206
Devine-Wright, P.: and Walker, G. 28
Dewey, J. 18–19, 23
diagnostic knowledge 269
Diagnostic and Statistical Manual of Mental Disorders (DSM IV) 269
dialogic democracy 70
dialogical processes 216–30
A dialogue (Macedo) 214
Dickson, D.: and Hargie, O. 62

Index

differentiation and power 255
disability 117
discrimination 51
dominant epistemology 243
Dominican Republic 206
Dubar, C. 191–2
Duke, C. 96

economic rationales 268
economic recession 106
economics 232
education 5, 84
education encounters 188
Education Matters (website) 254
education model 232
Education Participation Scale 145
education policy 289
education and race issues 222
Education for Sustainable Development (ESD) 19–22
education and training policy areas 111
education-related social justice 220
eldercare 172–3; transnational 173
embodied learning 244
empirical studies 157
employability 148
Employment and Support Allowance (ESA) 121
Empowering education (Shor) 214
English language 246
epistemological understandings 210
equal educational opportunities 206
Equal Opportunities Commission for Northern Ireland 71
equality 43–4; and inequalities 49–50
equality dimensions 47
equality framework 52–3
equality perspectives 45–6
established learning theory 240
ethics approval 225
ethnic communities 75
EU Peace and Reconciliation Programmes 65
European Association for the Education of Adults (EAEA) 21
European policies 111
European Social Fund (ESF) 110
European tertiary institutions 231
European Union (EU) 45–6, 107

European Union Sixth Framework Project 134

Falls Women's Centre 59
farmers markets 27
Fegan, T. 50
feminism 62–4
feminist politics 16
feminist scholars 158
Field, J. 3, 21, 139
filial piety 172
film industry 18
Firth, M. 93
Flexible New Deal (FND) 122, 123; regulations (2009) 117
food preparation 162
foreign language education 194–201
Foucault, M. 87, 286
foundational certainty 255
Frank, A.W. 267
Fraser, G.: and Morgan, V. 65
Freire, P. 4, 43, 213, 222; *Mentoring the mentor* 214; *A pedagogy for liberation* 214; *Pedagogy of the Oppressed* 44, 213–14; and Shor, I. 214
Freirean approach to empowerment 5
Freirean dialogical processes 216
Freirean pedagogy 218
Freud, D. 113
Freud Report (2007) 114–17
further education colleges 146

Galbraith, J.K. 84
Gasper, D. 25
gender 173–4, 247; and rurality 251
gender equality 156
gentrification 34
geographies of power 2
Gherardi, S.: and Nicolini, D. 245
global carbon intensity 29
global community 206
global language 181
globalisation 6, 102, 185
globalised knowledge economy 3
globalised world 289
Glor, M.: and Kanu, Y. 221
Golding, B.: *et al* 258
Government Economic Strategy 150
government legislation 122

Index

Greater Toronto Area 160
Greece 125
green economy 26–37
Green New Deal Group 28
Greene, M. 50
Gregg, P. 113
Gregg Report (2008) 117–20, 123

Habermas, J. 93
habitus 77
Hake, B.J. 139
Hall, S. 186
Halpern, D. 22
Halpin, D. 277
Hamber, B.: and Kelly, G. 53
Hanna's House 61
Haraway, D. 253
Hargie, O.: and Dickson, D. 62
Haymes, S.N. 32
hegemonic ways of being 288
Held, D. 198
Hesketh, A.: and Brown, P. 88
heterogeneous actors 253
'hidden wealth of nations' 22
Higher Education 16, 19
Higher Education Funding Council for England (HEFCE) 89, 95
Hoggett, P. 269; social justice 277
Holland, B. 24
Hornstein, G.: *Bibliography of First Person Narratives of Madness in English* 266
household work 156, 159; WALL survey 160–2
housework literature 160
Hudson, J. 139
human agency 25
human capabilities 193
human capital 141, 287; learning aspects 147
human capital theory 86
human dignity threshold capabilities 23–4, 31

identities 185, 218, 252; transformations 284
identity formation 246, 254, 284
identity formulation 230
identity and learning 238–41
identity poststructuralist understanding 238

identity renewal 192
'identity work' 270
illegal immigrants 195, 199
Imagined Communities (Anderson) 195
immaterialisation 27
immigration 194–5
individualism 8
inequalities 284
inequality dimensions 47
inequality of opportunities 207
inequality regimes 106
informal atmospheres 217
informal learning 106, 158, 240; WALL survey 160–2
innovative practice 149
Institute of Lifelong Learning 256
institutional funding 211
institutional structures 49
intellectual development 204
intellectuality 220
inter-cultural communication 186
International Adult Literacy Survey 44
International Standard Classification of Education (ISCED) 135
International Women's Day 59
interpersonal interaction 201
intersectionalities of disadvantage 181
intra-cultural research process 51–2
IRA 75
Ireland 15; Roman Catholic and Protestant communities 54

Jackson, S. 1–8, 13–16, 102, 105–29, 181, 185–8, 284, 285–9
Jackson, T. 29
Jamison, A. 36–7
Jamme Masjid Mosque 34
Jarvis, P. 286
Jobcentre Plus 116, 119; and FND **124**; and 'the customer' 127
Jobseekers benefit 121
John Dewey and Environmental Philosophy (McDonald) 31
Jones, A. 212

Kanu, Y.: and Glor, M. 221
Kelly, G.: and Hamber, B. 53
Keynesian welfare state economy 211
Kincheloe, J. 224; and Steinberg, S. 230

Index

Klein, M. 278
knowledge 27; limitations 224; theoretical and research 218; theory-related 221
knowledge economy 105, 129, 139

Labour government 126, 140
labour market 119; participation 152
labour movements 93
Lakeview Learning Centre 249
Lakeview Shire 258
Land Grant universities 82
Language Instruction for Newcomers to Canada (LINC) 168
Laplanchce, J.: and Pontalis, J. 267
Latinos 196
Lave, J.: *Situated Learning* 241; and Wenger, E. 241
Lawler, P. 90
learner identities 259
learner identity 237; constructed 256; decontextualised 240
learner location and study level *135*
mature learners 149
learning 242; initiatives 259; non-formal 254; opportunities 1; pillars 239; social aspects 147
Learning Connections 134, 141
Learning Skills Council 20
Lees, L. 34
legislative powers 117
Leitch Review 115
Lemke, J. 191; and van Helden, C. 202
Levitas, R. 134; three discourses 151
liberal intentions 229
Liberal–Conservative coalition government 112
Lichtenstein, R. 34
Lichun, W.L. 155–75
lifelong learning 1; manager interviews 136; rhetoric 237; and social justice 285–9
Likert scale 145
Lisbon Strategy 133, 138, 140
Lister, R. 66
literacy 5; definitions 44; and language 102; models 44–55
Literacy and Equality in Irish Society (LEIS) 42, 45
literacy skills: low 56

literature and policy: review of 136–8
Livingstone, D. 240
low socioeconomic community 212
low socioeconomic schools 227

McCartan, J. 66
McCauley, J. 76
McCormick, I. 64
McDonald, H.: *John Dewey and Environmental Philosophy* 31
Macedo, D.: *A dialogue* 214
McGrath, B. 74
McKeown, C. 60
McMinn, J. 64
Maguire, A. 60
Manzini, E. 33
Maori and Pasifika ways 228
Maori students 219
Marcus, G. 191
marginalised adult learner 277
marginalised groups 217
marginalised identities 216
Marginson, S. 85, 90
Margritte, R. 242
Mark, R. 42–57
Marx, K. 128, 286
masculinity 251
mass higher education system 92
Men's Sheds Movement 257
mental health: chronic depression 271; deteriorating 281
mental illness 185, 266–81
mentally ill adults 266
Mentoring the mentor (Freire) 214
Mezirow, J. 193; transformation 197
Mignolo, W. 193
Mills, V. 139
Ministry of Education 226
Mol, A. 244
Montesinos, P.: et al 90
Mooney, G.: and Scott, G. 133
moral underclass and dependency discourse (MUD) 136, 151
Morgan, V.: and Fraser, G. 65
Moser Report (1999) 268
Murphy, R.F. 278

National Adult Literacy Agency (NALA) 48

Index

National Institute of Adult and Continuing Education (NIACE) 21
neoliberal agenda 211
neoliberal based knowledge economy 221
neoliberal concerns 105
neoliberal market based economies 85
neoliberal policies 212, 219
neoliberalism 6, 102, 211
New Zealand 210; mainstream banking classes 228; urban school context 225
Newman, J.H. 90–1
Nicolini, D.: and Gherardi, S. 245
Nobel Prize jury 68
Nolan, P. 59–78
North America 159, 205
North American Culture 203
North American educator 191
North of England Council for Promoting the Higher Education of Women 94
Northern Ireland 15, 59–78, 61
Northern Ireland Assembly 60
Northern Ireland Troubles 62
Northern Ireland Women's Rights Movement 63
Norton, B. 192
Norton, M. 50
Nussbaum, M. 23–4

Ofsted 20
Olssen, M. 6; et al 285
Opportunity Scotland (Green Paper) 140
oppression 220
Organisation for Economic Co-operation and Development (OECD) 89, 158
Ostrander, S.A. 92
Ouane, A. 256

paid work 138
parenting 168
participation literature 244
Patterson, M. 67
Peace People 60
peacebuilding 54; and equality 46–9; process 42
Peacebuilding (Porter) 69
pedagogic approaches 280
pedagogical situations 219
pedagogy 223

A pedagogy for liberation (Shor and Freire) 214
Pedagogy of the Oppressed (Freire) 44, 213
personal limitation 129
personal renewal 204
Pew Hispanic Center 195
physical infirmity 274
place-identity-relations continuum 190–1
Pol, E. 30
policy texts 124–5
policymakers 289
political understandings 220
politics and theory 220–3
Pontalis, J.: and Laplanchce, J. 267
poor: deserving and undeserving 126
Poor Laws 110
Porter, E. 61; *Peacebuilding* 69
postcolonialism 7, 102
postgraduate class (PgC) 215
postgraduate study 224
Postlethwaite, P. 36
postmodern fragmented self 281
poverty 136, 150
power 285
power relations 284
prescriptive pedagogy 274
Prideaux, S. 127
Professional Development (PD) 204, 213
Protestant women 72–3
psychosocial analysis 270
psychoticism 271
public policy 3
public sphere 93
Puccini, G. 278
Putman, R. 287

qualification 143
Qualification and Curriculum Authority (QCA) 20

Raco, M. 14
Rasmussen Poll 197
recession 128
reconciliation process 53
recovery 276
redistribution (RED) 151
redistribution (RED) discourse 136
Registered Education Savings Plans (RESP) 171

relations of difference 289
relationship-forming 219
religious dogma 276
reparative culture 279
republican feminists 63
resources 48
Riddell, S.: and Weedon, E. 133–52
Robinson, M. 65
Roman Catholic and Protestant communities 55
Romantic narratives 271–4
Rooney, E. 60; and Woods, M. 65
rural community 249
rural discourses 251
rural femininity 247
Russell Group Universities 95

Sagan, O. 188, 266–81
Saito, M. 25
Sandhu, S. 35
Schuller, T. 257
sclerotic educational policy 275
Scotland: lifelong learning policy 140–2
Scott, G.: and Mooney, G. 133
Scottish economy 149
Scottish Funding Council 134, 151
Scottish lifelong learning policy 150
Scottish Nationalist Party (SNP) 133
semiotic thinking 243
Sen, A. 24
Shankill Women's Centre 59
Shattering Silence (Aretxaga) 59
Shor, I. 45, 227; *A pedagogy for liberation* 214; *Empowering education* 214; and Freire, P. 214
Shum, K.L.: and Watanabe, C. 28
Situated Learning (Lave and Wenger) 241
Skeffington, H.S. 61
Skills for Life Strategy 267, 274
Skills for Scotland (Scottish Government) 133
Snyder, L.: and Tcherepashenets, N. 186–7, 190–208
social capital 88, 219, 287
social control 129
social deprivation 29
social divisions of difference 288
social esteem 48
social inclusion and exclusion 107, 136–8

social integrationist discourse (SID) 138
social justice 4, 207, 226; issues 210, 231; and lifelong learning 285–9; principles 151
social networks 152
social relations 278
social relationship 287
Social Sciences and Humanities Research Council of Canada 159
social welfare 125
socialisation 191–2
Socialist Women's Group 63
societal inequalities 53
sociomaterial approach 243
sociomaterial farm-related practices 251
sociomaterial practices 255
solidarity and identity 230
Solomon, N.: and Boud, D. 240
Spanish language courses 196
Special Educational Needs and Disabilities Act (SENDA) 267–8
state benefit 118
State University of New York 194
Stehr, N. 26
Steinberg, S.: and Kincheloe, J. 230
student thinking and reflection time 229
sustainability 31
sustainable ecological capacity 24

Tcherepashenets, N.: and Snyder, L. 186–7, 190–208
Te Whakapakari project 215
Tett, L.: et al 147
textual confrontation 222
Times Higher Education Supplement (THES) 87
Tisdell, E. 50
Traditional Chinese Medicine 168
transition mechanisms 152
Transition Town Movement 33
Trickle-down economies 14

UK Centre for Economic and Environmental Development 27
UK Sustainable Development Commission 29
unconscious behaviours 270
'underclass' 126
undergraduate learners 232

UNESCO 158, 256
United Kingdom (UK): Coalition Agreement (Liberal/Conservative 2010) 126; legislative process 113; vocational skills and qualifications 239
United Nations University initiative 20–1
United States of America (USA): adult education 207; immigration policy 199; urban poverty 30
university education 229–30
university league tables 86
university norm and expectations 217
University of Sheffield 93
urban poverty: USA 30

van Helden, C.: and Lemke, J. 202
Venn, C. 7
Victorian Chooks Society 252
Victorian civic universities 82
VitalVoices conference 60
vocational education 3
vocational education and training (VET) 257
voluntary community organisations 188
voluntary organisations 135, 146
volunteering 248–52

Waiting for Godot (Beckett) 274
Walker, G.: and Devine-Wright, P. 28
Walker, M. 25
Watanabe, C.: and Shum, K.L. 28
Watson, D. 96
wealth redistribution 141
Webb, S. 82–97
Weedon, E.: and Riddell, S. 133–52
welfare 279
welfare managerialisation 278
welfare reform 122

Welfare Reform Act (2007) 114, 116
Welfare Reform Bill (2009) 122–3
Welfare-to-work papers 112
Wenger, E.: and Lave, J. 241; *Situated Learning* 242
White Paper on Adult Education in the Republic of Ireland 45
Williams, B. 68
Wilson, A. 64
Wisconsin 'W2' programme 121
Wolff, N. 281
Women Against Imperialism 63
women and non-traditional occupations 106
women in societies 205
Women Together 67
Women's Coalition 60
women's education 70–3
women's groups 248
women's informal learning 237, 243
Women's Information Group 71, 73–7
Women's Institutes in the UK 245
women's movements 16
Women's Peace Initiatives 67–70
Women's Support Network 59
Woods, M.: and Rooney, E. 65
work–life balance 29
Workers' Educational Association (WEA) 72, 138
workforce: skills and flexibility 3
working-class community 78
working-class people 77
working-class women 75
World Conference of the Associated Country Women of the World 243
world order perception 192–3

yuan (currency) 163